MW00885099

Table of contents

Introduction...6

Breakfast Recipes 6

Chia Oats..6
Almond Scones..6
Almond Cookies...6
Cinnamon Oats..7
Banana Muffins..7
Almond Pancakes..7
Berries Pancakes...7
Cashew Parfait..7
Almond Potato Waffles...7
Mozzarella Scramble 8
Cheddar Hash Browns...8
Chives Risotto...8
Coconut Quinoa..8
Cherries Bowls..8
Cinnamon Plums...8
Apples Bowls...8
Cheese Frittata...9
Eggs and Artichokes...9
Beans Bake...9
Rice Bowls...9
Hash Browns Casserole......................................9
Mushroom and Rice Mix......................................9
Coconut Berries 10
Apples Bowls...10
Cinnamon Porridge..10
Cauliflower Salad...10
Strawberry Oats..10
Almond Peach Mix...10
Dates Ric...10
Cherries Oatmeal..10
Pomegranate Yogurt..11
Coconut Cocoa Oats..11
Mango Oats..11
Pecan Bowls..11
Berries Rice...11
Coconut Rice..11
Baked Peache..11
Pomegranate Oats...11
Coconut Hash..12
Peppers Salad...12
Tomato Eggs..12
Lemon Chia Bowls...12
Cinnamon Tapioca Pudding...............................12
Quinoa Mix...12
Eggs Salad...12
Green Beans Hash...13
Chicken Hash...13
Mint Chickpeas Salad..13
Millet Pudding..13
Zucchini Almond Oatmeal..................................13
Maple Almonds Bowl..13
Coconut Porridge...13
Spring Omelet..14
Coconut Toast..14
Scallions Omelet..14
Carrots Hash..14
Carrot and Peas Salad 14
Apple Oats...14
Chia Bowls...15
Vanilla Rice and Cherries...................................15

Lunch Recipes 15

Corn and Beans Tortillas....................................15
Chicken and Spinach Mix...................................15
Garlic Chickpeas Fritters....................................15
Pork Soup...16
Shrimp and Spinach Salad.................................16
Raspberry Shrimp and Tomato Salad.................16
Cod Tacos..16
Zucchini Fritters...16
Chickpeas Stew..16
Lemon Chicken Salad..17
Asparagus Salad..17
Tomato Beef Stew..17
Chicken Stew...17
Turkey and Carrots Soup...................................17
Cilantro Chicken and Lentils..............................17
Balsamic Chicken and Cauliflower 18
Tomato Soup..18
Pork and Potatoes...18
Trout Soup..18
Garlic Turkey Stew...18
Tomato Eggplant Soup.......................................18
Potatoes Soup..19
Chili Chicken Soup...19
Salmon Skillet..19
Potato and Spinach Salad.................................19
Ground Beef Skillet..19
Shrimp and Arugula Salad.................................19
Coconut Broccoli Cream....................................20
Cabbage and Leek Soup....................................20
Dill Cauliflower Soup..20
Parsley Pork Soup...20
Minty Shrimp and Olives Salad..........................20
Shrimp Soup..20
Balsamic Shrimp..21
Spinach and Tomato Stew..................................21
Cilantro Peppers and Cauliflower Mix................21
Rosemary Carrot Stew.......................................21
Cabbage Stew..21
Mushroom Soup...21
Lime Turkey Stew...22
Beef and Beans Salad..22
Squash and Peppers Stew.................................22
Beef and Cabbage Stew.....................................22
Pork Stew...22
Turkey Tortillas..22
Cheddar Cauliflower Bowls................................23
Oregano Pork...23
Mushroom Salad..23
Beef and Scallions Mix.......................................23
Carrot Soup..23
Beef Soup...23
Chicken and Sauce..24
Turmeric Chicken Stew......................................24
Chickpeas Pan...24
Parsley Green Beans Soup................................24
Beef Skillet...24
Thyme Beef and Tomatoes................................24
Eggplant and Tomato Stew................................25
Chicken and Tomato Mix....................................25
Turmeric Chicken Mix..25
Zucchini Soup..25
Rosemary Pork Chops.......................................25
Chipotle Lentils..25
Salmon Salad 26

Shrimp Salad 26
Shrimp and Walnuts Salad 26
Avocado Salad 26
Balsamic Shrimp Salad 26
Salsa Seafood Bowls 26
Salmon and Olives Salad 26

Side Dishes **27**

Radish and Olives Salad 27
Spinach and Endives Salad 27
Arugula Salad 27
Lemon Spinach 27
Green Beans Salad 27
Endives Salad 27
Chives Edamame Salad 27
Grapes and Cucumber Salad 27
Parsley Beets 28
Tomato and Cabbage Mix 28
Cabbage Salad 28
Tomato Salsa 28
Pesto Zucchini Salad 28
Carrots Salad 28
Beet Salad 28
Chives Radishes 28
Balsamic Black Beans Mix 29
Cilantro and Spring Onions Endives 29
Tomatoes Salad 29
Peppers Salad 29
Garlic Tomatoes Mix 29
Paprika Brussels Sprouts 29
Turmeric Endives 29
Creamy Cauliflower Mash 29
Garlic Mushrooms 30
Paprika Green Beans 30
Lime Tomatoes 30
Caraway Cabbage Mix 30
Paprika Fennel Mix 30
Chili Squash Mix 30
Parsley Mushrooms 30
Spinach Sauté 30
Chili Broccoli 31
Hot Brussels Sprouts 31
Chili Corn Sauté 31
Almonds and Mango Salad 31
Spinach Mix 31
Garlic Potato Pan 31
Green Beans Mix 31
Garlic Potatoes 32
Creamy Brussels Sprouts 32
Paprika Carrots 32
Nutmeg Asparagus 32
Walnut Turnips Mix 32
Paprika Rice Mix 32
Basil Olives Mix 33
Balsamic Cabbage 33
Lime Carrots 33
Parmesan Eggplant Mix 33
Parmesan Endives 33
Lemon Asparagus 33
Parsley Artichokes Mix 34
Rosemary Tomatoes 34
Avocado, Tomato and Olives Salad 34
Greens Sauté 34
Balsamic Beets 34
Coconut Kale Sauté 34
Allspice Carrots 34

Dill Artichokes 34
Rice and Cranberries Mix 35
Thyme Black Beans Mix 35
Zucchini Salsa 35
Mint Peppers 35
Chives Cabbage Sauté 35
Avocado Mix 35
Roasted Sweet Potato Mix 36
Oregano Beans Mix 36
Coconut Beets 36
Broccoli Rice 36

Snacks **37**

Tahini Pumpkin Dip 37
Cheesy Spinach Dip 37
Olives Salsa 37
Chives Dip 37
Cucumber Salad 37
Chickpeas Spread 37
Coconut Olives Tapenade 37
Coconut Dip 37
Pine Nuts Dip 38
Cucumbers Salsa Bowls 38
Mint Cheesy Dip 38
Dill Dip 38
Cauliflower and Tomato Salsa 38
Shrimp Dip 38
Peach and Olives Salsa 38
Turmeric Carrot Chips 38
Asparagus Snack Bowls 39
Figs Bowls 39
Shrimp Salsa 39
Avocado Fries 39
Cilantro Lemon Dip 39
Sweet Potatoand and Coconut Dip 39
Beans and Tomato Salsa 39
Lime Beans Salsa 39
Coconut Peppers Dip 40
Lentils Dip 40
Chili Walnuts 40
Coconut Cranberry Crackers 40
Brussels Sprouts Bowls 40
Walnuts Bowls 40
Turmeric Radish Chips 40
Shrimp Salad 40
Cream Cheese and Leeks Dip 41
Bell Peppers Salsa 41
Avocado Dip 41
Corn Spread 41
Coconut Beans Bars 41
Pumpkin Seeds Bowls 41
Yogurt Dip 41
Rosemary Beet Bites 41
Mushrooms Bowls 42
Beans Dip 42
Chili Fennel Salsa 42
Pecans Bowls 42
Almonds Bowls 42
Paprika Potato Chips 42
Salmon and Spinach Bowls 42
Corn Salsa 42
Seeds Bowls 43
Coconut Carrot Spread 43
Tomato Spread 43
Dill Zucchini Spread 43
Salmon Muffins 43

Squash Bites 43
Almond Bars 44
Pearl Onions Snack 44
Oregano Broccoli Bars 44
Pineapple Salsa 44
Coconut Kale Spread 44
Cumin Beets Chips 44

Poultry 45

Creamy Turkey Mix 45
Turkey and Onion Mix 45
Balsamic Chicken 45
Turkey and Garlic Sauce 45
Coconut Chicken and Olives 45
Turkey and Peach 45
Paprika Chicken and Spinach 46
Chicken and Tomatoes Mix 46
Basil Turkey and Broccoli 46
Chicken with Green Beans and Sauce 46
Chicken with Zucchini 46
Lemon Chicken Mix 46
Ginger Turkey Mix 47
Chives Chicken 47
Turkey with Pepper and Rice 47
Chicken and Leeks 47
Turkey and Cabbage Mix 47
Spiced Chicken Mix 47
Mustard Chicken 48
Chili Chicken Mix 48
Turkey and Potatoes 48
Chicken and Greens 48
Herbed Chicken Mix 48
Cumin Chicken 48
Oregano Turkey and Tomato Mix 49
Ginger Chicken 49
Chicken and Green Onions 49
Parsley Turkey and Quinoa 49
Turkey and Parsnips 49
Turkey and Chickpeas 49
Buttery Cashew Turkey 50
Turkey and Cranberries Mix 50
Chicken Breast and Tomatoes 50
Turkey and Greens 50
Chicken and Almond Mushrooms 50
Chili Chicken 50
Parsley Chicken and Peas 51
Turkey and Broccoli 51
Paprika Chicken 51
Chicken and Artichokes 51
Peppercorn Turkey 51
Chicken and Veggies 51
Garlic Chicken Wings 52
Chicken and Cabbage 52
Turkey Sandwich 52
Turkey and Lentils 52
Turkey and Barley 52
Turkey with Radishes 52
Rosemary Chicken and Quinoa 53
Turkey Tortillas 53
Chicken with Peppers 53
Coconut Turkey 53
Chicken and Shrimp 53
Turkey and Asparagus 53
Chicken with Tomatoes and Grapes 54
Turkey and Olives 54
Balsamic Turkey 54

Cheesy Turkey 54
Chives Chicken and Beets 54
Turkey Salad 54

Meat 55

Paprika Pork Mix 55
Pork and Carrots 55
Cilantro Pork 55
Coriander Pork 55
Balsamic Pork 55
Cilantro Pork Skillet 55
Pork and Zucchinis 56
Nutmeg Pork 56
Peppercorn Pork 56
Parsley Pork and Tomatoes 56
Lemon Pork Chops 56
Coconut Pork Mix 56
Lime Pork 57
Coriander Pork 57
Basil Pork Mix 57
Pork and Tomatoes 57
Lamb and Cherry Tomatoes Mix 57
Pork with Green Beans 57
Lamb with Scallions and Mushrooms 58
Pork with Tomatoes and Spinach 58
Warm Pork Salad 58
Chili Pork and Apples 58
Hot Pork Chops 58
Creamy Pork Chops 58
Pork with Paprika Peaches 59
Lamb and Radish Skillet 59
Pork and Lemon Artichokes Mix 59
Parmesan Pork and Sauce 59
Pork with Mango and Tomatoes 59
Pork and Sweet Potatoes 59
Cilantro Pork and Chickpeas 60
Lamb Chops and Greens 60
Lamb and Red Onions Mix 60
Meatballs and Spinach 60
Creamy Meatballs Mix 60
Turmeric Pork Mix 60
Lamb with Veggies Mix 61
Coconut Pork with Beets 61
Thyme Lamb and Cabbage Stew 61
Lamb with Carrot and Bok Choy 61
Pork with Olives 61
Chives Pork and Barley 61
Simple Pork and Leeks 62
Pork with Parsley Peas 62
Oregano Lamb Chops 62
Pork Meatballs and Sauce 62
Pork with Chili Endives 62
Pork and Radish Hash 62
Pork and Green Beans 63
Coconut Lamb and Quinoa 63
Pork and Onions Bowls 63
Lamb with Okra 63
Pork with Spring Onions and Sprouts 63
Pork with Beans 63
Pork with Capers 64
Pork and Olives 64
Pork and Cilantro Rice 64
Lime Lamb 64
Minty Pork 64
Tarragon Pork Roast 64

Fish and Seafood..**65**

Coconut Flounder...65
Lime Salmon and Mango...................................65
Shrimp and Radish Mix......................................65
Salmon Spread..65
Salmon Soup...65
Cilantro and Nutmeg Shrimp.............................65
Shrimp and Strawberries...................................65
Baked Trout..65
Salmon Salad..66
Dill Salmon...66
Chives Salmon Salad..66
Chili Tuna..66
Lime Tuna...66
Citrus Cod..66
Cod and Coconut Asparagus..............................66
Trout and Avocado Salad...................................66
Thyme Shrimp..67
Hot Cod...67
Salmon with Scallions and Green Beans............67
Tuna and Chives Meatballs................................67
Salmon with Zucchini and Eggplant.................67
Turmeric Cod Mix..67
Balsamic Salmon..68
Cod and Coconut Sauce.....................................68
Cilantro Halibut and Radishes...........................68
Balsamic Scallops...68
Citrus Tuna...68
Creamy Salmon Curry..68
Chives Salmon and Olives..................................69
Lemon Fennel and Salmon.................................69
Chives Sea Bass..69
Shrimp and Black Beans.....................................69
Shrimp with Artichokes and Tomatoes.............69
Salmon and Veggies Mix....................................69
Balsamic Scallops and Scallions........................70
Garlic Cod and Tomatoes...................................70
Coconut Sea Bass Mix..70
Garlic Trout...70
Shrimp and Quinoa Bowls..................................70
Lemon and Mint Cod...70
Salmon and Spring Onions................................71
Trout and Arugula Salad....................................71
Saffron Salmon and Onion.................................71
Shrimp and Basil Salad......................................71
Crab and Tomatoes Salad..................................71
Allspice Shrimp..71
Shrimp and Sauce...71
Parsley Salmon Mix..71
Coconut Cod and Broccoli.................................72
Seafood and Tomato Bowls................................72
Cod and Green Onions Mix................................72
Ginger Sea Bass..72
Parsley Shrimp and Pineapple Bowls................72
Creamy Shrimp...72
Shrimp and Spinach Salad.................................72
Chives Tilapia...73
Sea Bass Pan...73
Paprika Scallops...73
Shrimp with Coconut Asparagus Mix...............73
Cod and Peas Pan...73

Desserts **74**

Lime Cream...74
Almond Berry Pudding......................................74

Almond Cookies...74
Cinnamon Peaches...74
Coconut Cake...74
Cinnamon Apple Cake..74
Coconut Cream...74
Strawberries and Yogurt Bowls.........................74
Pecan Cookies..75
Strawberries and Coconut Cake........................75
Almond Cocoa Pudding.....................................75
Walnuts Cream...75
Coconut Avocado Cream....................................75
Raspberries Cream Cheese Mix.........................75
Watermelon and Apples Salad...........................75
Lime Pears Mix...75
Orange Compote...76
Apricots Compote...76
Vanilla Cantaloupe Bowls..................................76
Blackberries Salad..76
Orange Bowls..76
Coconut Pumpkin Cream...................................76
Rhubarb and Figs Stew.......................................76
Nectarines Cocoa Squares..................................77
Grapes and Lime Compote.................................77
Mandarin Cream...77
Cherry Cream...77
Walnuts Pudding..77
Fruity Bread..77
Vanilla Rice Pudding..77
Lime Watermelon Compote...............................77
Ginger Chia Pudding..78
Lemon Cashew Cream..78
Coconut Hemp and Almond Cookies................78
Coconut Pomegranate Bowls............................78
Vanilla Chia Cream...78
Ginger Berries Bowls..78
Grapefruit and Coconut Cream.........................78
Rhubarb Cream..78
Mint Pineapple Mix..79
Berry Compote..79
Lime Coconut Pudding......................................79
Almond Cream..79
Sweet Plums Mix..79
Chia Apples Mix...79
Rice Pudding...79
Rhubarb Compote..79
Coconut Rhubarb Cream...................................80
Minty Fruit Salad..80
Dates Cream..80
Almond Plum Muffins..80
Coconut Plums Bowls..80
Seed Energy Bars..80
Nutmeg Baked Bananas.....................................80
Cocoa Avocado Smoothie...................................80
Banana and Avocado Bars..................................81
Cinnamon Bars...81
Vanilla Green Tea Bars.......................................81
Coconut Walnut Cream......................................81
Almond Lemon Cake..81

Recipe Index **82**

Introduction

Nowadays there is a massive amount of diets all over the world. All of them look very attractive and useful. Sometimes it is rather challenging to choose the perfect diet which will bring results. For now, the DASH diet is the healthiest diet that can be created. It is proven that the DASH diet really works! The meal plan has already demonstrated its effectiveness in maintaining health and making every day look amazing.

The DASH Diet is Dietary Approaches to stop hypertension. The main effect of it is in improving the immune system and overall health. The diet will help with weight loss too but it will help gradually. Other benefits of DASH eating are cholesterol-lowering ability, decreasing the risk of cancer, and diabetes. All these effects are possible to get by reducing the sodium intake to 2300mg per day.

The DASH diet can be called "light diet". You shouldn't restrict yourself strictly in your favorite types of dishes. Just bear in mind, that every meal should be in moderation.

The best food for the DASH diet is fresh veggies, beans, nuts, seeds, grains, cereals, low-fat and non-fat dairy, fish, seafood, poultry, and lean meats. It is recommended to not eat sugars and fatty food. Instead of them look for "no-salt-added" and "low-sodium" labels on food. The diet is pretty easy to follow and can be followed for everyone. Nevertheless, it is recommended to consult your doctor before the start. Like every diet it has exceptions!

This cookbook was created to help you in following the DASH diet. It has a lot of delicious and easy to cook recipes which come in handy every day!

If you were waiting for a sign, so know this is it! Today is exactly that time to start a new life and cook something not only super delicious but also very healthy!

Breakfast Recipes

Chia Oats

Prep time: 6 hours and 10 minutes | Cooking time: 0 minutes | Servings: 1

Ingredients:

- 1 tablespoon chia seeds
- ½ cup almond milk
- 2 tablespoons natural peanut butter
- 1 tablespoon stevia
- ½ cup gluten-free oats
- 2 tablespoons raspberries

Directions:

1. In a mason jar, combine the oats with the chia seeds and the other ingredients except the raspberries, stir a bit, cover and keep in the fridge for 6 hours.
2. Top with the raspberries and serve for breakfast.

Nutrition: 628 calories, 17.8g protein, 34g carbohydrates, 50.3g fat, 12g fiber, 0mg cholesterol, 31mg sodium, 396mg potassium.

Almond Scones

Prep time: 10 minutes | Cooking time: 12 minutes | Servings: 8

Ingredients:

- 2 cups almond flour
- ½ teaspoon baking soda
- ¼ cup cranberries, dried
- ¼ cup sunflower seeds
- ¼ cup apricots, chopped
- ¼ cup walnuts, chopped
- ¼ cup sesame seeds
- 2 tablespoons stevia
- 1 egg, whisked

Directions:

1. In a bowl, combine the flour with the baking soda, cranberries, and the other ingredients and stir well.
2. Shape a square dough, roll onto a floured working surface and cut into 16 squares.
3. Arrange the squares on a baking sheet lined with parchment paper and bake the scones at 350 degrees F for 12 minutes.
4. Serve the scones for breakfast.

Nutrition: 110 calories, 4.3g protein, 4.1g carbohydrates, 9.4g fat, 1.9g fiber, 20mg cholesterol, 90mg sodium, 77mg potassium.

Almond Cookies

Prep time: 10 minutes | Cooking time: 15 minutes | Servings: 12

Ingredients:

- 1 cup almond butter
- ¼ cup stevia
- 1 teaspoon vanilla extract
- 2 bananas, peeled and mashed
- 2 cups gluten-free oats
- 1 teaspoon cinnamon powder
- 1 cup almonds, chopped
- ½ cup raisins

Directions:

1. In a bowl, combine the butter with the stevia and the other ingredients and stir well using a hand mixer.
2. Scoop medium molds of this mix on a baking sheet lined with parchment paper and flatten them a bit.
3. Cook them at 325 degrees F for 15 minutes and serve for breakfast.

Nutrition: 166 calories, 4.9g protein, 24.8g carbohydrates, 6.3g fat, 4.9g fiber, 0mg cholesterol, 1mg sodium, 184mg potassium

Cinnamon Oats

Prep time: 10 minutes | Cooking time: 7 hours |
Servings: 5

Ingredients:

- 2 apples, cored, peeled and cubed
- 1 cup gluten-free oats
- 1 and ½ cups of water
- 1 and ½ cups of almond milk
- 2 tablespoons swerve
- 2 tablespoons almond butter
- ½ teaspoon cinnamon powder
- 1 tablespoon flax seed, ground
- Cooking spray

Directions:

1. Grease a slow cooker with the cooking spray and combine the oats with the water and the other ingredients inside.
2. Toss a bit and cook on Low for 7 hours.
3. Divide into bowls and serve for breakfast.

Nutrition: 201 calories, 5.2g protein, 38.5g carbohydrates, 6.8g fat, 6.8g fiber, 0mg cholesterol, 44mg sodium, 155mg potassium

Banana Muffins

Prep time: 10 minutes | Cooking time: 25 minutes |
Servings: 12

Ingredients:

- 2 bananas, peeled and mashed
- 1 cup almond milk
- 1 teaspoon vanilla extract
- ¼ cup pure maple syrup
- 1 teaspoon apple cider vinegar
- ¼ cup coconut oil, melted
- 2 cups almond flour
- 4 tablespoons coconut sugar
- 2 teaspoons cinnamon powder
- 2 teaspoons baking powder
- 2 cups blueberries
- ½ teaspoon baking soda
- ½ cup walnuts, chopped

Directions:

1. In a bowl, combine the bananas with the almond milk, vanilla, and the other ingredients and whisk well.
2. Divide the mix into 12 muffin tins and bake at 350 degrees F for 25 minutes.
3. Serve the muffins for breakfast.

Nutrition: 209 calories, 3.1g protein, 19.5g carbohydrates, 14.9g fat, 2.4g fiber, 0mg cholesterol, 59mg sodium, 267mg potassium

Almond Pancakes

Prep time: 10 minutes | Cooking time: 6 minutes |
Servings: 12

Ingredients:

- 1 cup almond flour
- 1 tablespoon flaxseed, ground
- 2 cups of coconut milk
- 2 tablespoons coconut oil,
- melted
- 1 teaspoon cinnamon powder
- 2 teaspoons stevia

Directions:

1. In a bowl, combine the flour with the flaxseed, milk, half of the oil, cinnamon, and stevia and whisk well.
2. Heat a pan with the rest of the oil over medium heat, add ¼ cup of the crepes batter, spread into the pan, cook for 2-3 minutes on each side and transfer to a plate.
3. Repeat with the rest of the crepes batter and serve them for breakfast.

Nutrition: 128 calories, 1.5g protein, 2.9g carbohydrates, 13.2g fat, 1.3g fiber, 0mg cholesterol, 7mg sodium, 110mg potassium

Berries Pancakes

Prep time: 10 minutes | Cooking time: 7 minutes |
Servings: 12

Ingredients:

- 2 eggs, whisked
- 4 tablespoons almond milk
- 1 cup full-fat yogurt
- 3 tablespoons coconut butter, melted
- ½ teaspoon vanilla extract
- 1 and ½ cups almond flour
- 2 tablespoons stevia
- 1 cup blueberries
- 1 tablespoon avocado oil

Directions:

1. In a bowl, combine the eggs with the almond milk and the other ingredients except the oil and whisk well.
2. Heat a pan with the oil over medium heat, add ¼ cup of the batter, spread into the pan, cook for 4 minutes, flip, cook for 3 minutes more and transfer to a plate.
3. Repeat with the rest of the batter and serve the pancakes for breakfast.

Nutrition: 82 calories, 2.6g protein, 5.1g carbohydrates, 6.1g fat, 1.5g fiber, 28mg cholesterol, 20mg sodium, 57mg potassium

Cashew Parfait

Prep time: 10 minutes | Cooking time: 0 minutes |
Servings: 4

Ingredients:

- ¼ cup cashews
- ½ cup of water
- 2 teaspoons pumpkin pie spice
- 2 cups pumpkin puree
- 2 tablespoons maple syrup
- 1 pear, cored, peeled and chopped
- 2 cups of coconut yogurt

Directions:

1. In a blender, combine the cashews with the water and the other ingredients except the yogurt and pulse well.
2. Divide the yogurt into bowls, also divide the pumpkin cream on top and serve.

Nutrition: 200 calories, 5.5g protein, 32.9g carbohydrates, 6.4g fat, 5.1g fiber, 0mg cholesterol, 10mg sodium, 367mg potassium

Almond Potato Waffles

Prep time: 10 minutes | Cooking time: 10 minutes |
Servings: 6

Ingredients:

- ½ cup sweet potato, cooked, peeled and grated
- 1 cup almond milk
- 1 cup gluten-free oats
- 2 eggs, whisked
- 1 tablespoon honey
- ¼ teaspoon baking powder
- 1 tablespoon olive oil
- Cooking spray

Directions:

1. In a bowl, combine the sweet potato with the almond milk and the rest of the ingredients except the cooking spray and whisk well.
2. Grease the waffle iron with the cooking spray and pour 1/3 of the batter in each mold.
3. Cook the waffles for 3-4 minutes and serve them for breakfast.

Nutrition: 234 calories, 5.6g protein, 22.3g carbohydrates, 14.9g fat, 5.1g fiber, 55mg cholesterol, 33mg sodium, 227mg potassium

Mozzarella Scramble

Prep time: 10 minutes | Cooking time: 15 minutes |
Servings: 4

Ingredients:

- 3 tablespoons low-fat mozzarella, shredded
- A pinch of black pepper
- 4 eggs, whisked
- 1 red bell pepper, chopped
- 1 teaspoon turmeric powder
- 1 tablespoon olive oil
- 2 shallots, chopped

Directions:

1. Heat up a pan with the oil over medium heat, add the shallots and the bell pepper, stir and sauté for 5 minutes.
2. Add the eggs mixed with the rest of the ingredients, stir, cook for 10 minutes, divide everything between plates and serve.

Nutrition: 133 calories, 10.2g protein, 5.6g carbohydrates, 8g fat, 1g fiber, 166mg cholesterol, 184mg sodium, 171mg potassium

Cheddar Hash Browns

Prep time: 10 minutes | Cooking time: 20 minutes |
Servings: 4

Ingredients:

- 1 tablespoon olive oil
- 4 eggs, whisked
- 1 cup hash browns
- ½ cup fat-free cheddar cheese, shredded
- 1 small yellow onion, chopped
- A pinch of black pepper
- ½ green bell pepper, chopped
- ½ red bell pepper, chopped
- 1 carrot, chopped
- 1 tablespoon cilantro, chopped

Directions:

1. Heat up a pan with the oil over medium-high heat, add the onion and the hash browns and cook for 5 minutes.
2. Add the bell peppers and the carrots, toss and cook for 5 minutes more.
3. Add the eggs, black pepper and the cheese, stir and cook for another 10 minutes.
4. Add the cilantro, stir, cook for a couple more seconds, divide everything between plates and serve for breakfast.

Nutrition: 274 calories, 10.8g protein, 19.1g carbohydrates, 17.5g fat, 2.3g fiber, 179mg cholesterol, 295mg sodium, 415mg potassium

Chives Risotto

Prep time: 10 minutes | Cooking time: 25 minutes |
Servings: 4

Ingredients:

- 3 slices bacon, low-sodium, chopped
- 1 tablespoon avocado oil
- 1 cup white rice
- 1 red onion, chopped
- 2 cups low-sodium chicken stock
- 2 tablespoons low-fat parmesan, grated
- 1 tablespoon chives, chopped
- A pinch of black pepper

Directions:

1. Heat up a pan with the oil over medium-high heat, add the onion and the bacon, stir and cook for 5 minutes.
2. Add the rice and the other ingredients, toss, bring to a simmer and cook over medium heat for 20 minutes.
3. Stir the mix, divide into bowls and serve for breakfast.

Nutrition: 220 calories, 6.4g protein, 39.9g carbohydrates, 3.3g fat, 1.4g fiber, 7mg cholesterol, 219mg sodium, 137mg potassium

Coconut Quinoa

Prep time: 5 minutes | Cooking time: 10 minutes |
Servings: 4

Ingredients:

- 1 and ½ cups water
- 1 teaspoon cinnamon powder
- 1 and ½ cups quinoa
- 1 cup almond milk
- 1 tablespoon coconut sugar
- ¼ cup pistachios, chopped

Directions:

1. Put the water and the almond milk in a pot, bring to a boil over medium heat, add the quinoa and the other ingredients, whisk, cook for 10 minutes, divide in to bowls, cool down and serve for breakfast.

Nutrition: 404 calories, 11.1g protein, 48.2g carbohydrates, 19.9g fat, 6.2g fiber, 0mg cholesterol, 32mg sodium, 555mg potassium

Cherries Bowls

Prep time: 10 minutes | Cooking time: 0 minutes |
Servings: 4

Ingredients:

- 4 cups non-fat yogurt
- 1 cup cherries, pitted and halved
- 4 tablespoons coconut sugar
- ½ teaspoon vanilla extract

Directions:

1. In a bowl, combine the yogurt with the cherries, sugar and vanilla, toss and keep in the fridge for 10 minutes.
2. Divide into bowls and serve f breakfast.

Nutrition: 205 calories, 14.1g protein, 361.g carbohydrates, 0.5g fat, 0.1g fiber, 5mg cholesterol, 192mg sodium, 645mg potassium

Cinnamon Plums

Prep time: 10 minutes | Cooking time: 15 minutes |
Servings: 4

Ingredients:

- 4 plums, pitted and halved
- 3 tablespoons coconut oil, melted
- ½ teaspoon cinnamon powder
- 1 cup coconut cream
- ¼ cup unsweetened coconut, shredded
- 2 tablespoons sunflower seeds, toasted

Directions:

1. In a baking dish, combine the plums with the oil, cinnamon and the other ingredients, introduce in the oven and bake at 380 degrees F for 15 minutes.
2. Divide everything into bowls and serve.

Nutrition: 282 calories, 2.3g protein, 12.4g carbohydrates, 27.1g fat, 2.8g fiber, 0mg cholesterol, 10mg sodium, 289mg potassium

Apples Bowls

Prep time: 10 minutes | Cooking time: 0 minutes |
Servings: 4

Ingredients:

- 6 apples, cored and pureed
- 1 cup natural apple juice
- 2 tablespoons coconut sugar
- 2 cups non-fat yogurt
- 1 teaspoon cinnamon powder

Directions:

1. In a bowl, combine the apples with the apple juice and the other ingredients, stir, divide into bowls and keep in the fridge for 10 minutes before serving.

Nutrition: 279 calories, 4.4g protein, 69.5g carbohydrates, 0.6g fat, 8.9g fiber, 3mg cholesterol, 56mg sodium, 379mg potassium

Cheese Frittata

Prep time: 10 minutes | Cooking time: 20 minutes |
Servings: 4

Ingredients:

- A pinch of black pepper
- 4 eggs, whisked
- 2 tablespoons parsley, chopped
- 1 tablespoon low-fat cheese, shredded
- 1 red onion, chopped
- 1 tablespoon olive oil

Directions:

1. Heat up a pan with the oil over medium heat, add the onion and the black pepper, stir and sauté for 5 minutes.
2. Add the eggs mixed with the other ingredients, spread into the pan, introduce in the oven and cook at 360 degrees F for 15 minutes.
3. Divide the frittata between plates and serve.

Nutrition: 112 calories, 6.3g protein, 3.1g carbohydrates, 8.5g fat, 0.7g fiber, 166mg cholesterol, 75mg sodium, 111mg potassium

Eggs and Artichokes

Prep time: 5 minutes | Cooking time: 20 minutes |
Servings: 4

Ingredients:

- 4 eggs
- 4 slices low-fat cheddar, shredded
- 1 yellow onion, chopped
- 1 tablespoon avocado oil
- 1 tablespoon cilantro, chopped
- 1 cup canned no-salt-added artichokes, drained and chopped

Directions:

1. Grease 4 ramekins with the oil, divide the onion in each, crack an egg in each ramekin, add the artichokes and top with cilantro and cheddar cheese.
2. Introduce the ramekins in the oven and bake at 380 degrees F for 20 minutes.
3. Serve the baked eggs for breakfast.

Nutrition: 178 calories, 14.2g protein, 8.4g carbohydrates, 10.9g fat, 2.9g fiber, 184mg cholesterol, 331mg sodium, 261mg potassium

Beans Bake

Prep time: 10 minutes | Cooking time: 30 minutes |
Servings: 8

Ingredients:

- 8 eggs, whisked
- 2 red onions, chopped
- 1 red bell pepper, chopped
- 4 ounces canned black beans, no-salt-added, drained and
- rinsed
- ½ cup green onions, chopped
- 1 cup low-fat mozzarella cheese, shredded
- Cooking spray

Directions:

1. Grease a baking pan with the cooking spray and spread the black beans, onions, green onions and bell pepper into the pan.
2. Add the eggs mixed with the cheese, introduce in the oven and bake at 380 degrees F for 30 minutes.
3. Divide the mix between plates and serve for breakfast.

Nutrition: 171 calories, 12.3g protein, 13.7g carbohydrates, 7.8g fat, 3.1g fiber, 175mg cholesterol, 153mg sodium, 365mg potassium

Rice Bowls

Prep time: 10 minutes | Cooking time: 25 minutes |
Servings: 4

Ingredients:

- 1 cup white rice
- 2 cups almond milk
- 1 tablespoon ginger, grated
- 3 tablespoons coconut sugar
- 1 teaspoon cinnamon powder

Directions:

1. Put the milk in a pot, bring to a simmer over medium heat, add the rice and the other ingredients, stir, cook for 25 minutes, divide into bowls and serve.

Nutrition: 483 calories, 6.2g protein, 53.6g carbohydrates, 29g fat, 3.4g fiber, 0mg cholesterol, 21mg sodium, 387mg potassium

Hash Browns Casserole

Prep time: 10 minutes | Cooking time: 35 minutes |
Servings: 4

Ingredients:

- 1 pound hash browns
- 4 eggs, whisked
- 1 red onion, chopped
- 1 chili pepper, chopped
- 1 tablespoon olive oil
- 6 ounces loëw-sodium sausage, chopped
- ¼ teaspoon chili powder
- A pinch of black pepper

Directions:

1. Heat up a pan with the oil over medium heat, add the onion and the sausage, stir and brown for 5 minutes.
2. Add the hash browns and the other ingredients except the eggs and pepper, stir and cook for 5 minutes more.
3. Pour the eggs mixed with the black pepper over the sausage mix, introduce the pan in the oven and bake at 370 degrees F for 25 minutes.
4. Divide the mix between plates and serve for breakfast,

Nutrition: 357 calories, 15.2g protein, 19.4g carbohydrates, 24.8g fat, 1.7g fiber, 204mg cholesterol, 241mg sodium, 522mg potassium

Mushroom and Rice Mix

Prep time: 10 minutes | Cooking time: 30 minutes |
Servings: 4

Ingredients:

- 1 red onion, chopped
- 1 cup white rice
- 2 garlic cloves, minced
- 2 tablespoons olive oil
- 2 cups low-sodium chicken stock
- 1 tablespoon cilantro, chopped
- ½ cup fat-free cheddar cheese, grated
- ½ pound white mushroom, sliced
- Black pepper to the taste

Directions:

1. Heat up a pan with the oil over medium heat, add the onion, garlic and mushrooms, stir and cook for 5-6 minutes.
2. Add the rice and the rest of the ingredients, bring to a simmer and cook over medium heat for 25 minutes stirring often.
3. Divide the rice mix between bowls and serve for breakfast.

Nutrition: 314 calories, 9.5g protein, 42.1g carbohydrates, 12.2g fat, 1.8g fiber, 15mg cholesterol, 162mg sodium, 295mg potassium

Coconut Berries

Prep time: 5 minutes | Cooking time: 15 minutes | Servings: 4

Ingredients:

- 3 tablespoons coconut sugar
- 1 cup coconut cream
- 1 cup blueberries
- 1 cup blackberries
- 1 cup strawberries
- 1 teaspoon vanilla extract

Directions:

1. Put the cream in a pot, heat it up over medium heat, add the sugar and the other ingredients, toss, cook for 15 minutes, divide into bowls and serve for breakfast.

Nutrition: 223 calories, 2.4g protein, 23.9g carbohydrates, 14.7g fat, 4.8g fiber, 0mg cholesterol, 10mg sodium, 301mg potassium

Apples Bowls

Prep time: 5 minutes | Cooking time: 15 minutes | Servings: 4

Ingredients:

- 1 cup blueberries
- 1 teaspoon cinnamon powder
- 1 and ½ cups almond milk
- ¼ cup raisins
- 2 apples, cored, peeled and cubed
- 1 cup coconut cream

Directions:

1. Put the milk in a pot, bring to a simmer over medium heat, add the berries and the other ingredients, toss, cook for 15 minutes, divide into bowls and serve for breakfast.

Nutrition: 266 calories, 2.6g protein, 3g14. carbohydrates, 15.6g fat, 5.2g fiber, 0mg cholesterol, 64mg sodium, 373mg potassium

Cinnamon Porridge

Prep time: 10 minutes | Cooking time: 25 minutes | Servings: 4

Ingredients:

- 1 cup buckwheat
- 3 cups coconut milk
- ½ teaspoon vanilla extract
- 1 tablespoon coconut sugar
- 1 teaspoon ginger powder
- 1 teaspoon cinnamon powder

Directions:

1. Put the milk and the sugar in a pot, bring to a simmer over medium heat, add the buckwheat and the other ingredients, cook for 25 minutes, stirring often, divide into bowls and serve for breakfast.

Nutrition: 577 calories, 9.8g protein, 44.5g carbohydrates, 44.4g fat, 8.3g fiber, 0mg cholesterol, 36mg sodium, 676mg potassium

Cauliflower Salad

Prep time: 10 minutes | Cooking time: 20 minutes | Servings: 4

Ingredients:

- 1 pound cauliflower florets
- 1 tablespoon olive oil
- 2 spring onions, chopped
- 1 red bell pepper, sliced
- 1 yellow bell pepper, sliced
- 1 green bell pepper, sliced
- 1 tablespoon cilantro, chopped
- A pinch of black pepper

Directions:

1. Heat up a pan with the oil over medium heat, add the spring onions, stir and sauté for 2 minutes.
2. Add the cauliflower and the other ingredients, toss, cook for 16 minutes, divide into bowls and serve for breakfast.

Nutrition: 79 calories, 3g protein, 10.8g carbohydrates, 3.7g fat, 4.1g fiber, 0mg cholesterol, 36mg sodium, 430 potassium

Strawberry Oats

Prep time: 10 minutes | Cooking time: 20 minutes | Servings: 4

Ingredients:

- 1 and ½ cups gluten-free oats
- 2 and ¼ cups almond milk
- ½ teaspoon vanilla extract
- 2 cups strawberries, sliced
- 2 tablespoons coconut sugar

Directions:

1. Put the milk in a pot, bring to a simmer over medium heat, add the oats and the other ingredients, stir, cook for 20 minutes, divide into bowls and serve for breakfast.

Nutrition: 226 calories, 6.4g protein, 42.5g carbohydrates, 3.6g fat, 8.4g fiber, 0mg cholesterol, 46mg sodium, 158mg potassium

Almond Peach Mix

Prep time: 10 minutes | Cooking time: 15 minutes | Servings: 4

Ingredients:

- 4 peaches, cored and cut into wedges
- ¼ cup maple syrup
- ¼ teaspoon almond extract
- ½ cup almond milk

Directions:

1. Put the almond milk in a pot, bring to a simmer over medium heat, add the peaches and the other ingredients, toss, cook for 15 minutes, divide into bowls and serve for breakfast.

Nutrition: 180 calories, 2.1g protein, 28.9g carbohydrates, 7.6g fat, 3g fiber, 0mg cholesterol, 6mg sodium, 404mg potassium

Dates Ric

Prep time: 10 minutes | Cooking time: 20 minutes | Servings: 4

Ingredients:

- 1 cup white rice
- 2 cups almond milk
- 4 dates, chopped
- 2 tablespoons cinnamon powder
- 2 tablespoons coconut sugar

Directions:

1. In a pot, combine the rice with the milk and the other ingredients, bring to a simmer and cook over medium heat for 20 minutes.
2. Stir the mix again, divide into bowls and serve for breakfast.

Nutrition: 231 calories, 3.8g protein, 51.2g carbohydrates, 1g fat, 1.5g fiber, 0mg cholesterol, 40mg sodium, 108mg potassium

Cherries Oatmeal

Prep time: 10 minutes | Cooking time: 10 minutes | Servings: 6

Ingredients:

- 2 cups old-fashioned oats
- 3 cups almond milk
- 2 and ½ tablespoons cocoa powder
- 1 teaspoon vanilla extract
- 10 ounces cherries, pitted
- 2 pears, cored, peeled and cubed

Directions:

1. In your pressure cooker, combine the oats with the milk and the other ingredients, toss, cover and cook on High for 10 minutes.
2. Release the pressure naturally for 10 minutes, stir the oatmeal one more time, divide it into bowls and serve.

Nutrition: 483 calories, 7.5g protein, 51.1g carbohydrates, 31.1g fat, 9.1g fiber, 0mg cholesterol, 30mg sodium, 657mg potassium

Pomegranate Yogurt

Prep time: 10 minutes | Cooking time: 0 minutes |
Servings: 4

Ingredients:

- 1 cup figs, halved
- 1 pear, cored and cubed
- ½ cup pomegranate seeds
- ½ cup coconut sugar
- 2 cups non-fat yogurt

Directions:

1. In a bowl, combine the figs with the yogurt and the other ingredients, toss, divide into bowls and serve for breakfast.

Nutrition: 315 calories, 8.9g protein, 73.5g carbohydrates, 0.7g fat, 6.1g fiber, 2mg cholesterol, 100mg sodium, 691mg potassium

Coconut Cocoa Oats

Prep time: 10 minutes | Cooking time: 20 minutes |
Servings: 4

Ingredients:

- 2 cups almond milk
- 1 cup old-fashioned oats
- 2 tablespoons coconut sugar
- 1 teaspoon cocoa powder
- 2 teaspoons vanilla extract

Directions:

1. Heat up a pot with the milk over medium heat, add the oats and the other ingredients, bring to a simmer and cook for 20 minutes.
2. Divide the oats into bowls and serve warm for breakfast.

Nutrition: 381 calories, 5.5g protein, 26.7g carbohydrates, 30g fat, 4.8g fiber, 0mg cholesterol, 19mg sodium, 403mg potassium

Mango Oats

Prep time: 10 minutes | Cooking time: 20 minutes |
Servings: 4

Ingredients:

- 2 cups coconut milk
- 1 cup old-fashioned oats
- 1 cup mango, peeled and cubed
- 3 tablespoons almond butter
- 2 tablespoons coconut sugar
- ½ teaspoon vanilla extract

Directions:

1. Put the milk in a pot, heat it up over medium heat, add the oats and the other ingredients, stir, bring to a simmer and cook for 20 minutes.
2. Stir the oatmeal, divide it into bowls and serve.

Nutrition: 473 calories, 8.3g protein, 34.7g carbohydrates, 36.8g fat, 6.5g fiber, 0mg cholesterol, 20mg sodium, 548mg potassium

Pecan Bowls

Prep time: 10 minutes | Cooking time: 20 minutes |
Servings: 4

Ingredients:

- 1 cup steel cut oats
- 2 cups orange juice
- 2 tablespoons coconut butter, melted
- 2 tablespoons stevia
- 3 tablespoons pecans, chopped
- ¼ teaspoon vanilla extract

Directions:

1. Heat up a pot with the orange juice over medium heat, add the oats, the butter and the other ingredients, whisk, simmer for 20 minutes, divide into bowls and serve for breakfast.

Nutrition: 238 calories, 4.8g protein, 29.8g carbohydrates, 11.8g fat, 4.6g fiber, 0mg cholesterol, 2mg sodium, 351mg potassium

Berries Rice

Prep time: 10 minutes | Cooking time: 20 minutes |
Servings: 4

Ingredients:

- 1 cup brown rice
- 2 cups coconut milk
- 1 tablespoon cinnamon powder
- 1 cup blackberries
- ½ cup coconut cream, unsweetened

Directions:

1. Put the milk in a pot, bring to a simmer over medium heat, add the rice and the other ingredients, cook for 20 minutes, and divide into bowls.
2. Serve warm for breakfast.

Nutrition: 463 calories, 6.8g protein, 46.3g carbohydrates, 30.1g fat, 6.2g fiber, 0mg cholesterol, 20mg sodium, 501mg potassium

Coconut Rice

Prep time: 10 minutes | Cooking time: 20 minutes |
Servings: 6

Ingredients:

- 2 cups coconut milk
- 1 cup basmati rice
- 2 tablespoons coconut sugar
- ¾ cup coconut cream
- 1 teaspoon vanilla extract

Directions:

1. In a pot, combine the milk with the rice and the other ingredients, stir, bring to a simmer and cook over medium heat for 20 minutes.
2. Stir the mix again, divide into bowls and serve for breakfast.

Nutrition: 317 calories, 4g protein, 34.2g carbohydrates, 19.3g fat, 2.2g fiber, 0mg cholesterol, 25mg sodium, 247mg potassium

Baked Peach

Prep time: 10 minutes | Cooking time: 20 minutes |
Servings: 4

Ingredients:

- 2 cups coconut cream
- 1 teaspoon cinnamon powder
- 1/3 cup palm sugar
- 4 peaches, stones removed and cut into wedges
- Cooking spray

Directions:

1. Grease a baking pan with the cooking spray and combine the peaches with the other ingredients inside.
2. Bake this at 360 degrees F for 20 minutes, divide into bowls and serve for breakfast.

Nutrition: 395 calories, 4.2g protein, 36.7g carbohydrates, 29g fat, 4.6g fiber, 4.9mg cholesterol, 54mg sodium, 601mg potassium

Pomegranate Oats

Prep time: 10 minutes | Cooking time: 20 minutes |
Servings: 4

Ingredients:

- 3 cups almond milk
- 1 cup steel cut oats
- 1 tablespoon cinnamon powder
- 1 mango, peeled, and cubed
- ½ teaspoon vanilla extract
- 3 tablespoons pomegranate seeds

Directions:

1. Put the milk in a pot and heat it up over medium heat.
2. Add the oats, cinnamon and the other ingredients, toss, simmer for 20 minutes, divide into bowls and serve for breakfast.

Nutrition: 546 calories, 7.5g protein, 37.1g carbohydrates, 44.6g fat, 7.4g fiber, 0mg cholesterol, 29mg sodium, 689mg potassium

Coconut Hash

Prep time: 10 minutes | Cooking time: 25 minutes |
Servings: 4

Ingredients:

- 1 pound hash browns
- 1 tablespoon avocado oil
- 1/3 cup coconut cream
- 1 yellow onion, chopped
- 1 cup fat-free cheddar cheese, grated
- Black pepper to the taste
- 4 eggs, whisked

Directions:

1. Heat up a pan with the oil over medium heat, add the hash browns and the onion, stir and sauté for 5 minutes.
2. Add the rest of the ingredients except the cheese, toss and cook for 5 minutes more.
3. Sprinkle the cheese on top, introduce the pan in the oven and cook at 390 degrees F for 15 minutes.
4. Divide the mix between plates and serve for breakfast.

Nutrition: 238 calories, 18.1g protein, 11g carbohydrates, 13.4g fat, 1.2g fiber, 170mg cholesterol, 518mg sodium, 163mg potassium

Peppers Salad

Prep time: 5 minutes | Cooking time: 15 minutes |
Servings: 4

Ingredients:

- 1 cup black olives, pitted and halved
- ½ cup green olives, pitted and halved
- 1 tablespoon olive oil
- 2 scallions, chopped
- 1 red bell pepper, cut into strips
- 1 green bell pepper, cut into strips
- Zest of 1 lime, grated
- Juice of 1 lime
- 1 bunch parsley, chopped
- 1 tomato, chopped

Directions:

1. Heat up a pan with the oil over medium heat, add the scallions, stir and sauté for 2 minutes.
2. Add the olives, peppers and the other ingredients, stir and cook for 13 minutes more.
3. Divide into bowls and serve for breakfast.

Nutrition: 107 calories, 1.g 7protein, 9.5g carbohydrates, 8g fat, 15.1g fiber, 0mg cholesterol, 376mg sodium, 257mg potassium

Tomato Eggs

Prep time: 10 minutes | Cooking time: 20 minutes |
Servings: 4

Ingredients:

- ½ cup low-fat milk
- Black pepper to the taste
- 8 eggs, whisked
- 1 cup baby spinach, chopped
- 1 yellow onion, chopped
- 1 tablespoon olive oil
- 1 cup cherry tomatoes, cubed
- ¼ cup fat-free cheddar, grated

Directions:

1. Heat up a pan with the oil over medium heat, add the onion, stir and cook for 2-3 minutes.
2. Add the spinach and tomatoes, stir and cook for 2 minutes more.
3. Add the eggs mixed with the milk and black pepper and toss gently.
4. Sprinkle the cheddar on top, introduce the pan in the oven and cook at 390 degrees F for 15 minutes.
5. Divide between plates and serve.

Nutrition: 201 calories, 15.3g protein, 7g carbohydrates, 12.7g fat, 1.3g fiber, 330mg cholesterol, 216mg sodium, 352mg potassium

Lemon Chia Bowls

Prep time: 15 minutes | Cooking time: 0 minutes |
Servings: 4

Ingredients:

- 2 cups almond milk
- ½ cup chia seeds
- 2 tablespoons coconut sugar
- Zest of ½ lemon, grated
- 1 teaspoon vanilla extract
- ½ teaspoon ginger powder

Directions:

1. In a bowl, combine the chia seeds with the milk and the other ingredients, toss and leave aside for 15 minutes before serving.

Nutrition: 375 calories, 52.g protein, 19.5g carbohydrates, 33g fat 7.7g fiber, 0mg cholesterol, 21mg sodium, 387mg potassium

Cinnamon Tapioca Pudding

Prep time: 2 hours | Cooking time: 0 minutes |
Servings: 4

Ingredients:

- ½ cup tapioca pearls
- 2 cups coconut milk, hot
- 4 teaspoons coconut sugar
- ½ teaspoon cinnamon powder

Directions:

1. In a bowl, combine the tapioca with the hot milk and the other ingredients, stir and leave aside for 2 hours before serving.
2. Divide into small bowls and serve for breakfast.

Nutrition: 359 calories, 2.8g protein, 27.5g carbohydrates, 28.6g fat 2.8g fiber, 0mg cholesterol, 18mg sodium, 318mg potassium

Quinoa Mix

Prep time: 10 minutes | Cooking time: 20 minutes |
Servings: 6

Ingredients:

- 1 red onion, chopped
- 1 tablespoon olive oil
- 15 ounces canned chickpeas, no-salt-added and drained
- 14 ounces coconut milk
- ¼ cup quinoa
- 1 tablespoon ginger, grated
- 2 garlic cloves, minced
- 1 tablespoon turmeric powder
- 1 tablespoon cilantro, chopped

Directions:

1. Heat up a pan with the oil over medium heat, add the onion, stir and sauté for 5 minutes.
2. Add the chickpeas, quinoa and the other ingredients, stir, bring to a simmer and cook for 15 minutes.
3. Divide the mix into bowls and serve for breakfast.

Nutrition: 472 calories, 16.6g protein, 54.6g carbohydrates, 23g fat 15.1g fiber, 0mg cholesterol, 29mg sodium, 906mg potassium

Eggs Salad

Prep time: 10 minutes | Cooking time: 0 minutes |
Servings: 4

Ingredients:

- 2 carrots, cubed
- 2 green onions, chopped
- 1 bunch of parsley, chopped
- 2 tablespoons olive oil
- 4 eggs, hard boiled, peeled
- and cubed
- 1 tablespoon balsamic vinegar
- 1 tablespoon chives, chopped
- A pinch of black pepper

Directions:

1. In a bowl, combine the carrots with the eggs and the other ingredients, toss and serve for breakfast.

Nutrition: 144 calories, 6.4g protein, 4.9g carbohydrates, 11.5g fat 1.5g fiber, 164mg cholesterol, 92mg sodium, 265mg potassium

Green Beans Hash

Prep time: 10 minutes | Cooking time: 15 minutes |
Servings: 4

Ingredients:

- 1 garlic clove, minced
- 1 red onion, chopped
- 1 tablespoon avocado oil
- 1 pound green beans, trimmed

- and halved
- 8 eggs, whisked
- 1 tablespoon cilantro, chopped
- A pinch of black pepper

Directions:

1. Heat up a pan with the oil over medium heat, add the onion and the garlic and sauté for 2 minutes.
2. Add the green beans and cook for 2 minutes more.
3. Add the eggs, black pepper and cilantro, toss, spread into the pan and cook for 10 minutes.
4. Divide the mix between plates and serve.

Nutrition: 178 calories, 13.5g protein, 11.8g carbohydrates, 9.4g fat, 4.6g fiber, 327mg cholesterol, 131mg sodium, 410mg potassium

Chicken Hash

Prep time: 10 minutes | Cooking time: 25 minutes |
Servings: 4

Ingredients:

- 2 tablespoons olive oil
- 1 yellow onion, chopped
- 2 garlic cloves, minced
- 1 teaspoon Cajun seasoning
- 8 ounces chicken breast,

- skinless, boneless and ground
- ½ pound hash browns
- 2 tablespoons veggie stock, no-salt-added
- 1 green bell pepper, chopped

Directions:

1. Heat up a pan with the oil over medium heat, add the onion, garlic and the meat and brown for 5 minutes.
2. Add the hash browns and the other ingredients, stir, and cook over medium heat for 20 minutes stirring often.
3. Divide between plates and serve for breakfast.

Nutrition: 298 calories, 14.4g protein, 25.2g carbohydrates, 15.6g fat, 2.8g fiber, 36mg cholesterol, 237mg sodium, 639mg potassium

Mint Chickpeas Salad

Prep time: 5 minutes | Cooking time: 15 minutes |
Servings: 4

Ingredients:

- 2 garlic cloves, minced
- 2 tomatoes, roughly cubed
- 1 cucumber, roughly cubed
- 2 shallots, chopped
- 2 cups canned chickpeas, no-salt-added, drained
- 1 tablespoon parsley, chopped

- 1/3 cup mint, chopped
- 1 avocado, pitted, peeled and diced
- 2 tablespoons olive oil
- Juice of 1 lime
- Black pepper to the taste

Directions:

1. Heat up a pan with the oil over medium heat, add the garlic and the shallots, stir and cook for 2 minutes.
2. Add the chickpeas and the other ingredients, toss, cook for 13 minutes more, divide into bowls and serve for breakfast.

Nutrition: 563 calories, 21.9g protein, 73g carbohydrates, 23.1g fat, 22.5g fiber, 0mg cholesterol, 36mg sodium, 1455mg potassium

Millet Pudding

Prep time: 10 minutes | Cooking time: 30 minutes |
Servings: 4

Ingredients:

- 14 ounces coconut milk
- 1 cup millet

- 1 tablespoon cocoa powder
- ½ teaspoon vanilla extract

Directions:

1. Put the milk in a pot, bring to a simmer over medium heat, add the millet and the other ingredients, and cook for 30 minutes stirring often.
2. Divide into bowls and serve for breakfast.

Nutrition: 422 calories, 8g protein, 42.7g carbohydrates, 25.9g fat, 6.8g fiber, 0mg cholesterol, 18mg sodium, 393mg potassium

Zucchini Almond Oatmeal

Prep time: 5 minutes | Cooking time: 20 minutes |
Servings: 4

Ingredients:

- 1 cup steel cut oats
- 3 cups almond milk
- 1 tablespoon fat-free butter

- 2 teaspoons cinnamon powder
- 1 teaspoon pumpkin pie spice
- 1 cup zucchinis, grated

Directions:

1. Heat up a pan with the milk over medium heat, add the oats and the other ingredients, toss, bring to a simmer and cook for 20 minutes, stirring from time to time.
2. Divide the oatmeal into bowls and serve for breakfast.

Nutrition: 508 calories, 7.5g protein, 27.2g carbohydrates, 44.5g fat, 6.7g fiber, 0mg cholesterol, 63mg sodium, 624mg potassium

Maple Almonds Bowl

Prep time: 5 minutes | Cooking time: 20 minutes |
Servings: 4

Ingredients:

- 2 cups coconut milk
- 1 cup coconut, shredded
- ½ cup maple syrup

- 1 cup raisins
- 1 cup almonds
- ½ teaspoon vanilla extract

Directions:

1. Put the milk in a pot, bring to a simmer over medium heat, add the coconut and the other ingredients, and cook for 20 minutes, stirring from time to time.
2. Divide the mix into bowls and serve warm for breakfast.

Nutrition: 697 calories, 9g .6protein, 70g carbohydrates, 47.4g fat, 8.8g fiber, 0mg cholesterol, 30mg sodium, 914mg potassium

Coconut Porridge

Prep time: 10 minutes | Cooking time: 20 minutes |
Servings: 4

Ingredients:

- 4 cups coconut milk
- 1 cup cornmeal
- 1 teaspoon vanilla extract

- 1 cup strawberries, halved
- ½ teaspoon nutmeg, ground

Directions:

1. Put the milk in a pot, bring to a simmer over medium heat, add the cornmeal and the other ingredients, toss, cook for 20 minutes, and take off the heat.
2. Divide the porridge between plates and serve for breakfast.

Nutrition: 678 calories, 8.2g protein, 39.8g carbohydrates, 58.5g fat, 8.3g fiber, 0mg cholesterol, 47mg sodium, 776mg potassium

Spring Omelet

Prep time: 10 minutes | Cooking time: 15 minutes |
Servings: 4

Ingredients:

- 4 eggs, whisked
- A pinch of black pepper
- ¼ cup low-sodium bacon, chopped
- 1 tablespoon olive oil
- 1 cup red bell peppers, chopped
- 4 spring onions, chopped
- ¾ cup low-fat cheese, shredded

Directions:

1. Heat up a pan with the oil over medium heat, add the spring onions and the bell peppers, toss and cook for 5 minutes.
2. Add the eggs and the other ingredients, toss, spread into the pan, cook for 5 minutes, flip, cook for another 5 minutes, divide between plates and serve.

Nutrition: 236 calories, 13.9g protein, 4g carbohydrates, 18.8g fat, 0.8g fiber, 205mg cholesterol, 365mg sodium, 178mg potassium

Coconut Toast

Prep time: 10 minutes | Cooking time: 5 minutes |
Servings: 2

Ingredients:

- 4 whole-wheat bread slices
- 2 tablespoons coconut sugar
- ½ cup of coconut milk
- 2 eggs, whisked
- 1 teaspoon vanilla extract
- Cooking spray

Directions:

1. In a bowl, combine the sugar with the milk, eggs, and the vanilla and whisk well.
2. Dip each bread slice in this mix.
3. Heat a pan greased with cooking spray over medium heat, add the French toast, cook for 2-3 minutes on each side, divide between plates and serve for breakfast.

Nutrition: 390 calories, 14.2g protein, 39.1g carbohydrates, 20.6g fat, 5.1g fiber, 164mg cholesterol, 335mg sodium, 359mg potassium

Scallions Omelet

Prep time: 5 minutes | Cooking time: 15 minutes |
Servings: 4

Ingredients:

- 4 eggs, whisked
- A pinch of black pepper
- 1 tablespoon olive oil
- 1 teaspoon sesame seeds
- 2 scallions, chopped
- 1 teaspoon sweet paprika
- 1 tablespoon cilantro, chopped

Directions:

1. Heat up a pan with the oil over medium heat, add the scallions, stir and sauté for 2 minutes.
2. Add the eggs mixed with the other ingredients, toss a bit, spread the omelet into the pan and cook for 7 minutes.
3. Flip, cook the omelet for 6 minutes more, divide between plates and serve.

Nutrition: 101 calories, 5.9g protein, 1.4g carbohydrates, 8.3g fat, 0.5g fiber, 164mg cholesterol, 63mg sodium, 97mg potassium

Carrots Hash

Prep time: 10 minutes | Cooking time: 20 minutes |
Servings: 4

Ingredients:

- 2 carrots, peeled and cubed
- 1 tablespoon olive oil
- 1 yellow onion, chopped
- 1 cup low-fat cheddar cheese, shredded
- 8 eggs, whisked
- 1 cup coconut milk
- A pinch of salt and black pepper

Directions:

1. Heat up a pan with the oil over medium heat, add the onion and the carrots, toss and brown for 5 minutes.
2. Add the eggs and the other ingredients, toss, cook for 15 minutes stirring often, divide between plates and serve.

Nutrition: 431 calories, 20g protein, 9.9g carbohydrates, 35.9g fat, 2.7g fiber, 357mg cholesterol, 330mg sodium, 441mg potassium

Carrot and Peas Salad

Prep time: 10 minutes | Cooking time: 20 minutes |
Servings: 4

Ingredients:

- 3 garlic cloves, minced
- 1 yellow onion, chopped
- 1 tablespoon olive oil
- 1 carrot, chopped
- 1 tablespoon balsamic vinegar
- 2 cups snow peas, halved
- ½ cup veggie stock, no-salt-added
- 2 tablespoons scallions, chopped
- 1 tablespoon cilantro, chopped

Directions:

1. Heat up a pan with the oil over medium heat, add the onion and the garlic, stir and cook for 5 minutes.
2. Add the snow peas and the other ingredients, toss and cook over medium heat for 15 minutes.
3. Divide the mix into bowls and serve warm for breakfast.

Nutrition: 89 calories, 3.4g protein, 11.2g carbohydrates, 3.7g fat, 3.5g fiber, 0mg cholesterol, 33mg sodium, 318mg potassium

Apple Oats

Prep time: 10 minutes | Cooking time: 15 minutes |
Servings: 4

Ingredients:

- 1 cup steel cut oats
- 1 and ½ cups almond milk
- 1 cup non-fat yogurt
- ¼ cup maple syrup
- 2 apples, cored, peeled and chopped
- ½ teaspoon cinnamon powder

Directions:

1. In a pot, combine the oats with the m ilk and the other ingredients except the yogurt, toss, bring to a simmer and cook over medium-high heat for 15 minutes.
2. Divide the yogurt into bowls, divide the apples and oats mix on top and serve for breakfast.

Nutrition: 303 calories, 6g protein, 64g carbohydrates, 3.3g fat, 4.8g fiber, 3mg cholesterol, 161mg sodium, 234mg potassium

Chia Bowls

Prep time: 10 minutes | Cooking time: 20 minutes | Servings: 4

Ingredients:

- ½ cup steel cut oats
- 2 cups almond milk
- ¼ cup pomegranate seeds
- 4 tablespoons chia seeds
- 1 teaspoon vanilla extract

Directions:

1. Put the milk in a pot, bring to a simmer over medium heat, add the oats and the other ingredients, bring to a simmer and cook for 20 minutes.
2. Divide the mix into bowls and serve for breakfast.

Nutrition: 393 calories, 6.5g protein, 21.2g carbohydrates, 33.6g fat, 8.6g fiber, 0mg cholesterol, 21mg sodium, 412mg potassium

Vanilla Rice and Cherries

Prep time: 10 minutes | Cooking time: 25 minutes | Servings: 4

Ingredients:

- 1 tablespoon coconut, shredded
- 2 tablespoons coconut sugar
- 1 cup white rice
- 2 cups coconut milk
- ½ teaspoon vanilla extract
- ¼ cup cherries, pitted and halved
- Cooking spray

Directions:

1. Put the milk in a pot, add the sugar and the coconut, stir and bring to a simmer over medium heat.
2. Add the rice and the other ingredients, simmer for 25 minutes stirring often, divide into bowls and serve.

Nutrition: 484 calories, 6.1g protein, 52.7g carbohydrates, 29.3g fat, 3.4g fiber, 0mg cholesterol, 38mg sodium, 379mg potassium

Lunch Recipes

Corn and Beans Tortillas

Prep time: 5 minutes | Cooking time: 12 minutes | Servings: 4

Ingredients:

- 1 cup canned black beans, no-salt-added, drained and rinsed
- 1 green bell pepper, chopped
- 1 carrots, peeled and grated
- 1 tablespoon olive oil
- 1 red onion, sliced
- ½ cup corn
- 1 cup low-fat cheddar, shredded
- 6 whole wheat tortillas
- 1 cup non-fat yogurt

Directions:

1. Heat up a pan with the oil over medium heat, add the onion and sauté for 2 minutes.
2. Add the beans, carrot, bell pepper and the corn, stir, and cook for 10 minutes more.
3. Arrange the tortillas on a working surface, divide the beans mix on each, also divide the cheese and the yogurt, roll and serve for lunch.

Nutrition: 478 calories, 24.9g protein, 78.4g carbohydrates, 9.1g fat, 13.8g fiber, 11mg cholesterol, 375mg sodium, 1072mg potassium

Chicken and Spinach Mix

Prep time: 10 minutes | Cooking time: 20 minutes | Servings: 4

Ingredients:

- 2 chicken breasts, skinless, boneless and cubed
- ¼ cup low-sodium chicken stock
- ½ cup celery, chopped
- 1 cup baby spinach
- 1 mango, peeled, and cubed
- 2 spring onions, chopped
- 1 tablespoon olive oil
- 1 teaspoon thyme, dried
- ¼ teaspoon garlic powder
- A pinch of black pepper

Directions:

1. Heat up a pan with the oil over medium-high heat, add the spring onions and the chicken and brown for 5 minutes.
2. Add the celery and the other ingredients except the spinach, toss and cook for 12 minutes more.
3. Add the spinach, toss, cook for 2-3 minutes, divide everything between plates and serve.

Nutrition: 227 calories, 22.4g protein, 14.1g carbohydrates, 9.3g fat, 2g fiber, 65mg cholesterol, 89mg sodium, 418mg potassium

Garlic Chickpeas Fritters

Prep time: 10 minutes | Cooking time: 10 minutes | Servings: 4

Ingredients:

- 2 garlic cloves, minced
- 15 ounces canned chickpeas, no-salt-added, drained and rinsed
- 1 teaspoon chili powder
- 1 teaspoon cumin, ground
- 1 egg
- 1 tablespoon olive oil
- 1 tablespoon lime juice
- 1 tablespoon lime zest, grated
- 1 tablespoon cilantro, chopped

Directions:

1. In a blender, combine the chickpeas with the garlic and the other ingredients except the egg and pulse well.
2. Shape medium cakes out of this mix.
3. Heat up a pan with the oil over medium-high heat, add the chickpeas cakes, cook for 5 minutes on each side, divide between plates and serve for lunch with a side salad.

Nutrition: 440 calories, 22.2g protein, 65.9g carbohydrates, 11.3g fat, 19g fiber, 41mg cholesterol, 49mg sodium, 977mg potassium

Pork Soup

Prep time: 10 minutes | Cooking time: 25 minutes |
Servings: 4

Ingredients:

- 1 tablespoon olive oil
- 1 red onion, chopped
- 1 pound pork stew meat, cubed
- 1 quart low-sodium beef stock
- 1 pound carrots, sliced
- 1 cup tomato puree
- 1 tablespoon cilantro, chopped

Directions:

1. Heat up a pot with the oil over medium-high heat, add the onion and the meat and brown for 5 minutes.
2. Add the rest of the ingredients except the cilantro, bring to a simmer, reduce heat to medium, and boil the soup for 20 minutes.
3. Ladle into bowls and serve for lunch with the cilantro sprinkled on top.

Nutrition: 354 calories, 36g protein, 19.3g carbohydrates, 14.6g fat, 4.6g fiber, 98mg cholesterol, 199mg sodium, 1104mg potassium

Shrimp and Spinach Salad

Prep time: 5 minutes | Cooking time: 7 minutes |
Servings: 4

Ingredients:

- 1 cup corn
- 1 endive, shredded
- 1 cup baby spinach
- 1 pound shrimp, peeled and deveined
- 2 garlic cloves, minced
- 1 tablespoon lime juice
- 2 cups strawberries, halved
- 2 tablespoons olive oil
- 2 tablespoons balsamic vinegar
- 1 tablespoon cilantro, chopped

Directions:

1. Heat up a pan with the oil over medium-high heat, add the garlic and brown for 1 minute.
2. Add the shrimp and lime juice, toss and cook for 3 minutes on each side.
3. In a salad bowl, combine the shrimp with the corn, endive and the other ingredients, toss and serve for lunch.

Nutrition: 257 calories, 28g protein, 15.6g carbohydrates, 9.6g fat, 2.9g fiber, 239mg cholesterol, 291mg sodium, 481mg potassium

Raspberry Shrimp and Tomato Salad

Prep time: 5 minutes | Cooking time: 10 minutes |
Servings: 4

Ingredients:

- 1 pound green beans, trimmed and halved
- 2 tablespoons olive oil
- 2 pounds shrimp, peeled and deveined
- 1 tablespoon lemon juice
- 2 cups cherry tomatoes, halved
- ¼ cup raspberry vinegar
- A pinch of black pepper

Directions:

1. Heat up a pan with the oil over medium-high heat, add the shrimp, toss and cook for 2 minutes.
2. Add the green beans and the other ingredients, toss, cook for 8 minutes more, divide into bowls and serve for lunch.

Nutrition: 379 calories, 53.9g protein, 13g carbohydrates, 11.1g fat, 4g fiber, 478mg cholesterol, 574mg sodium, 613mg potassium

Cod Tacos

Prep time: 10 minutes | Cooking time: 10 minutes |
Servings: 2

Ingredients:

- 4 whole wheat taco shells
- 1 tablespoon light mayonnaise
- 1 tablespoon salsa
- 1 tablespoon low-fat mozzarella, shredded
- 1 tablespoon olive oil
- 1 red onion, chopped
- 1 tablespoon cilantro, chopped
- 2 cod fillets, boneless, skinless and cubed
- 1 tablespoon tomato puree

Directions:

1. Heat up a pan with the oil over medium heat, add the onion, stir and cook for 2 minutes.
2. Add the fish and tomato puree, toss gently and cook for 5 minutes more.
3. Spoon this into the taco shells, also divide the mayo, salsa and the cheese and serve for lunch.

Nutrition: 454 calories, 31.7g protein, 56.1g carbohydrates, 14.5g fat, 7.5g fiber, 38mg cholesterol, 487mg sodium, 142mg potassium

Zucchini Fritters

Prep time: 10 minutes | Cooking time: 10 minutes |
Servings: 4

Ingredients:

- 1 yellow onion, chopped
- 2 zucchinis, grated
- 2 tablespoons almond flour
- 1 egg, whisked
- 1 garlic clove, minced
- A pinch of black pepper
- 1/3 cup carrot, shredded
- 1/3 cup low-fat cheddar, grated
- 1 tablespoon cilantro, chopped
- 1 teaspoon lemon zest, grated
- 2 tablespoons olive oil

Directions:

1. In a bowl, combine the zucchinis with the garlic, onion and the other ingredients except the oil, stir well and shape medium cakes out of this mix.
2. Heat up a pan with the oil over medium-high heat, add the zucchini cakes, cook for 5 minutes on each side, divide between plates and serve with a side salad.

Nutrition: 204 calories, 8.3g protein, 10.4g carbohydrates, 16g fat, 3.5g fiber, 43mg cholesterol, 96mg sodium, 353mg potassium

Chickpeas Stew

Prep time: 10 minutes | Cooking time: 20 minutes |
Servings: 4

Ingredients:

- 1 tablespoon olive oil
- 1 yellow onion, chopped
- 2 teaspoons chili powder
- 14 ounces canned chickpeas, no-salt-added, drained and rinsed
- 14 ounces canned tomatoes, no-salt-added, cubed
- 1 cup low-sodium chicken stock
- 1 tablespoon cilantro, chopped
- A pinch of black pepper

Directions:

1. Heat up a pot with the oil over medium-high heat, add the onion and chili powder, stir and cook for 5 minutes.
2. Add the chickpeas and the other ingredients, toss, cook for 15 minutes over medium heat, divide into bowls and serve for lunch.

Nutrition: 425 calories, 20.7g protein, 67.3g carbohydrates, 9.9g fat, 19.5g fiber, 0mg cholesterol, 77mg sodium, 1170mg potassium

Lemon Chicken Salad

Prep time: 10 minutes | Cooking time: 0 minutes |
Servings: 4

Ingredients:

- 1 tablespoon olive oil
- A pinch of black pepper
- 2 rotisserie chicken, skinless, boneless, shredded
- 1 pound cherry tomatoes, halved
- 1 red onion, chopped
- 4 cups baby spinach
- ¼ cup walnuts, chopped
- ½ teaspoon lemon zest, grated
- 2 tablespoons lemon juice

Directions:

1. In a salad bowl, combine the chicken with the tomato and the other ingredients, toss and serve for lunch.

Nutrition: 199 calories, 21.6g protein, 10.6g carbohydrates, 9.1g fat, 3.2g fiber, 53mg cholesterol, 292mg sodium, 527mg potassium

Asparagus Salad

Prep time: 10 minutes | Cooking time: 20 minutes |
Servings: 4

Ingredients:

- 3 garlic cloves, minced
- 2 tablespoons olive oil
- 1 red onion, chopped
- 3 carrots, sliced
- ½ cup low-sodium chicken stock
- 2 cups baby spinach
- 1 pound asparagus, trimmed
- and halved
- 1 red bell pepper, cut into strips
- 1 yellow bell pepper, cut into strips
- 1 green bell pepper, cut into strips
- A pinch of black pepper

Directions:

1. Heat up a pan with the oil over medium-high heat, add the onion and the garlic, stir and sauté for 2 minutes.
2. Add the asparagus and the other ingredients except the spinach, toss, and cook for 15 minutes.
3. Add the spinach, cook everything for 3 minutes more, divide into bowls and serve for lunch.

Nutrition: 141 calories, 4.7g protein, 17.8g carbohydrates, 7.4g fat, 5.9g fiber, 0mg cholesterol, 66mg sodium, 669mg potassium

Tomato Beef Stew

Prep time: 10 minutes | Cooking: 1 hour and 20 minutes |
Servings: 4

Ingredients:

- 1 pound beef stew meat, cubed
- 1 cup no-salt-added tomato sauce
- 1 cup low-sodium beef stock
- 1 tablespoon olive oil
- 1 yellow onion, chopped
- ¼ teaspoon hot sauce
- 1 teaspoon onion powder
- 1 teaspoon garlic powder
- 1 tablespoon cilantro, chopped

Directions:

1. Heat up a pot with the oil over medium-high heat, add the meat and the onion, stir and brown for 5 minutes.
2. Add the tomato sauce and the rest of the ingredients, bring to a simmer and cook over medium heat for 1 hour and 15 minutes.
3. Divide into bowls and serve for lunch.

Nutrition: 273 calories, 36.2g protein, 6.9g carbohydrates, 10.7g fat, 1.6g fiber, 101mg cholesterol, 440mg sodium, 715mg potassium

Chicken Stew

Prep time: 5 minutes | Cooking time: 20 minutes |
Servings: 4

Ingredients:

- 1 pound chicken thighs, boneless, skinless and cubed
- 2 endives, shredded
- 1 cup low-sodium chicken stock
- 1 tablespoon olive oil
- 1 yellow onion, chopped
- 1 carrot, sliced
- 2 garlic cloves, minced
- 8 ounces canned tomatoes, no-salt-added, chopped
- 1 tablespoon chives, chopped

Directions:

1. Heat up a pan with the oil over medium-high heat, add the onion and garlic and sauté for 5 minutes.
2. Add the chicken and brown for 5 minutes more.
3. Add the rest of the ingredients, bring to a simmer, cook for 10 minutes more, divide between plates and serve.

Nutrition: 279 calories, 34.3g protein, 7.2g carbohydrates, 12.1g fat, 2.1g fiber, 101mg cholesterol, 149mg sodium, 546mg potassium

Turkey and Carrots Soup

Prep time: 10 minutes | Cooking time: 40 minutes |
Servings: 4

Ingredients:

- 1 turkey breast, skinless, boneless, cubed
- 1 tablespoon tomato sauce, no-salt-added
- 1 tablespoon olive oil
- 2 yellow onions, chopped
- 1 quart low-sodium chicken
- stock
- 1 tablespoon oregano, chopped
- 2 carrots, sliced
- 3 garlic cloves, minced
- A pinch of black pepper

Directions:

1. Heat up a pot with the oil over medium heat, add the onions and the garlic and sauté for 5 minutes.
2. Add the meat and brown it for 5 minutes more.
3. Add the rest of the ingredients, bring to a simmer and cook over medium heat for 30 minutes.
4. Ladle the soup into bowls and serve.

Nutrition: 79 calories, 2.5g protein, 9.8g carbohydrates, 3.7g fat, 2.5g fiber, 0mg cholesterol, 215mg sodium, 219mg potassium

Cilantro Chicken and Lentils

Prep time: 10 minutes | Cooking time: 25 minutes |
Servings: 4

Ingredients:

- 1 cup canned tomatoes, no-salt-added, chopped
- Black pepper to the taste
- 1 tablespoon chipotle paste
- 1 pound chicken breast, skinless, boneless and cubed
- 2 cups canned lentils, no-salt-added, drained and rinsed
- ½ tablespoon olive oil
- 1 yellow onion, chopped
- 2 tablespoons cilantro, chopped

Directions:

1. Heat up a pan with the oil over medium heat, add the onion and chipotle paste, stir and sauté for 5 minutes.
2. Add the chicken, toss and brown for 5 minutes.
3. Add the rest of the ingredients, toss, cook everything for 15 minutes, divide into bowls and serve.

Nutrition: 515 calories, 49.8g protein, 63.5g carbohydrates, 6.4g fat, 30.4g fiber, 74mg cholesterol, 112mg sodium, 1486mg potassium

Balsamic Chicken and Cauliflower

Prep time: 5 minutes | Cooking time: 25 minutes | Servings: 4

Ingredients:

- 1 pound chicken breast, skinless, boneless and cubed
- 2 cups cauliflower florets
- 1 tablespoon olive oil
- 1 red onion, chopped
- 1 tablespoon balsamic vinegar
- ½ cup red bell pepper, chopped
- A pinch of black pepper
- 2 garlic cloves, minced
- ½ cup low-sodium chicken stock
- 1 cup canned tomatoes, no-salt-added, chopped

Directions:

1. Heat up a pan with the oil over medium-high heat, add the onion, garlic and the meat and brown for 5 minutes.
2. Add the rest of the ingredients, toss and cook over medium heat for 20 minutes.
3. Divide everything into bowls and serve for lunch.

Nutrition: 200 calories, 26g protein, 8.7g carbohydrates, 6.6g fat, 2.6g fiber, 73mg cholesterol, 94mg sodium, 755mg potassium

Tomato Soup

Prep time: 10 minutes | Cooking time: 20 minutes | Servings: 4

Ingredients:

- 3 garlic cloves, minced
- 1 yellow onion, chopped
- 3 carrots, chopped
- 1 tablespoon olive oil
- 20 ounces roasted tomatoes, no-salt-added
- 2 cup low-sodium vegetable stock
- 1 tablespoon basil, dried
- 1 cup coconut cream
- A pinch of black pepper

Directions:

1. Heat up a pot with the oil over medium heat, add the onion and the garlic and sauté for 5 minutes.
2. Add the rest of the ingredients, stir, bring to a simmer, cook for 15 minutes, blend the soup using an immersion blender, divide into bowls and serve for lunch.

Nutrition: 241 calories, 3.3g protein, 18.6g carbohydrates, 17.8g fat, 4.2g fiber, 0mg cholesterol, 253mg sodium, 355mg potassium

Pork and Potatoes

Prep time: 10 minutes | Cooking time: 30 minutes | Servings: 4

Ingredients:

- 4 pork chops, boneless
- 1 pound sweet potatoes, peeled and cut into wedges
- 1 tablespoon olive oil
- 1 cup vegetable stock, low-
- sodium
- A pinch of black pepper
- 1 teaspoon oregano, dried
- 1 teaspoon rosemary, dried
- 1 teaspoon basil, dried

Directions:

1. Heat up a pan with the oil over medium-high heat, add the pork chops and cook them for 4 minutes on each side.
2. Add the sweet potatoes and the rest of the ingredients, put the lid on and cook over medium heat for 20 minutes more stirring from time to time.
3. Divide everything between plates and serve.

Nutrition: 426 calories, 19.8g protein, 33.1g carbohydrates, 23.7g fat, 4.9g fiber, 69mg cholesterol, 164mg sodium, 1210mg potassium

Trout Soup

Prep time: 10 minutes | Cooking time: 25 minutes | Servings: 4

Ingredients:

- 1 yellow onion, chopped
- 12 cups low-sodium fish stock
- 1 pound carrots, sliced
- 1 pound trout fillets, boneless, skinless and cubed
- 1 tablespoon sweet paprika
- 1 cup tomatoes, cubed
- 1 tablespoon olive oil
- Black pepper to the taste

Directions:

1. Heat up a pot with the oil over medium-high heat, add the onion, stir and sauté for 5 minutes.
2. Add the fish, carrots and the rest of the ingredients, bring to a simmer and cook over medium heat for 20 minutes.
3. Ladle the soup into bowls and serve.

Nutrition: 31 c6alories, 32.1g protein, 16.4g carbohydrates, 13.4g fat, 4.6g fiber, 84mg cholesterol, 158mg sodium, 1075mg potassium

Garlic Turkey Stew

Prep time: 10 minutes | Cooking time: 45 minutes | Servings: 4

Ingredients:

- 1 turkey breast, skinless, boneless and cubed
- 2 fennel bulbs, sliced
- 1 tablespoon olive oil
- 2 bay leaves
- 1 yellow onion, chopped
- 1 cup canned tomatoes, no-salt-added
- 2 low-sodium beef stock
- 3 garlic cloves, chopped
- Black pepper to the taste

Directions:

1. Heat up a pan with the oil over medium heat, add the onion and the meat and brown for 5 minutes.
2. Add the fennel and the rest of the ingredients, bring to a simmer and cook over medium heat for 40 minutes, stirring from time to time.
3. Divide the stew into bowls and serve.

Nutrition: 96 c6alories, 3.4g protein, 14g carbohydrates, 3.9g fat, 4.9g fiber, 0mg cholesterol, 137mg sodium, 644mg potassium

Tomato Eggplant Soup

Prep time: 10 minutes | Cooking time: 30 minutes | Servings: 4

Ingredients:

- 2 big eggplants, roughly cubed
- 1 quart low-sodium vegetable stock
- 2 tablespoons no-salt-added
- tomato paste
- 1 red onion, chopped
- 1 tablespoon olive oil
- 1 tablespoon cilantro, chopped
- A pinch of black pepper

Directions:

1. Heat up a pot with the oil over medium heat, add the onion, stir and sauté for 5 minutes.
2. Add the eggplants and the other ingredients, bring to a simmer over medium heat, cook for 25 minutes, divide into bowls and serve.

Nutrition: 102 c6alories, 3g protein, 16.2g carbohydrates, 3.8g fat, 6.8g fiber, 0mg cholesterol, 152mg sodium, 566mg potassium

Potatoes Soup

Prep time: 10 minutes | Cooking time: 25 minutes | Servings: 4

Ingredients:

- 4 cups veggie stock
- 2 tablespoons avocado oil
- 2 sweet potatoes, peeled and cubed
- 2 yellow onions, chopped
- 2 garlic cloves, minced
- 1 cup coconut milk
- A pinch of black pepper
- ½ teaspoon basil, chopped

Directions:

1. Heat up a pot with the oil over medium heat, add the onion and the garlic, stir and sauté for 5 minutes.
2. Add the sweet potatoes and the rest of the ingredients, bring to a simmer and cook over medium heat for 20 minutes.
3. Blend the soup using an immersion blender, ladle into bowls and serve for lunch.

Nutrition: 236 calories, 3.7g protein, 23.8g carbohydrates, 15.3g fat, 5.4g fiber, 0mg cholesterol, 155mg sodium, 703mg potassium

Chili Chicken Soup

Prep time: 10 minutes | Cooking time: 30 minutes | Servings: 4

Ingredients:

- 1 quart veggie stock, low-sodium
- 1 tablespoon ginger, grated
- 1 yellow onion, chopped
- 1 tablespoon olive oil
- 1 pound chicken breast, skinless, boneless and cubed
- ½ pound white mushrooms, sliced
- 4 Thai chilies, chopped
- ¼ cup lime juice
- ¼ cup cilantro, chopped
- A pinch of black pepper

Directions:

1. Heat up a pot with the oil over medium heat, add the onion, ginger, chilies and the meat, stir and brown for 5 minutes.
2. Add the mushrooms, stir and cook for 5 minutes more.
3. Add the rest of the ingredients, bring to a simmer and cook over medium heat for 20 minutes more.
4. Ladle the soup into bowls and serve right away.

Nutrition: 197 calories, 26.5g protein, 7.4g carbohydrates, 6.6g fat, 1.6g fiber, 73mg cholesterol, 173mg sodium, 696mg potassium

Salmon Skillet

Prep time: 10 minutes | Cooking time: 20 minutes | Servings: 4

Ingredients:

- 4 salmon fillet, boneless
- 3 garlic cloves, minced
- 1 yellow onion, chopped
- Black pepper to the taste
- 2 tablespoons olive oil
- Juice of 1 lime
- 1 tablespoon lime zest, grated
- 1 tablespoon thyme, chopped

Directions:

1. Heat up a pan with the oil over medium-high heat, add the onion and garlic, stir and sauté for 5 minutes.
2. Add the fish and cook it for 3 minutes on each side.
3. Add the rest of the ingredients, cook everything for 10 minutes more, divide between plates and serve for lunch.

Nutrition: 253 calories, 35.1g protein, 4.1g carbohydrates, 11.1g fat, 1.1g fiber, 78mg cholesterol, 80mg sodium, 741mg potassium

Potato and Spinach Salad

Prep time: 10 minutes | Cooking time: 20 minutes | Servings: 4

Ingredients:

- 2 tomatoes, chopped
- 2 avocados, pitted and chopped
- 2 cups baby spinach
- 2 scallions, chopped
- 1 pound gold potatoes, boiled, peeled and cut into wedges
- 1 tablespoon olive oil
- 1 tablespoon lemon juice
- 1 yellow onion, chopped
- 2 garlic cloves, minced
- Black pepper to the taste
- 1 bunch cilantro, chopped

Directions:

1. Heat up a pan with the oil over medium-high heat, add the onion, scallions and the garlic, stir and sauté for 5 minutes.
2. Add the potatoes, toss gently and cook for 5 minutes more.
3. Add the rest of the ingredients, toss, cook over medium heat for 10 minutes more, divide into bowls and serve for lunch.

Nutrition: 342 calories, 5g protein, 33.5g carbohydrates, 23.4g fat, 11.7g fiber, 0mg cholesterol, 25mg sodium, 1262mg potassium

Ground Beef Skillet

Prep time: 10 minutes | Cooking time: 20 minutes | Servings: 4

Ingredients:

- 1 pound beef, ground
- 1 red onion, chopped
- 1 tablespoon olive oil
- 1 cup cherry tomatoes, halved
- ½ red bell pepper, chopped
- Black pepper to the taste
- 1 tablespoon chives, chopped
- 1 tablespoon rosemary, chopped
- 3 tablespoons low-sodium beef stock

Directions:

1. Heat up a pan with the oil over medium heat, add the onion and the bell pepper, stir and sauté for 5 minutes.
2. Add the meat, stir and brown it for another 5 minutes.
3. Add the rest of the ingredients, toss, cook for 10 minutes, divide into bowls and serve for lunch.

Nutrition: 265 calories, 35.3g protein, 5.5g carbohydrates, 10.7g fat, 1.4g fiber, 101mg cholesterol, 85mg sodium, 634mg potassium

Shrimp and Arugula Salad

Prep time: 5 minutes | Cooking time: 0 minutes | Servings: 4

Ingredients:

- 1 orange, peeled and cut into segments
- 1 pound shrimp, cooked, peeled and deveined
- 2 cups baby arugula
- 1 avocado, pitted, peeled and
- cubed
- 2 tablespoons olive oil
- 2 tablespoons balsamic vinegar
- Juice of ½ orange
- Salt and black pepper

Directions:

1. In a salad bowl, mix combine the shrimp with the oranges and the other ingredients, toss and serve for lunch.

Nutrition: 323 calories, 27.5g protein, 11.9g carbohydrates, 18.9g fat, 4.6g fiber, 239mg cholesterol, 283mg sodium, 561mg potassium

Coconut Broccoli Cream

Prep time: 10 minutes | Cooking time: 40 minutes | Servings: 4

Ingredients:

- 2 pounds broccoli florets
- 1 yellow onion, chopped
- 1 tablespoon olive oil
- Black pepper to the taste
- 2 garlic cloves, minced
- 3 cups low-sodium beef stock
- 1 cup coconut milk
- 2 tablespoons cilantro, chopped

Directions:

1. Heat up a pot with the oil over medium heat, add the onion and the garlic, stir and sauté for 5 minutes.
2. Add the broccoli and the other ingredients except the coconut milk, bring to a simmer and cook over medium heat for 35 minutes more.
3. Blend the soup using an immersion blender, add the coconut milk, pulse again, divide into bowls and serve.

Nutrition: 275 calories, 12.5g protein, 21g carbohydrates, 18.6g fat, 7.8g fiber, 0mg cholesterol, 648mg sodium, 918mg potassium

Cabbage and Leek Soup

Prep time: 10 minutes | Cooking time: 40 minutes | Servings: 4

Ingredients:

- 1 big green cabbage head, roughly shredded
- 1 yellow onion, chopped
- 1 tablespoon olive oil
- Black pepper to the taste
- 1 leek, chopped
- 2 cups canned tomatoes, low-sodium
- 4 cups chicken stock, low-sodium
- 1 tablespoon cilantro, chopped

Directions:

1. Heat up a pot with the oil over medium heat, add the onion and the leek, stir and cook for 5 minutes.
2. Add the cabbage and the rest of the ingredients except the cilantro, bring to a simmer and cook over medium heat for 35 minutes.
3. Ladle the soup into bowls, sprinkle the cilantro on top and serve.

Nutrition: 125 calories, 4.4g protein, 20.3g carbohydrates, 4.5g fat, 6.5g fiber, 0mg cholesterol, 806mg sodium, 613mg potassium

Dill Cauliflower Soup

Prep time: 10 minutes | Cooking time: 40 minutes | Servings: 4

Ingredients:

- 2 pounds cauliflower florets
- 1 red onion, chopped
- 1 tablespoon olive oil
- 1 cup tomato puree
- Black pepper to the taste
- 1 cup celery, chopped
- 6 cups low-sodium chicken stock
- 1 tablespoon dill, chopped

Directions:

1. Heat up a pot with the oil over medium-high heat, add the onion and the celery, stir and sauté for 5 minutes.
2. Add the cauliflower and the rest of the ingredients, bring to a simmer and cook over medium heat for 35 minutes more.
3. Divide the soup into bowls and serve.

Nutrition: 150 calories, 9.5g protein, 22.4g carbohydrates, 3.9g fat, 7.6g fiber, 0mg cholesterol, 211mg sodium, 1028mg potassium

Parsley Pork Soup

Prep time: 10 minutes | Cooking time: 40 minutes | Servings: 4

Ingredients:

- 1 pound pork stew meat, cubed
- Black pepper to the taste
- 5 leeks, chopped
- 1 yellow onion, chopped
- 2 tablespoons olive oil
- 1 tablespoon parsley, chopped
- 6 cups low-sodium beef stock

Directions:

1. Heat up a pot with the oil over medium-high heat, add the onion and the leeks, stir and sauté for 5 minutes.
2. Add the meat, stir and brown for 5 minutes more.
3. Add the rest of the ingredients, bring to a simmer and cook over medium heat for 30 minutes.
4. Ladle the soup into bowls and serve.

Nutrition: 402 calories, 41.2g protein, 18.4g carbohydrates, 18.3g fat, 2.6g fiber, 98mg cholesterol, 766mg sodium, 671mg potassium

Minty Shrimp and Olives Salad

Prep time: 5 minutes | Cooking time: 20 minutes | Servings: 4

Ingredients:

- 1/3 cup low-sodium vegetable stock
- 2 tablespoons olive oil
- 2 cups broccoli florets
- 1 pound shrimp, peeled and deveined
- Black pepper to the taste
- 1 yellow onion, chopped
- 4 cherry tomatoes, halved
- 2 garlic cloves, minced
- Juice of ½ lemon
- ½ cup kalamata olives, pitted and cut into halves
- 1 tablespoon mint, chopped

Directions:

1. Heat up a pan with the oil over medium-high heat, add the onion and the garlic, stir and sauté for 3 minutes.
2. Add the shrimp, toss and cook for 2 minutes more.
3. Add the broccoli and the other ingredients, toss, cook everything for 10 minutes, divide into bowls and serve for lunch.

Nutrition: 267 calories, 28.9g protein, 13.8g carbohydrates, 11.2g fat, 3.9g fiber, 239mg cholesterol, 452mg sodium, 682mg potassium

Shrimp Soup

Prep time: 10 minutes | Cooking time: 20 minutes | Servings: 4

Ingredients:

- 1 quart low-sodium chicken stock
- ½ pound shrimp, peeled and deveined
- ½ pound cod fillets, boneless, skinless and cubed
- 2 tablespoons olive oil
- 2 teaspoons chili powder
- 1 teaspoon sweet paprika
- 2 shallots, chopped
- A pinch of black pepper
- 1 tablespoon dill, chopped

Directions:

1. Heat up a pot with the oil over medium heat, add the shallots stir and sauté for 5 minutes.
2. Add the shrimp and the cod, and cook for 5 minutes more.
3. Add the rest of the ingredients, bring to a simmer and cook over medium heat for 10 minutes.
4. Divide the soup into bowls and serve.

Nutrition: 190 calories, 24.8g protein, 3.2g carbohydrates, 8.8g fat, 0.8g fiber, 147mg cholesterol, 358mg sodium, 176mg potassium

Balsamic Shrimp

Prep time: 10 minutes | Cooking time: 10 minutes | Servings: 4

Ingredients:

- 2 pounds shrimp, peeled and deveined
- 1 cup cherry tomatoes, halved
- 1 tablespoon olive oil
- 4 green onion, chopped
- 1 tablespoon balsamic vinegar
- 1 tablespoon chives, chopped

Directions:

1. Heat up a pan with the oil over medium heat, add the onion, and the cherry tomatoes, stir and sauté for 4 minutes.
2. Add the shrimp and the other ingredients, cook for 6 minutes more, divide between plates and serve.

Nutrition: 313 calories, 52.4g protein, 6.4g carbohydrates, 7.5g fat, 1g fiber, 478mg cholesterol, 558mg sodium, 537mg potassium

Spinach and Tomato Stew

Prep time: 10 minutes | Cooking time: 15 minutes | Servings: 4

Ingredients:

- 1 tablespoons olive oil
- 1 teaspoon ginger, grated
- 2 garlic cloves, minced
- 1 yellow onion, chopped
- 2 tomatoes, chopped
- 1 cup canned tomatoes, no-
- salt-added
- 1 teaspoon cumin, ground
- A pinch of black pepper
- 1 cup low-sodium vegetable stock
- 2 pounds spinach leaves

Directions:

1. Heat up a pot with the oil over medium heat, add the ginger, garlic and the onion, stir and sauté for 5 minutes.
2. Add the tomatoes, canned tomatoes and the other ingredients, toss gently, bring to a simmer and cook for 10 minutes more.
3. Divide the stew into bowls and serve.

Nutrition: 120 calories, 8.1g protein, 14.5g carbohydrates, 4.7g fat, 6.5g fiber, 0mg cholesterol, 207mg sodium, 1473mg potassium

Cilantro Peppers and Cauliflower Mix

Prep time: 10 minutes | Cooking time: 25 minutes | Servings: 4

Ingredients:

- 1 red onion, chopped
- 1 tablespoon olive oil
- 2 garlic cloves, minced
- 1 red bell pepper, chopped
- 1 green bell pepper, chopped
- 1 tablespoon lime juice
- 1 pound cauliflower florets
- 14 ounces canned tomatoes, chopped
- 2 teaspoons curry powder
- A pinch of black pepper
- 2 cups coconut cream
- 1 tablespoon cilantro, chopped

Directions:

1. Heat up a pot with the oil over medium heat, add the onion and the garlic, stir and cook for 5 minutes.
2. Add the bell peppers and the other ingredients, bring everything to a simmer and cook over medium heat for 20 minutes.
3. Divide everything into bowls and serve.

Nutrition: 384 calories, 7g protein, 23.8g carbohydrates, 32.7g fat, 8.5g fiber, 0mg cholesterol, 60mg sodium, 1065mg potassium

Rosemary Carrot Stew

Prep time: 10 minutes | Cooking time: 30 minutes | Servings: 4

Ingredients:

- 1 yellow onion, chopped
- 2 tablespoons olive oil
- 2 garlic cloves, minced
- 4 zucchinis, sliced
- 2 carrots, sliced
- 1 teaspoon sweet paprika
- ¼ teaspoon chili powder
- A pinch of black pepper
- ½ cup tomatoes, chopped
- 2 cups low-sodium vegetable stock
- 1 tablespoon chives, chopped
- 1 tablespoon rosemary, chopped

Directions:

1. Heat up a pot with the oil over medium heat, add the onion and the garlic, stir and sauté for 5 minutes.
2. Add the zucchinis, carrots and the other ingredients, bring to a simmer and cook for 25 minutes more.
3. Divide the stew in to bowls and serve right away for lunch.

Nutrition: 134 calories, 4.4g protein, 15g carbohydrates, 7.7g fat, 4.4g fiber, 0mg cholesterol, 80mg sodium, 737mg potassium

Cabbage Stew

Prep time: 10 minutes | Cooking time: 25 minutes | Servings: 4

Ingredients:

- 2 tablespoons olive oil
- 1 red cabbage head, shredded
- 1 red onion, chopped
- 1 pound green beans, trimmed and halved
- 2 garlic cloves, minced
- 7 ounces canned tomatoes, no-salt-added chopped
- 2 cups low-sodium vegetable stock
- A pinch of black pepper
- 1 tablespoon dill, chopped

Directions:

1. Heat up a pot with the oil, over medium heat, add the onion and the garlic, stir and sauté for 5 minutes.
2. Add the cabbage and the other ingredients, stir, cover and simmer over medium heat for 20 minutes.
3. Divide into bowls and serve for lunch.

Nutrition: 171 calories, 6.3g protein, 24.4g carbohydrates, 7.5g fat, 9.7g fiber, 0mg cholesterol, 79mg sodium, 730mg potassium

Mushroom Soup

Prep time: 5 minutes | Cooking time: 30 minutes | Servings: 4

Ingredients:

- 1 yellow onion, chopped
- 1 tablespoon olive oil
- 1 red chili pepper, chopped
- 1 teaspoon chili powder
- ½ teaspoon hot paprika
- 4 garlic cloves, minced
- 1 pound white mushrooms,
- sliced
- 6 cups low-sodium vegetable stock
- 1 cup tomatoes, chopped
- ½ tablespoon parsley, chopped

Directions:

1. Heat up a pot with the oil, over medium heat, add the onion, chili pepper, hot paprika, chili powder and the garlic, stir and sauté for 5 minutes.
2. Add the mushrooms, stir and cook for 5 minutes more.
3. Add the rest of the ingredients, bring to a simmer and cook over medium heat for 20 minutes.
4. Divide the soup into bowls and serve.

Nutrition: 103 calories, 7.5g protein, 11g carbohydrates, 4.1g fat, 2.6g fiber, 0mg cholesterol, 122mg sodium, 537mg potassium

Lime Turkey Stew

Prep time: 5 minutes | Cooking time: 30 minutes |
Servings: 4

Ingredients:

- 2 tablespoons olive oil
- 1 turkey breast, skinless, boneless and cubed
- 1 cup low-sodium beef stock
- 1 cup tomato puree
- ¼ teaspoon lime zest, grated
- 1 yellow onion, chopped
- 1 tablespoon sweet paprika
- 1 tablespoon cilantro, chopped
- 2 tablespoons lime juice
- ¼ teaspoon ginger, grated

Directions:

1. Heat up a pot with the oil over medium-high heat, add the onion and the meat and brown for 5 minutes.
2. Add the stock and the other ingredients, bring to a simmer and cook over medium heat for 25 minutes.
3. Divide the mix into bowls and serve for lunch.

Nutrition: 147 calories, 9.5g protein, 11.1g carbohydrates, 8.1g fat, 2.7g fiber, 18mg cholesterol, 491mg sodium, 488mg potassium

Beef and Beans Salad

Prep time: 10 minutes | Cooking time: 30 minutes |
Servings: 4

Ingredients:

- 1 pound beef stew meat, cut into strips
- 1 tablespoon sage, chopped
- 1 tablespoon olive oil
- A pinch of black pepper
- ½ teaspoon cumin, ground
- 2 cups cherry tomatoes, cubed
- 1 avocado, peeled, pitted and cubed
- 1 cup canned black beans, no-salt-added, drained and rinsed
- ½ cup green onions, chopped
- 2 tablespoons lime juice
- 2 tablespoons balsamic vinegar
- 2 tablespoons cilantro, chopped

Directions:

1. Heat up a pan with the oil over medium-high heat, add the meat and brown for 5 minutes.
2. Add the sage, black pepper and the cumin, toss and cook for 5 minutes more.
3. Add the rest of the ingredients, toss, reduce heat to medium and cook the mix for 20 minutes.
4. Divide the salad into bowls and serve for lunch.

Nutrition: 533 calories, 47g protein, 39.5g carbohydrates, 21.4g fat, 12.4g fiber, 101mg cholesterol, 88mg sodium, 1686mg potassium

Squash and Peppers Stew

Prep time: 10 minutes | Cooking time: 20 minutes |
Servings: 4

Ingredients:

- 1 pound squash, peeled and roughly cubed
- 1 cup low-sodium chicken stock
- 1 cup canned tomatoes, no-salt-added, crushed
- 1 tablespoon olive oil
- 1 red onion, chopped
- 2 orange sweet peppers, chopped
- ½ cup quinoa
- ½ tablespoon chives, chopped

Directions:

1. Heat up a pot with the oil over medium heat, add the onion, stir and sauté for 2 minutes.
2. Add the squash and the other ingredients, bring to a simmer, and cook for 15 minutes.
3. Stir the stew, divide into bowls and serve for lunch.

Nutrition: 156 calories, 5.8g protein, 23.7g carbohydrates, 5.2g fat, 4.3g fiber, 0mg cholesterol, 52mg sodium, 601mg potassium

Beef and Cabbage Stew

Prep time: 10 minutes | Cooking time: 20 minutes |
Servings: 4

Ingredients:

- 1 green cabbage head, shredded
- ¼ cup low-sodium beef stock
- 2 tomatoes, cubed
- 2 yellow onions, chopped
- ¾ cup red bell peppers, chopped
- 1 tablespoon olive oil
- 1 pound beef, ground
- ¼ cup cilantro, chopped
- ¼ cup green onions, chopped
- ¼ teaspoon red pepper, crushed

Directions:

1. Heat up a pan with the oil over medium heat, add the meat and the onions, stir and brown for 5 minutes.
2. Add the cabbage and the other ingredients, toss, cook for 15 minutes, divide into bowls and serve for lunch.

Nutrition: 329 calories, 38.4g protein, 20.1g carbohydrates, 11g fat, 6.9g fiber, 101mg cholesterol, 142mg sodium, 1081mg potassium

Pork Stew

Prep time: 5 minutes | Cooking time: 8 hours and 10 minutes |
Servings: 4

Ingredients:

- 1 pound pork stew meat, cubed
- 1 tablespoon olive oil
- ½ pound green beans, trimmed and halved
- 2 yellow onions, chopped
- 2 garlic cloves, minced
- 2 cups low-sodium beef stock
- 8 ounces tomato sauce
- A pinch of black pepper
- A pinch of allspice, ground
- 1 tablespoon rosemary, chopped

Directions:

1. Heat up a pan with the oil over medium-high heat, add the meat, garlic and onion, stir and brown for 10 minutes.
2. Transfer this to a slow cooker, add the other ingredients as well, put the lid on and cook on Low for 8 hours.
3. Divide the stew into bowls and serve.

Nutrition: 357 calories, 38g protein, 16.9g carbohydrates, 14.8g fat, 6.2g fiber, 98mg cholesterol, 587mg sodium, 1139mg potassium

Turkey Tortillas

Prep time: 10 minutes | Cooking time: 3 minutes |
Servings: 2

Ingredients:

- 2 whole wheat tortillas
- 2 teaspoons mustard
- 2 teaspoons mayonnaise
- 1 turkey breast, skinless, boneless and cut into strips
- 1 tablespoons olive oil
- 1 red onion, chopped
- 1 red bell peppers, cut into strips
- 1 green bell pepper, cut into strips
- ¼ cup low-fat mozzarella, shredded

Directions:

1. Heat up a pan with the oil over medium heat, add the meat and the onion and brown for 5 minutes
2. Add the peppers, toss and cook for 10 minutes more.
3. Arrange the tortillas on a working surface, divide the turkey mix on each, also divide the mayo, mustard and the cheese, wrap and serve for lunch.

Nutrition: 303 calories, 15.9g protein, 37.8g carbohydrates, 11.1g fat, 7g fiber, 15mg cholesterol, 620mg sodium, 394mg potassium

Cheddar Cauliflower Bowls

Prep time: 10 minutes | Cooking time: 10 minutes | Servings: 4

Ingredients:

- 1 tablespoon avocado oil
- 1 cup red bell peppers, cubed
- 1 pound cauliflower florets
- 1 red onion, chopped
- 3 tablespoons salsa
- 2 tablespoons low-fat cheddar, shredded
- 2 tablespoons coconut cream

Directions:

1. Heat up a pan with the oil over medium-high heat, add the onion and peppers, and sauté for 2 minutes.
2. Add the cauliflower and the other ingredients, toss, cook for 8 minutes more, divide into bowls and serve.

Nutrition: 79 calories, 4.4g protein, 12.5g carbohydrates, 2.5g fat, 4.3g fiber, 1mg cholesterol, 134mg sodium, 506mg potassium

Oregano Pork

Prep time: 10 minutes | Cooking time: 30 minutes | Servings: 4

Ingredients:

- 2 pounds pork stew meat, cubed
- 2 tablespoons chili paste
- 1 yellow onion, chopped
- 2 garlic cloves, minced
- 1 tablespoon olive oil
- 2 cups low-sodium beef stock
- 1 tablespoon oregano, chopped

Directions:

1. Heat up a pot with the oil, over medium-high heat, add the onion and the garlic, stir and sauté for 5 minutes.
2. Add the meat and brown it for 5 minutes more.
3. Add the rest of the ingredients, bring to a simmer and cook over medium heat for 20 minutes more.
4. Divide the mix into bowls and serve.

Nutrition: 565 calories, 69.4g protein, 7.8g carbohydrates, 26.8g fat, 1.1g fiber, 198mg cholesterol, 475mg sodium, 916mg potassium

Mushroom Salad

Prep time: 10 minutes | Cooking time: 20 minutes | Servings: 4

Ingredients:

- 10 ounces smoked salmon, low-sodium, boneless, skinless and cubed
- 2 green onions, chopped
- 2 red chili peppers, chopped
- 1 tablespoon olive oil
- ½ teaspoon oregano, dried
- ½ teaspoon smoked paprika
- A pinch of black pepper
- 8 ounces white mushrooms, sliced
- 1 tablespoon lemon juice
- 1 cup black olives, pitted and halved
- 1 tablespoon parsley, chopped

Directions:

1. Heat up a pan with the oil over medium heat, add the onions and chili peppers, stir and cook for 4 minutes.
2. Add the mushrooms, stir and sauté them for 5 minutes.
3. Add the salmon and the other ingredients, toss, cook everything for 10 minutes more, divide into bowls and serve for lunch.

Nutrition: 95 calories, 3.7g protein, 5.1g carbohydrates, 7.7g fat, 2.2g fiber, 2mg cholesterol, 355mg sodium, 240mg potassium

Beef and Scallions Mix

Prep time: 10 minutes | Cooking time: 30 minutes | Servings: 4

Ingredients:

- 1 and ¼ cups low-sodium beef stock
- 1 yellow onion, chopped
- 1 tablespoon olive oil
- 2 cups peas
- 1 pound beef stew meat, cubed
- 1 cup canned tomatoes, no-salt-added and chopped
- 1 cup scallions, chopped
- ¼ cup parsley, chopped
- Black pepper to the taste

Directions:

1. Heat up a pot with the oil over medium-high heat, add the onion and the meat and brown for 5 minutes.
2. Add the peas and the other ingredients, stir, bring to a simmer and cook over medium heat for 25 minutes more.
3. Divide the mix into bowls and serve for lunch.

Nutrition: 331 calories, 41.2g protein, 16.9g carbohydrates, 11.1g fat, 5.6g fiber, 101mg cholesterol, 131mg sodium, 870mg potassium

Carrot Soup

Prep time: 5 minutes | Cooking time: 25 minutes | Servings: 4

Ingredients:

- 2 tablespoons olive oil
- 1 yellow onion, chopped
- 1 pound carrots, peeled and chopped
- 1 teaspoon turmeric powder
- 4 celery stalks, chopped
- 5 cups low-sodium chicken stock
- A pinch of black pepper
- 1 tablespoon cilantro, chopped

Directions:

1. Heat up a pot with the oil over medium heat, add the onion, stir and sauté for 2 minutes.
2. Add the carrots and the other ingredients, bring to a simmer and cook over medium heat for 20 minutes.
3. Blend the soup using an immersion blender, ladle into bowls and serve.

Nutrition: 128 calories, 2.7g protein, 14.6g carbohydrates, 7.1g fat, 3.8g fiber, 0mg cholesterol, 262mg sodium, 462mg potassium

Beef Soup

Prep time: 10 minutes | Cooking time: 1 hour and 40 minutes | Servings: 4

Ingredients:

- 1 cup canned black beans, no-salt-added and drained
- 7 cups low-sodium beef stock
- 1 green bell pepper, chopped
- 1 tablespoon olive oil
- 1 pound beef stew meat, cubed
- 1 yellow onion, chopped
- 3 garlic cloves, minced
- 1 chili pepper, chopped
- 1 potato, cubed
- A pinch of black pepper
- 1 tablespoon cilantro, chopped

Directions:

1. Heat up a pot with the oil over medium heat, add the onion, garlic and the meat, and brown for 5 minutes.
2. Add the beans and the rest of the ingredients except the cilantro, bring to a simmer and cook over medium heat for 1 hour and 35 minutes.
3. Add the cilantro, ladle the soup into bowls and serve.

Nutrition: 489 calories, 51.8g protein, 45.1g carbohydrates, 11.4g fat, 9.4g fiber, 101mg cholesterol, 327mg sodium, 1464mg potassium

Chicken and Sauce

Prep time: 5 minutes | Cooking time: 20 minutes | Servings: 4

Ingredients:

- 1 tablespoon olive oil
- 1 yellow onion, chopped
- A pinch of black pepper
- 1 pound chicken breasts, skinless, boneless and cubed
- 4 garlic cloves, minced
- 1 cup low-sodium chicken stock
- 2 cups coconut cream
- 1 tablespoon basil, chopped
- 1 tablespoon chives, chopped

Directions:

1. Heat up a pan with the oil over medium-high heat, add the garlic, onion and the meat, toss and brown for 5 minutes.
2. Add the stock and the rest of the ingredients, bring to a simmer and cook over medium heat for 15 minutes.
3. Divide the mix between plates and serve.

Nutrition: 539 calories, 36.3g protein, 10.3g carbohydrates, 40.6g fat, 3.3g fiber, 101mg cholesterol, 151mg sodium, 648mg potassium

Turmeric Chicken Stew

Prep time: 5 minutes | Cooking time: 20 minutes | Servings: 4

Ingredients:

- 1 pound chicken breasts, skinless, boneless and cubed
- 2 shallots, chopped
- 1 tablespoon olive oil
- 1 eggplant, cubed
- 1 cup canned tomatoes, no-
- salt-added and crushed
- 1 tablespoon lime juice
- A pinch of black pepper
- ¼ teaspoon ginger, ground
- 1 tablespoon cilantro, chopped

Directions:

1. Heat up a pot with the oil over medium heat, add the shallots and the chicken and brown for 5 minutes.
2. Add the rest of the ingredients, bring to a simmer and cook over medium heat for 15 minutes more.
3. Divide into bowls and serve for lunch.

Nutrition: 286 calories, 34.5g protein, 9.4g carbohydrates, 12.2g fat, 4.6g fiber, 101mg cholesterol, 103mg sodium, 664mg potassium

Chickpeas Pan

Prep time: 10 minutes | Cooking time: 30 minutes | Servings: 4

Ingredients:

- 2 tablespoons olive oil
- 1 cup canned chickpeas, no-salt-added, drained and rinsed
- 1 pound sweet potatoes, peeled and cut into wedges
- 4 garlic cloves, minced
- 2 shallots, chopped
- 1 cup canned tomatoes, no-
- salt-added and chopped
- 1 teaspoon coriander, ground
- 2 tomatoes, chopped
- 1 cup low-sodium vegetable stock
- A pinch of black pepper
- 1 tablespoon lemon juice
- 1 tablespoon cilantro, chopped

Directions:

1. Heat up a pot with the oil over medium heat, add the shallots and the garlic, stir and sauté for 5 minutes.
2. Add the chickpeas, potatoes and the other ingredients, bring to a simmer and cook over medium heat for 25 minutes.
3. Divide everything into bowls and serve for lunch.

Nutrition: 450 calories, 15g protein, 78.5g carbohydrates, 10.7g fat, 16.7g fiber, 0mg cholesterol, 126mg sodium, 2169mg potassium

Parsley Green Beans Soup

Prep time: 5 minutes | Cooking time: 25 minutes | Servings: 4

Ingredients:

- 2 teaspoons olive oil
- 2 garlic cloves, minced
- 1 pound green beans, trimmed and halved
- 1 yellow onion, chopped
- 2 tomatoes, cubed
- 1 teaspoon sweet paprika
- 1 quart low-sodium chicken stock
- 2 tablespoons parsley, chopped

Directions:

1. Heat up a pot with the oil over medium-high heat, add the garlic and the onion, stir and sauté for 5 minutes.
2. Add the green beans and the other ingredients except the parsley, stir, bring to a simmer and cook for 20 minutes.
3. Add the parsley, stir, divide the soup into bowls and serve.

Nutrition: 87 calories, 4.1g protein, 14g carbohydrates, 2.7g fat, 5.5g fiber, 0mg cholesterol, 147mg sodium, 452mg potassium

Beef Skillet

Prep time: 5 minutes | Cooking time: 20 minutes | Servings: 4

Ingredients:

- 1 pound beef, ground
- ½ cup yellow onion, chopped
- 1 tablespoon olive oil
- 1 cup zucchini, cubed
- 2 garlic cloves, minced
- 14 ounces canned tomatoes,
- no-salt-added, chopped
- 1 teaspoon Italian seasoning
- ¼ cup low-fat parmesan, shredded
- 1 tablespoon chives, chopped
- 1 tablespoon cilantro, chopped

Directions:

1. Heat up a pan with the oil over medium heat, add the garlic, onion and the beef and brown for 5 minutes.
2. Add the rest of the ingredients, toss, cook for 15 minutes more, divide into bowls and serve for lunch.

Nutrition: 300 calories, 37.2g protein, 9.3g carbohydrates, 12.5g fat, 1.9g fiber, 108mg cholesterol, 184mg sodium, 797mg potassium

Thyme Beef and Tomatoes

Prep time: 10 minutes | Cooking time: 25 minutes | Servings: 4

Ingredients:

- ½ pound beef, ground
- 3 tablespoons olive oil
- 1 and ¾ pounds red potatoes, peeled and roughly cubed
- 1 yellow onion, chopped
- 2 teaspoons thyme, dried
- 1 cup canned tomatoes, no-salt-added, and chopped
- A pinch of black pepper

Directions:

1. Heat up a pan with the oil over medium-high heat, add the onion and the beef, stir and brown for 5 minutes.
2. Add the potatoes and the rest of the ingredients, toss, bring to a simmer, cook for 20 minutes more, divide into bowls and serve for lunch.

Nutrition: 355 calories, 21.7g protein, 36.2g carbohydrates, 14.5g fat, 4.7g fiber, 51mg cholesterol, 53mg sodium, 1282mg potassium

Eggplant and Tomato Stew

Prep time: 5 minutes | Cooking: 20 minutes | Servings: 4

Ingredients:

- 1 pound eggplants, roughly cubed
- 2 garlic cloves, minced
- 2 tablespoons olive oil
- 1 yellow onion, chopped
- 1 teaspoon sweet paprika
- ½ cup cilantro, chopped
- 14 ounces low-sodium canned tomatoes, chopped
- 1 tablespoon cilantro, chopped

Directions:

1. Heat up a pan with the oil over medium-high heat, add the onion and the garlic and sauté for 2 minutes.
2. Add the eggplant and the other ingredients except the cilantro, bring to a simmer and cook for 18 minutes.
3. Divide into bowls and serve with the cilantro sprinkled on top.

Nutrition: 153 calories, 2.9g protein, 18.4g carbohydrates, 8.6g fat, 6.2g fiber, 3mg cholesterol, 35mg sodium, 329mg potassium

Chicken and Tomato Mix

Prep time: 10 minutes | Cooking time: 20 minutes | Servings: 4

Ingredients:

- 1 tablespoon olive oil
- 1 pound chicken breast, skinless, boneless and cubed
- ½ pound kale, torn
- 2 cherry tomatoes, halved
- 1 yellow onion, chopped
- ½ cup low-sodium chicken stock
- ¼ cup low-fat mozzarella, shredded

Directions:

1. Heat up a pan with the oil over medium heat, add the chicken and the onion and brown for 5 minutes.
2. Add the kale and the other ingredients except the mozzarella, toss, and cook for 12 minutes more.
3. Sprinkle the cheese on top, cook the mix for 2-3 minutes, divide between plates and serve for lunch.

Nutrition: 230 calories, 28.2g protein, 11.1g carbohydrates, 7.7g fat, 2.2g fiber, 78mg cholesterol, 158mg sodium, 884mg potassium

Turmeric Chicken Mix

Prep time: 10 minutes | Cooking time: 30 minutes | Servings: 4

Ingredients:

- 1 tablespoon olive oil
- 1 pound chicken breast, skinless, boneless and cubed
- 1 shallot, chopped
- 1 tablespoon ginger, grated
- 2 garlic cloves, minced
- 1 teaspoon cardamom, ground
- ½ teaspoon turmeric powder
- 1 teaspoon lime juice
- 1 cup low-sodium chicken stock
- 1 tablespoon cilantro, chopped

Directions:

1. Heat up a pot with the oil over medium-high heat, add the shallot, ginger, garlic, cardamom and the turmeric, stir and sauté for 5 minutes.
2. Add the meat and brown it for 5 minutes.
3. Add the rest of the ingredients, bring everything to a simmer and cook for 20 minutes.
4. Divide the mix into bowls and serve.

Nutrition: 176 calories, 25g protein, 3.1g carbohydrates, 6.5g fat, 0.4g fiber, 73mg cholesterol, 77mg sodium, 474mg potassium

Zucchini Soup

Prep time: 10 minutes | Cooking time: 20 minutes | Servings: 4

Ingredients:

- 1 tablespoon olive oil
- 1 yellow onion, chopped
- 1 teaspoon ginger, grated
- 1 pound zucchinis, chopped
- 32 ounces low-sodium chicken stock
- 1 cup coconut cream
- 1 tablespoon dill, chopped

Directions:

1. Heat up a pot with the oil over medium heat, add the onion and ginger, stir and cook for 5 minutes.
2. Add the zucchinis and the other ingredients, bring to a simmer and cook over medium heat for 15 minutes.
3. Blend using an immersion blender, divide into bowls and serve.

Nutrition: 205 calories, 4.2g protein, 10.5g carbohydrates, 18.1g fat, 3.3g fiber, 0mg cholesterol, 151mg sodium, 527mg potassium

Rosemary Pork Chops

Prep time: 5 minutes | Cooking: 8 hours and 10 minutes | Servings: 4

Ingredients:

- 4 pork chops
- 1 tablespoon olive oil
- 2 shallots, chopped
- 1 pound white mushrooms, sliced
- ½ cup low-sodium beef stock
- 1 tablespoon rosemary, chopped
- ¼ teaspoon garlic powder
- 1 teaspoon sweet paprika

Directions:

1. Heat up a pan with the oil over medium-high heat, add the pork chops and the shallots, toss, brown for 10 minutes and transfer to a slow cooker.
2. Add the rest of the ingredients, put the lid on and cook on Low for 8 hours.
3. Divide the pork chops and mushrooms between plates and serve for lunch.

Nutrition: 324 calories, 22.2g protein, 6.4g carbohydrates, 23.9g fat, 1.7g fiber, 69mg cholesterol, 82mg sodium, 692mg potassium

Chipotle Lentils

Prep time: 10 minutes | Cooking time: 35 minutes | Servings: 6

Ingredients:

- 1 green bell pepper, chopped
- 1 tablespoon olive oil
- 2 spring onions, chopped
- 2 garlic cloves, minced
- 24 ounces canned lentils, no-salt-added, drained and rinsed
- 2 cups veggie stock
- 2 tablespoons chili powder, mild
- ½ teaspoon chipotle powder
- 30 ounces canned tomatoes, no-salt-added, chopped
- A pinch of black pepper

Directions:

1. Heat up a pot with the oil over medium heat, add the onions and the garlic, stir and sauté for 5 minutes.
2. Add the bell pepper, lentils and the other ingredients, bring to a simmer and cook over medium heat for 30 minutes.
3. Divide the chili into bowls and serve for lunch.

Nutrition: 476 calories, 32.8g protein, 77.5g carbohydrates, 4.8g fat, 37.6g fiber, 0mg cholesterol, 295mg sodium, 1591mg potassium

Salmon Salad

Prep time: 5 minutes | Cooking time: 0 minutes | Servings: 4

Ingredients:

- 1 cup canned salmon, drained and flaked
- 1 tablespoon lime zest, grated
- 1 tablespoon lime juice
- 3 tablespoons fat-free yogurt
- 1 cup baby spinach
- 1 teaspoon capers, drained and chopped
- 1 red onion, chopped
- A pinch of black pepper
- 1 tablespoon chives, chopped

Directions:

1. In a bowl, combine the salmon with lime zest, lime juice and the other ingredients, toss and serve cold for lunch.

Nutrition: 67 calories, 9.2g protein, 4.1g carbohydrates, 1.5g fat, 1g fiber, 21mg cholesterol, 64mg sodium, 245mg potassium

Shrimp Salad

Prep time: 5 minutes | Cooking time: 10 minutes | Servings: 4

Ingredients:

- 1 tablespoon olive oil
- 1 pound shrimp, peeled and deveined
- 1 tablespoon basil pesto
- 1 cup baby arugula
- 1 yellow onion, chopped
- 1 cucumber, sliced
- 1 cup carrots, shredded
- 1 tablespoon cilantro, chopped

Directions:

1. Heat up a pan with the oil over medium heat, add the onion and carrots, stir and cook for 3 minutes.
2. Add the shrimp and the other ingredients, toss, cook for 7 minutes more, divide into bowls and serve.

Nutrition: 200 calories, 27g protein, 9.9g carbohydrates, 5.6g fat, 1.8g fiber, 239mg cholesterol, 300mg sodium, 452mg potassium

Shrimp and Walnuts Salad

Prep time: 5 minutes | Cooking time: 0 minutes | Servings: 4

Ingredients:

- 2 tablespoons low-fat mayonnaise
- 2 teaspoons chili powder
- A pinch of black pepper
- 1 pound shrimp, cooked, peeled and deveined
- 1 cup red grapes, halved
- ½ cup scallions, chopped
- ¼ cup walnuts, chopped
- 1 tablespoon cilantro, chopped

Directions:

1. In a salad bowl, combine shrimp with the chili powder and the other ingredients, toss and serve for lunch.

Nutrition: 250 calories, 28.7g protein, 12.9g carbohydrates, 9.2g fat, 1.8g fiber, 241mg cholesterol, 344mg sodium, 369mg potassium

Avocado Salad

Prep time: 5 minutes | Cooking time: 0 minutes | Servings: 4

Ingredients:

- 2 tablespoons balsamic vinegar
- 2 tablespoons mint, chopped
- A pinch of black pepper
- 1 avocado, peeled, pitted and sliced
- 4 cups baby spinach
- 1 cup black olives, pitted and halved
- 1 cucumber, sliced
- 1 tablespoon olive oil

Directions:

1. In a salad bowl, combine the avocado with the spinach and the other ingredients, toss and serve for lunch.

Nutrition: 192 calories, 2.7g protein, 10.6g carbohydrates, 17.1g fat, 5.7g fiber, 0mg cholesterol, 322mg sodium, 543mg potassium

Balsamic Shrimp Salad

Prep time: 10 minutes | Cooking time: 8 minutes | Servings: 4

Ingredients:

- 1 tablespoon olive oil
- 1 red onion, sliced
- 1 pound shrimp, peeled and deveined
- 2 cups baby arugula
- 1 tablespoon balsamic vinegar
- 1 tablespoon lemon juice
- 1 tablespoon coriander, chopped
- A pinch of black pepper

Directions:

1. Heat up a pan with the oil over medium heat, add the onion, stir and sauté for 2 minutes.
2. Add the shrimp and the other ingredients, toss, cook for 6 minutes, divide into bowls and serve for lunch.

Nutrition: 180 calories, 26.4g protein, 4.8g carbohydrates, 5.6g fat, 0.8g fiber, 239mg cholesterol, 282mg sodium, 278mg potassium

Salsa Seafood Bowls

Prep time: 10 minutes | Cooking time: 13 minutes | Servings: 4

Ingredients:

- ½ pound smoked salmon, boneless, skinless and cubed
- ½ pound shrimp, peeled and deveined
- 1 tablespoon olive oil
- 1 red onion, chopped
- ¼ cup tomatoes, cubed
- ½ cup mild salsa
- 2 tablespoons cilantro, chopped

Directions:

1. Heat up a pan with the oil over medium-high heat, add the salmon, toss and cook for 5 minutes.
2. Add the onion, shrimp and the other ingredients, cook for 7 minutes more, divide into bowls and serve.

Nutrition: 185 calories, 24g protein, 5.3g carbohydrates, 7.1g fat, 0.8g fiber, 132mg cholesterol, 1453mg sodium, 265mg potassium

Salmon and Olives Salad

Prep time: 10 minutes | Cooking time: 0 minutes | Servings: 4

Ingredients:

- 6 ounces canned salmon, drained and cubed
- 1 tablespoon balsamic vinegar
- 1 tablespoon olive oil
- 2 shallots, chopped
- ½ cup black olives, pitted and halved
- 2 cups baby arugula
- A pinch of black pepper

Directions:

1. In a bowl, combine the salmon with the shallots and the other ingredients, toss and keep in the fridge for 10 minutes before serving for lunch.

Nutrition: 116 calories, 8.9g protein, 3.1g carbohydrates, 8g fat, 0.7g fiber, 19mg cholesterol, 169mg sodium, 238mg potassium

Side Dishes

Radish and Olives Salad

Prep time: 5 minutes | Cooking time: 0 minutes |
Servings: 4

Ingredients:

- 2 green onions, sliced
- 1 pound radishes, cubed
- 2 tablespoons balsamic vinegar
- 2 tablespoon olive oil
- 1 teaspoon chili powder
- 1 cup black olives, pitted and halved
- A pinch of black pepper

Directions:

1. In a large salad bowl, combine radishes with the onions and the other ingredients, toss and serve as a side dish.

Nutrition: 123 calories, 1.3g protein, 6.9g carbohydrates, 10.8g fat, 3.3g fiber, 0mg cholesterol, 345mg sodium, 306mg potassium

Spinach and Endives Salad

Prep time: 5 minutes | Cooking time: 0 minutes |
Servings: 4

Ingredients:

- 2 endives, roughly shredded
- 1 tablespoon dill, chopped
- ¼ cup lemon juice
- ¼ cup olive oil
- 2 cups baby spinach
- 2 tomatoes, cubed
- 1 cucumber, sliced
- ½ cups walnuts, chopped

Directions:

1. In a large bowl, combine the endives with the spinach and the other ingredients, toss and serve as a side dish.

Nutrition: 238 calories, 5.7g protein, 8.4g carbohydrates, 22.3g fat, 3.1g fiber, 0mg cholesterol, 24mg sodium, 506mg potassium

Arugula Salad

Prep time: 5 minutes | Cooking time: 0 minutes |
Servings: 4

Ingredients:

- ¼ cup pomegranate seeds
- 5 cups baby arugula
- 6 tablespoons green onions, chopped
- 1 tablespoon balsamic vinegar
- 2 tablespoons olive oil
- 3 tablespoons pine nuts
- ½ shallot, chopped

Directions:

1. In a salad bowl, combine the arugula with the pomegranate and the other ingredients, toss and serve.

Nutrition: 120 calories, 1.8g protein, 4.2g carbohydrates, 11.6g fat, 0.9g fiber, 0mg cholesterol, 9mg sodium, 163mg potassium

Lemon Spinach

Prep time: 10 minutes | Cooking time: 0 minutes |
Servings: 4

Ingredients:

- 2 tablespoons olive oil
- 2 avocados, peeled, pitted and cut into wedges
- 3 cups baby spinach
- ¼ cup almonds, toasted and chopped
- 1 tablespoon lemon juice
- 1 tablespoon cilantro, chopped

Directions:

1. In a bowl, combine the avocados with the almonds, spinach and the other ingredients, toss and serve as a side dish.

Nutrition: 306 calories, 3.9g protein, 10.8g carbohydrates, 29.7g fat, 8g fiber, 0mg cholesterol, 25mg sodium, 663mg potassium

Green Beans Salad

Prep time: 4 minutes | Cooking time: 0 minutes |
Servings: 4

Ingredients:

- Juice of 1 lime
- 2 cups romaine lettuce, shredded
- 1 cup corn
- ½ pound green beans, blanched and halved
- 1 cucumber, chopped
- 1/3 cup chives, chopped

Directions:

1. In a bowl, combine the green beans with the corn and the other ingredients, toss and serve.

Nutrition: 67 calories, 3g protein, 15g carbohydrates, 0.7g fat, 3.6g fiber, 0mg cholesterol, 12mg sodium, 384mg potassium

Endives Salad

Prep time: 4 minutes | Cooking time: 0 minutes |
Servings: 4

Ingredients:

- 3 tablespoons olive oil
- 2 endives, trimmed and shredded
- 2 tablespoons lime juice
- 1 tablespoon lime zest, grated
- 1 red onion, sliced
- 1 tablespoon balsamic vinegar
- 1 pound kale, torn
- A pinch of black pepper

Directions:

1. In a bowl, combine the endives with the kale and the other ingredients, toss well and serve cold as a side salad.

Nutrition: 160 calories, 3.9g protein, 15.1g carbohydrates, 10.6g fat, 2.8g fiber, 0mg cholesterol, 53mg sodium, 641mg potassium

Chives Edamame Salad

Prep time: 5 minutes | Cooking time: 6 minutes |
Servings: 4

Ingredients:

- 2 tablespoons olive oil
- 2 tablespoons balsamic vinegar
- 2 garlic cloves, minced
- 3 cups edamame, shelled
- 1 tablespoon chives, chopped
- 2 shallots, chopped

Directions:

1. Heat up a pan with the oil over medium heat, add the edamame, the garlic and the other ingredients, toss, cook for 6 minutes, divide between plates and serve.

Nutrition: 350 calories, 25.1g protein, 22.7g carbohydrates, 20.1g fat, 8.1g fiber, 0mg cholesterol, 30mg sodium, 1221mg potassium

Grapes and Cucumber Salad

Prep time: 5 minutes | Cooking time: 0 minutes |
Servings: 4

Ingredients:

- 2 cups baby spinach
- 2 avocados, peeled, pitted and roughly cubed
- 1 cucumber, sliced
- 1 and ½ cups green grapes, halved
- 2 tablespoons avocado oil
- 1 tablespoon cider vinegar
- 2 tablespoons parsley, chopped
- A pinch of black pepper

Directions:

1. In a salad bowl, combine the baby spinach with the avocados and the other ingredients, toss and serve.

Nutrition: 274 calories, 3.1g protein, 18g carbohydrates, 23.4g fat, 7.8g fiber, 0mg cholesterol, 21mg sodium, 761mg potassium

Parsley Beets

Prep time: 10 minutes | Cooking time: 30 minutes |
Servings: 4

Ingredients:

- 4 beets, peeled and cut into wedges
- 2 tablespoons olive oil
- 2 garlic cloves, minced
- A pinch of black pepper
- ¼ cup parsley, chopped
- ¼ cup walnuts, chopped

Directions:

1. In a baking dish, combine the beets with the oil and the other ingredients, toss to coat, introduce in the oven at 420 degrees F, bake for 30 minutes, divide between plates and serve as a side dish.

Nutrition: 156 calories, 3.8g protein, 11.5g carbohydrates, 11.8g fat, 2.7g fiber, 0mg cholesterol, 80mg sodium, 373mg potassium

Tomato and Cabbage Mix

Prep time: 10 minutes | Cooking time: 15 minutes |
Servings: 4

Ingredients:

- 1 pound green cabbage, shredded
- 1 yellow onion, chopped
- 1 tomato, cubed
- 1 tablespoon dill, chopped
- A pinch of black pepper
- 1 tablespoon olive oil

Directions:

1. Heat up a pan with the oil over medium heat, add the onion and sauté for 5 minutes.
2. Add the cabbage and the rest of the ingredients, toss, cook over medium heat for 10 minutes, divide between plates and serve.

Nutrition: 74 calories, 2.1g protein, 10.2g carbohydrates, 3.7g fat, 3.7g fiber, 0mg cholesterol, 24mg sodium, 295mg potassium

Cabbage Salad

Prep time: 5 minutes | Cooking time: 0 minutes |
Servings: 4

Ingredients:

- 2 shallots, chopped
- 2 carrots, grated
- 1 big red cabbage head, shredded
- 1 tablespoon olive oil
- 1 tablespoon red vinegar
- A pinch of black pepper
- 1 tablespoon lime juice

Directions:

1. In a bowl, mix the cabbage with the shallots and the other ingredients, toss and serve as a side salad.

Nutrition: 59 calories, 0.9g protein, 6.9g carbohydrates, 3.5g fat, 1.8g fiber, 0mg cholesterol, 34mg sodium, 224mg potassium

Tomato Salsa

Prep time: 10 minutes | Cooking time: 0 minutes |
Servings: 6

Ingredients:

- 1 pound cherry tomatoes, halved
- 2 tablespoons olive oil
- 1 cup kalamata olives, pitted and halved
- A pinch of black pepper
- 1 red onion, chopped
- 1 tablespoon balsamic vinegar
- ¼ cup cilantro, chopped

Directions:

1. In a bowl, mix the tomatoes with the olives and the other ingredients, toss and serve as a side salad.

Nutrition: 87 calories, 1.1g protein, 6.1g carbohydrates, 7.2g fat, 2g fiber, 0mg cholesterol, 20mg sodium, 213mg potassium

Pesto Zucchini Salad

Prep time: 4 minutes | Cooking time: 0 minutes |
Servings: 4

Ingredients:

- 2 zucchinis, cut with a spiralizer
- 1 red onion, sliced
- 1 tablespoon basil pesto
- 1 tablespoon lemon juice
- 1 tablespoon olive oil
- ½ cup cilantro, chopped
- Black pepper to the taste

Directions:

1. In a salad bowl, mix the zucchinis with the onion and the other Ingredients, toss and serve.

Nutrition: 58 calories, 1.6g protein, 6g carbohydrates, 3.8g fat, 1.8g fiber, 0mg cholesterol, 13mg sodium, 314mg potassium

Carrots Salad

Prep time: 4 minutes | Cooking time: 0 minutes |
Servings: 4

Ingredients:

- 1 pound carrots, peeled and roughly grated
- 2 tablespoons avocado oil
- 2 tablespoons lemon juice
- 3 tablespoons sesame seeds
- ½ teaspoon curry powder
- 1 teaspoon rosemary, dried
- ½ teaspoon cumin, ground

Directions:

1. In a bowl, mix the carrots with the oil, lemon juice and the other ingredients, toss and serve cold as a side salad.

Nutrition: 99 calories, 2.4g protein, 13.7g carbohydrates, 4.4g fat, 4.2g fiber, 0mg cholesterol, 81mg sodium, 437mg potassium

Beet Salad

Prep time: 5 minutes | Cooking time: 0 minutes |
Servings: 4

Ingredients:

- 1 tablespoon ginger, grated
- 2 garlic cloves, minced
- 4 cups romaine lettuce, torn
- 1 beet, peeled and grated
- 2 green onions, chopped
- 1 tablespoon balsamic vinegar
- 1 tablespoon sesame seeds

Directions:

1. In a bowl, combine the lettuce with the ginger, garlic and the other ingredients, toss and serve as a side dish.

Nutrition: 42 calories, 1.4g protein, 6.7g carbohydrates, 1.4g fat, 1.5g fiber, 0mg cholesterol, 25mg sodium, 212mg potassium

Chives Radishes

Prep time: 5 minutes | Cooking time: 0 minutes |
Servings: 4

Ingredients:

- 1 pound red radishes, roughly cubed
- 1 tablespoon chives, chopped
- 1 tablespoon parsley, chopped
- 1 tablespoon oregano, chopped
- 2 tablespoons olive oil
- 1 tablespoon lime juice
- Black pepper to the taste

Directions:

1. In a salad bowl, mix the radishes with the chives and the other ingredients, toss and serve.

Nutrition: 82 calories, 0.9g protein, 4.7g carbohydrates, 7.3g fat, 2.3g fiber, 0mg cholesterol, 45mg sodium, 291mg potassium

Balsamic Black Beans Mix

Prep time: 4 minutes | Cooking time: 0 minutes |
Servings: 4

Ingredients:

- 3 cups canned black beans, no-salt-added, drained and rinsed
- 1 cup cherry tomatoes, halved
- 2 shallots, chopped
- 3 tablespoons olive oil
- 1 tablespoon balsamic vinegar
- Black pepper to the taste
- 1 tablespoon chives, chopped

Directions:

1. In a bowl, combine the beans with the tomatoes and the other ingredients, toss and serve cold as a side dish.

Nutrition: 602 calories, 32.1g protein, 94.2g carbohydrates, 12.7g fat, 22.7g fiber, 0mg cholesterol, 11mg sodium, 2303mg potassium

Cilantro and Spring Onions Endives

Prep time: 4 minutes | Cooking time: 0 minutes |
Servings: 4

Ingredients:

- 2 spring onions, chopped
- 2 endives, shredded
- 1 cup black olives, pitted and sliced
- ½ cup kalamata olives, pitted
- and sliced
- ¼ cup apple cider vinegar
- 2 tablespoons olive oil
- 1 tablespoons cilantro, chopped

Directions:

1. In a bowl, mix the endives with the olives and the other ingredients, toss and serve.

Nutrition: 127 calories, 0.6g protein, 4.1g carbohydrates, 12.7g fat, 1.7g fiber, 0mg cholesterol, 498mg sodium, 75mg potassium

Tomatoes Salad

Prep time: 5 minutes | Cooking time: 0 minutes |
Servings: 4

Ingredients:

- ½ pound tomatoes, cubed
- 2 cucumber, sliced
- 1 tablespoon olive oil
- 2 spring onions, chopped
- Black pepper to the taste
- Juice of 1 lime
- ½ cup basil, chopped

Directions:

1. In a salad bowl, combine the tomatoes with the cucumber and the other ingredients, toss and serve cold.

Nutrition: 71 calories, 2g protein, 10.1g carbohydrates, 3.8g fat, 2.2g fiber, 0mg cholesterol, 7mg sodium, 404mg potassium

Peppers Salad

Prep time: 5 minutes | Cooking time: 0 minutes |
Servings: 4

Ingredients:

- 1 cup cherry tomatoes, halved
- 1 yellow bell pepper, chopped
- 1 red bell pepper, chopped
- 1 green bell pepper, chopped
- ½ pound carrots, shredded
- 3 tablespoons red wine vinegar
- 2 tablespoons olive oil
- 1 tablespoon cilantro, chopped
- Black pepper to the taste

Directions:

1. In a salad bowl, mix the tomatoes with the peppers, carrots and the other ingredients, toss and serve as a side salad.

Nutrition: 115 calories, 1.7g protein, 12.5g carbohydrates, 7.3g fat, 3.3g fiber, 0mg cholesterol, 44mg sodium, 458mg potassium

Garlic Tomatoes Mix

Prep time: 10 minutes | Cooking time: 20 minutes |
Servings: 4

Ingredients:

- 2 pounds tomatoes, halved
- 1 tablespoon basil, chopped
- 3 tablespoons olive oil
- Zest of 1 lemon, grated
- 3 garlic cloves, minced
- ¼ cup low-fat parmesan, grated
- A pinch of black pepper

Directions:

1. In a baking pan, combine the tomatoes with the basil and the other ingredients except the cheese and toss.
2. Sprinkle the parmesan on top, introduce in the oven at 375 degrees F for 20 minutes, divide between plates and serve as a side dish.

Nutrition: 136 calories, 2.3g protein, 10g carbohydrates, 11g fat, 2.9g fiber, 0mg cholesterol, 20mg sodium, 553mg potassium

Paprika Brussels Sprouts

Prep time: 10 minutes | Cooking time: 25 minutes |
Servings: 4

Ingredients:

- 2 tablespoons olive oil
- 1 pound Brussels sprouts, trimmed and halved
- 3 green onions, chopped
- 2 garlic cloves, minced
- 1 tablespoon balsamic vinegar
- 1 tablespoon sweet paprika
- A pinch of black pepper

Directions:

1. In a baking pan, combine the Brussels sprouts with the oil and the other ingredients, toss and bake at 400 degrees F for 25 minutes.
2. Divide the mix between plates and serve.

Nutrition: 121 calories, 4.4g protein, 12.6g carbohydrates, 7.6g fat, 5.2g fiber, 0mg cholesterol, 31mg sodium, 521mg potassium

Turmeric Endives

Prep time: 10 minutes | Cooking time: 20 minutes |
Servings: 4

Ingredients:

- 2 endives, halved lengthwise
- 2 tablespoons olive oil
- 1 teaspoon rosemary, dried
- ½ teaspoon turmeric powder
- A pinch of black pepper

Directions:

3. In a baking pan, combine the endives with the oil and the other ingredients, toss gently, introduce in the oven and bake at 400 degrees F for 20 minutes.
4. Divide between plates and serve as a side dish.

Nutrition: 64 calories, 0.2g protein, 0.8g carbohydrates, 7.1g fat, 0.6g fiber, 0mg cholesterol, 3mg sodium, 50mg potassium

Creamy Cauliflower Mash

Prep time: 10 minutes | Cooking time: 25 minutes |
Servings: 4

Ingredients:

- 2 pounds cauliflower florets
- ½ cup coconut milk
- A pinch of black pepper
- ½ cup low-fat sour cream
- 1 tablespoon cilantro, chopped
- 1 tablespoon chives, chopped

Directions:

1. Put the cauliflower in a pot, add water to cover, bring to a boil over medium heat, cook for 25 minutes and drain.
2. Mash the cauliflower, add the milk, black pepper and the cream, whisk well, divide between plates, sprinkle the rest of the ingredients on top and serve.

Nutrition: 188 calories, 6.1g protein, 15g carbohydrates, 13.4g fat, 6.4g fiber, 13mg cholesterol, 88mg sodium, 811mg potassium

Garlic Mushrooms

Prep time: 10 minutes | Cooking time: 20 minutes |
Servings: 4

Ingredients:

- 1 pound white mushrooms, halved
- 2 cups corn
- 2 tablespoons olive oil
- 4 garlic cloves, minced
- 1 cup canned tomatoes, no-salt-added, chopped
- A pinch of black pepper
- ½ teaspoon chili powder

Directions:

1. Heat up a pan with the oil over medium heat, add the mushrooms, garlic and the corn, stir and sauté for 10 minutes.
2. Add the rest of the ingredients, toss, cook over medium heat for 10 minutes more, divide between plates and serve.

Nutrition: 164 calories, 6.7g protein, 21.2g carbohydrates, 8.4g fat, 4g fiber, 0mg cholesterol, 24mg sodium, 694mg potassium

Paprika Green Beans

Prep time: 10 minutes | Cooking time: 15 minutes |
Servings: 4

Ingredients:

- 2 tablespoons basil pesto
- 2 teaspoons sweet paprika
- 1 pound green beans, trimmed and halved
- Juice of 1 lemon
- 2 tablespoons olive oil
- 1 red onion, sliced
- A pinch of black pepper

Directions:

1. Heat up a pan with the oil over medium-high heat, add the onion, stir and sauté for 5 minutes.
2. Add the beans and the rest of the ingredients, toss, cook over medium heat fro 10 minutes, divide between plates and serve.

Nutrition: 114 calories, 2.7g protein, 12.6g carbohydrates, 7.4g fat, 5.3g fiber, 0mg cholesterol, 9mg sodium, 326mg potassium

Lime Tomatoes

Prep time: 5 minutes | Cooking time: 0 minutes |
Servings: 4

Ingredients:

- 1 and ½ tablespoon olive oil
- 1 pound tomatoes, cut into wedges
- 1 tablespoon lime juice
- 1 tablespoon lime zest, grated
- 2 tablespoons tarragon, chopped
- A pinch of black pepper

Directions:

1. In a bowl, combine the tomatoes with the other ingredients, toss and serve as a side salad.

Nutrition: 69 calories, 1.2g protein, 5.1g carbohydrates, 5.6g fat, 1.6g fiber, 0mg cholesterol, 6mg sodium, 298mg potassium

Caraway Cabbage Mix

Prep time: 5 minutes | Cooking time: 0 minutes |
Servings: 4

Ingredients:

- 2 green apples, cored and cubed
- 1 red cabbage head, shredded
- 2 tablespoons balsamic
- vinegar
- ½ teaspoon caraway seeds
- 2 tablespoons olive oil
- Black pepper to the taste

Directions:

1. In a bowl, combine the cabbage with the apples and the other ingredients, toss and serve as a side salad.

Nutrition: 165 calories, 2.6g protein, 26g carbohydrates, 7.3g fiber, 0mg cholesterol, 34mg sodium, 432mg potassium

Paprika Fennel Mix

Prep time: 5 minutes | Cooking time: 20 minutes |
Servings: 4

Ingredients:

- 2 fennel bulbs, sliced
- 1 teaspoon sweet paprika
- 1 small red onion, sliced
- 2 tablespoons olive oil
- 2 tablespoons lime juice
- 2 tablespoons dill, chopped
- Black pepper to the taste

Directions:

1. In a roasting pan, combine the fennel with the paprika and the other ingredients, toss, and bake at 380 degrees F for 20 minutes.
2. Divide the mix between plates and serve.

Nutrition: 109 calories, 2g protein, 11.3g carbohydrates, 7.4g fat, 4.4g fiber, 0mg cholesterol, 65mg sodium, 574mg potassium

Chili Squash Mix

Prep time: 10 minutes | Cooking time: 45 minutes |
Servings: 4

Ingredients:

- 2 tablespoons olive oil
- 2 pounds butternut squash, peeled, and cut into wedges
- 1 tablespoon lemon juice
- 1 teaspoon chili powder
- 1 teaspoon garlic powder
- 2 teaspoons cilantro, chopped
- A pinch of black pepper

Directions

1. In a roasting pan, combine the squash with the oil and the other ingredients, toss gently, bake in the oven at 400 degrees F for 45 minutes, divide between plates and serve as a side dish.

Nutrition: 167 calories, 2.5g protein, 27.5g carbohydrates, 7.4g fat, 4.9g fiber, 0mg cholesterol, 17mg sodium, 824mg potassium

Parsley Mushrooms

Prep time: 10 minutes | Cooking time: 30 minutes |
Servings: 4

Ingredients:

- 2 pounds white mushrooms, halved
- 4 garlic cloves, minced
- 2 tablespoons olive oil
- 1 tablespoon thyme, chopped
- 2 tablespoons parsley, chopped
- Black pepper to the taste

Directions:

1. In a baking pan, combine the mushrooms with the garlic and the other ingredients, toss, introduce in the oven and cook at 400 degrees F for 30 minutes.
2. Divide between plates and serve as a side dish.

Nutrition: 116 calories, 7.4g protein, 9g carbohydrates, 7.7g fat, 2.6g fiber, 0mg cholesterol, 15mg sodium, 749mg potassium

Spinach Sauté

Prep time: 10 minutes | Cooking time: 15 minutes |
Servings: 4

Ingredients:

- 1 cup corn
- 1 pound spinach leaves
- 1 teaspoon sweet paprika
- 1 tablespoon olive oil
- 1 yellow onion, chopped
- ½ cup basil, torn
- A pinch of black pepper
- ½ teaspoon red pepper flakes

Directions:

1. Heat up a pan with the oil over medium-high heat, add the onion, stir and sauté for 5 minutes.
2. Add the corn, spinach and the other ingredients, toss, cook over medium heat for 10 minutes more, divide between plates and serve.

Nutrition: 102 calories, 5g protein, 14.3g carbohydrates, 4.5g fat, 4.4g fiber, 0mg cholesterol, 97mg sodium, 798mg potassium

Chili Broccoli

Prep time: 10 minutes | Cooking time: 30 minutes | Servings: 4

Ingredients:

- 2 tablespoons olive oil
- 1 pound broccoli florets
- 2 garlic cloves, minced
- 2 tablespoons chili sauce
- 1 tablespoon lemon juice
- A pinch of black pepper
- 2 tablespoons cilantro, chopped

Directions:

1. In a baking pan, combine the broccoli with the oil, garlic and the other ingredients, toss a bit, introduce in the oven and bake at 400 degrees F for 30 minutes.
2. Divide the mix between plates and serve as a side dish.

Nutrition: 103 calories, 3.4g protein, 8.3g carbohydrates, 7.4g fat, 3g fiber, 0mg cholesterol, 229mg sodium, 383mg potassium

Hot Brussels Sprouts

Prep time: 10 minutes | Cooking time: 25 minutes | Servings: 4

Ingredients:

- 1 tablespoon olive oil
- 1 pound Brussels sprouts, trimmed and halved
- 2 garlic cloves, minced
- ½ cup low-fat mozzarella, shredded
- A pinch of pepper flakes, crushed

Directions:

1. In a baking dish, combine the sprouts with the oil and the other ingredients except the cheese and toss.
2. Sprinkle the cheese on top, introduce in the oven and bake at 400 degrees F for 25 minutes.
3. Divide between plates and serve as a side dish.

Nutrition: 111 calories, 10g protein, 11.6g carbohydrates, 3.9g fat, 5g fiber, 4mg cholesterol, 209mg sodium, 447mg potassium

Chili Corn Sauté

Prep time: 10 minutes | Cooking time: 15 minutes | Servings: 4

Ingredients:

- 4 cups corn
- 1 tablespoon avocado oil
- 2 shallots, chopped
- 1 teaspoon chili powder
- 2 tablespoons tomato paste, no-salt-added
- 3 scallions, chopped
- A pinch of black pepper

Directions:

1. Heat up a pan with the oil over medium-high heat, add the scallions and chili powder, stir and sauté for 5 minutes.
2. Add the corn and the other ingredients, toss, cook for 10 minutes more, divide between plates and serve as a side dish.

Nutrition: 156 calories, 5.9g protein, 33.6g carbohydrates, 2.4g fat, 5.2g fiber, 0mg cholesterol, 41mg sodium, 585mg potassium

Almonds and Mango Salad

Prep time: 10 minutes | Cooking time: 0 minutes | Servings: 4

Ingredients:

- 1 cup mango, peeled and cubed
- 4 cups baby spinach
- 1 tablespoon olive oil
- 2 spring onions, chopped
- 1 tablespoon lemon juice
- 1 tablespoon capers, drained, no-salt-added
- 1/3 cup almonds, chopped

Directions:

1. In a bowl, mix the spinach with the mango an d the other ingredients, toss and serve.

Nutrition: 111 calories, 3.1g protein, 9.7g carbohydrates, 7.8g fat, 2.6g fiber, 0mg cholesterol, 90mg sodium, 321mg potassium

Spinach Mix

Prep time: 5 minutes | Cooking time: 15 minutes | Servings: 4

Ingredients:

- 2 cups baby spinach
- 5 cups kale, torn
- 2 shallots, chopped
- 2 garlic cloves, minced
- 1 cup canned tomatoes, no-salt-added, chopped
- 1 tablespoon olive oil

Directions:

1. Heat up a pan with the oil over medium-high heat, add the shallots, stir and sauté for 5 minutes.
2. Add the spinach, kale and the other ingredients, toss, cook for 10 minutes more, divide between plates and serve as a side dish.

Nutrition: 89 calories, 3.6g protein, 12.4g carbohydrates, 3.7g fat, 2.2g fiber, 0mg cholesterol, 51mg sodium, 624mg potassium

Garlic Potato Pan

Prep time: 10 minutes | Cooking time: 1 hour | Servings: 8

Ingredients:

- 1 pound gold potatoes, peeled and cut into wedges
- 2 tablespoons olive oil
- 1 red onion, chopped
- 2 garlic cloves, minced
- 2 cups coconut cream
- 1 tablespoon thyme, chopped
- ¼ teaspoon nutmeg, ground
- ½ cup low-fat parmesan, grated

Directions:

1. Heat up a pan with the oil over medium heat, add the onion and the garlic and sauté for 5 minutes.
2. Add the potatoes and brown them for 5 minutes more.
3. Add the cream and the rest of the ingredients, toss gently, bring to a simmer and cook over medium heat for 40 minutes more.
4. Divide the mix between plates and serve as a side dish.

Nutrition: 230 calories, 3.6g protein, 14.3g carbohydrates, 19.1g fat, 3.3g fiber, 6mg cholesterol, 105mg sodium, 426mg potassium

Green Beans Mix

Prep time: 4 minutes | Cooking time: 40 minutes | Servings: 4

Ingredients:

- 1 pound green beans, trimmed and halved
- 1 small eggplant, cut into large chunks
- 1 yellow onion, chopped
- 2 tablespoons olive oil
- 2 tablespoons lime juice
- 1 teaspoon smoked paprika
- ¼ cup low-sodium vegetable stock
- Black pepper to the taste
- ½ teaspoon oregano, dried

Directions:

1. In a roasting pan, combine the green beans with the eggplant and the other ingredients, toss, introduce in the oven, bake at 390 degrees F for 40 minutes, divide between plates and serve as a side dish.

Nutrition: 137 calories, 3.6g protein, 17.8g carbohydrates, 7.5g fat, 8.8g fiber, 0mg cholesterol, 10mg sodium, 555mg potassium

Garlic Potatoes

Prep time: 5 minutes | Cooking time: 1 hour | Servings: 4

Ingredients:

- 1 pound gold potatoes, peeled and cut into wedges
- 2 tablespoons olive oil
- A pinch of black pepper
- 2 tablespoons rosemary, chopped
- 1 tablespoon Dijon mustard
- 2 garlic cloves, minced

Directions:

1. In a baking pan, combine the potatoes with the oil and the other ingredients, toss, introduce in the oven at 400 degrees F and bake for about 1 hour.
2. Divide between plates and serve as a side dish right away.

Nutrition: 146 calories, 1.9g protein, 19.9g carbohydrates, 7.4g fat, 3.9g fiber, 0mg cholesterol, 45mg sodium, 496mg potassium

Creamy Brussels Sprouts

Prep time: 5 minutes | Cooking time: 30 minutes | Servings: 4

Ingredients:

- 1 pound Brussels sprouts, trimmed and halved
- 1 cup coconut cream
- 1 tablespoon olive oil
- 2 shallots, chopped
- A pinch of black pepper
- ½ cup cashews, chopped

Directions:

1. In a roasting pan, combine the sprouts with the cream and the rest of the ingredients, toss, and bake in the oven for 30 minutes at 350 degrees F.
2. Divide between plates and serve as a side dish.

Nutrition: 323 calories, 8.1g protein, 20.9g carbohydrates, 26.1g fat, 6.1g fiber, 0mg cholesterol, 41mg sodium, 729mg potassium

Paprika Carrots

Prep time: 10 minutes | Cooking time: 30 minutes | Servings: 4

Ingredients:

- 2 tablespoons olive oil
- 2 teaspoons sweet paprika
- 1 pound carrots, peeled and roughly cubed
- 1 red onion, chopped
- 1 tablespoon sage, chopped
- A pinch of black pepper

Directions:

1. In a baking pan, combine the carrots with the oil and the other ingredients, toss and bake at 380 degrees F for 30 minutes.
2. Divide between plates and serve.

Nutrition: 122 calories, 1.4g protein, 14.6g carbohydrates, 7.2g fat, 4g fiber, 0mg cholesterol, 80mg sodium, 433mg potassium

Nutmeg Asparagus

Prep time: 5 minutes | Cooking time: 20 minutes | Servings: 4

Ingredients:

- ½ teaspoon nutmeg, ground
- 1 pound asparagus, trimmed and halved
- 1 cup coconut cream
- 1 yellow onion, chopped
- 2 tablespoons olive oil
- 1 tablespoon lime juice
- 1 tablespoon cilantro, chopped

Directions:

1. Heat up a pan with the oil over medium heat, add the onion and the nutmeg, stir and sauté for 5 minutes.
2. Add the asparagus and the other ingredients, toss, bring to a simmer and cook over medium heat for 15 minutes.
3. Divide between plates and serve.

Nutrition: 233 calories, 4.2g protein, 10.4g carbohydrates, 21.6g fat, 4.4g fiber, 0mg cholesterol, 13mg sodium, 429mg potassium

Walnut Turnips Mix

Prep time: 10 minutes | Cooking time: 15 minutes | Servings: 4

Ingredients:

- 1 tablespoon avocado oil
- 4 turnips, sliced
- ¼ cup basil, chopped
- Black pepper to the taste
- ¼ cup low-sodium vegetable stock
- ½ cup walnuts, chopped
- 2 garlic cloves, minced

Directions:

1. Heat up a pan with the oil over medium-high heat, add the garlic and the turnips and brown for 5 minutes.
2. Add the rest of the ingredients, toss, cook for 10 minutes more, divide between plates and serve.

Nutrition: 140 calories, 5.1g protein, 10.4g carbohydrates, 9.7g fat, 3.3g fiber, 0mg cholesterol, 85mg sodium, 333mg potassium

Paprika Rice Mix

Prep time: 10 minutes | Cooking time: 20 minutes | Servings: 4

Ingredients:

- 1 cup white rice
- 1 tablespoon capers, chopped
- 2 cups low-sodium chicken stock
- 1 red onion, chopped
- 1 tablespoon avocado oil
- 1 tablespoon cilantro, chopped
- 1 teaspoon sweet paprika

Directions:

1. Heat up a pan with the oil over medium-high heat, add the onion, stir and sauté for 5 minutes.
2. Add the rice, capers and the other ingredients, toss, bring to a simmer and cook for 15 minutes.
3. Divide the mix between plates and serve as a side dish.

Nutrition: 189 calories, 4.3g protein, 40.2g carbohydrates, 0.9g fat, 1.6g fiber, 0mg cholesterol, 135mg sodium, 119mg potassium

Basil Olives Mix

Prep time: 5 minutes | Cooking time: 0 minutes |
Servings: 4

Ingredients:

- 2 tablespoons olive oil
- 1 tablespoon balsamic vinegar
- A pinch of black pepper
- 4 cups corn
- 2 cups black olives, pitted and halved
- 1 red onion, chopped
- ½ cup cherry tomatoes, halved
- 1 tablespoon basil, chopped
- 1 tablespoon jalapeno, chopped
- 2 cups romaine lettuce, shredded

Directions:

1. In a large bowl, combine the corn with the olives, lettuce and the other ingredients, toss well, divide between plates and serve as a side dish.

Nutrition: 290 calories, 6.2g protein, 37.6g carbohydrates, 16.1g fat, 7.4g fiber, 0mg cholesterol, 613mg sodium, 562mg potassium

Balsamic Cabbage

Prep time: 10 minutes | Cooking time: 20 minutes |
Servings: 4

Ingredients:

- 1 pound green cabbage, roughly shredded
- 2 tablespoons olive oil
- A pinch of black pepper
- 1 shallot, chopped
- 2 garlic cloves, minced
- 2 tablespoons balsamic vinegar
- 2 teaspoons hot paprika
- 1 teaspoon sesame seeds

Directions:

1. Heat up a pan with the oil over medium heat, add the shallot and the garlic and sauté for 5 minutes.
2. Add the cabbage and the other ingredients, toss, cook over medium heat for 15 minutes, divide between plates and serve.

Nutrition: 100 calories, 1.8g protein, 8.2g carbohydrates, 7.5g fat, 3g fiber, 0mg cholesterol, 22mg sodium, 225mg potassium

Lime Carrots

Prep time: 10 minutes | Cooking time: 30 minutes |
Servings: 4

Ingredients:

- 1 pound baby carrots, trimmed
- 1 tablespoon sweet paprika
- 1 teaspoon lime juice
- 3 tablespoons olive oil
- A pinch of black pepper
- 1 teaspoon sesame seeds

Directions:

1. Arrange the carrots on a lined baking sheet, add the paprika and the other ingredients except the sesame seeds, toss, introduce in the oven and bake at 400 degrees F for 30 minutes.
2. Divide the carrots between plates, sprinkle sesame seeds on top and serve as a side dish.

Nutrition: 139 calories, 1.1g protein, 10.5g carbohydrates, 11.2g fat, 4g fiber, 0mg cholesterol, 89mg sodium, 313mg potassium

Parmesan Eggplant Mix

Prep time: 10 minutes | Cooking time: 20 minutes |
Servings: 4

Ingredients:

- 2 big eggplants, roughly cubed
- 1 tablespoon oregano, chopped
- ½ cup low-fat parmesan, grated
- ¼ teaspoon garlic powder
- 2 tablespoons olive oil
- A pinch of black pepper

Directions:

1. In a baking pan combine the eggplants with the oregano and the other ingredients except the cheese and toss.
2. Sprinkle parmesan on top, introduce in the oven and bake at 370 degrees F for 20 minutes.
3. Divide between plates and serve as a side dish.

Nutrition: 154 calories, 4.9g protein, 14.5g carbohydrates, 10g fat, 8.6g fiber, 11mg cholesterol, 196mg sodium, 561mg potassium

Parmesan Endives

Prep time: 10 minutes | Cooking time: 20 minutes |
Servings: 4

Ingredients:

- 4 endives, halved lengthwise
- 1 tablespoon lemon juice
- 1 tablespoon lemon zest, grated
- 2 tablespoons fat-free parmesan, grated
- 2 tablespoons olive oil
- A pinch of black pepper

Directions:

1. In a baking dish, combine the endives with the lemon juice and the other ingredients except the parmesan and toss.
2. Sprinkle the parmesan on top, bake the endives at 400 degrees F for 20 minutes, divide between plates and serve as a side dish.

Nutrition: 71 calories, 0.9g protein, 2.2g carbohydrates, 7.1g fat, 0.9g fiber, 0mg cholesterol, 71mg sodium, 88mg potassium

Lemon Asparagus

Prep time: 10 minutes | Cooking time: 20 minutes |
Servings: 4

Ingredients:

- 1 pound asparagus, trimmed
- 2 tablespoons basil pesto
- 1 tablespoon lemon juice
- A pinch of black pepper
- 3 tablespoons olive oil
- 2 tablespoons cilantro, chopped

Directions:

1. Arrange the asparagus n a lined baking sheet, add the pesto and the other ingredients, toss, introduce in the oven and cook at 400 degrees F for 20 minutes.
2. Divide between plates and serve as a side dish.

Nutrition: 114 calories, 2.6g protein, 4.5g carbohydrates, 10.7g fat, 2.4g fiber, 0mg cholesterol, 3mg sodium, 240mg potassium

Parsley Artichokes Mix

Prep time: 5 minutes | Cooking time: 0 minutes |
Servings: 4

Ingredients:

- 10 ounces canned artichoke hearts, no-salt-added, drained and halved
- 1 cup black olives, pitted and sliced
- 1 tablespoon capers, drained
- 1 cup green olives, pitted and sliced
- 1 tablespoon parsley, chopped
- Black pepper to the taste
- 2 tablespoons olive oil
- 2 tablespoons red wine vinegar
- 1 tablespoon chives, chopped

Directions:

1. In a salad bowl, combine the artichokes with the olives and the other ingredients, toss and serve as a side dish.

Nutrition: 160 calories, 2.7g protein, 9.8g carbohydrates, 13.2g fat, 5g fiber, 0mg cholesterol, 704mg sodium, 279mg potassium

Rosemary Tomatoes

Prep time: 5 minutes | Cooking time: 0 minutes |
Servings: 4

Ingredients:

- 2 tablespoons mint, chopped
- 1 pound tomatoes, cut into wedges
- 2 cups corn
- 2 tablespoons olive oil
- 1 tablespoon rosemary vinegar
- A pinch of black pepper

Directions:

1. In a salad bowl, combine the tomatoes with the corn and the other ingredients, toss and serve.
2. Enjoy!

Nutrition: 166 calories, 3.8g protein, 21.3g carbohydrates, 9.2g fat, 3.9g fiber, 0mg cholesterol, 60mg sodium, 490mg potassium

Avocado, Tomato and Olives Salad

Prep time: 5 minutes | Cooking time: 0 minutes |
Servings: 4

Ingredients:

- 2 tablespoons olive oil
- 2 avocados, peeled, pitted and cut into wedges
- 1 cup kalamata olives, pitted and halved
- 1 cup tomatoes, cubed
- 1 tablespoon ginger, grated
- A pinch of black pepper
- 2 cups baby arugula
- 1 tablespoon balsamic vinegar

Directions:

1. In a bowl, combine the avocados with the kalamata and the other ingredients, toss and serve as a side dish.

Nutrition: 320 calories, 3g protein, 13.9g carbohydrates, 30.4g fat, 8.7g fiber, 0mg cholesterol, 305mg sodium, 655mg potassium

Greens Sauté

Prep time: 10 minutes | Cooking time: 12 minutes |
Servings: 4

Ingredients:

- 6 cups mustard greens
- 2 tablespoons olive oil
- 2 spring onions, chopped
- ½ cup coconut cream
- 2 tablespoons sweet paprika
- Black pepper to the taste

Directions:

1. Heat up a pan with the oil over medium-high heat, add the onions, paprika and black pepper, stir and sauté for 3 minutes.
2. Add the mustard greens and the other ingredients, toss, cook for 9 minutes more, divide between plates and serve as a side dish.

Nutrition: 163 calories, 3.6g protein, 8.3g carbohydrates, 14.8g fat, 4.9g fiber, 0mg cholesterol, 28mg sodium, 478mg potassium

Balsamic Beets

Prep time: 10 minutes | Cooking time: 30 minutes |
Servings: 4

Ingredients:

- 4 beets, peeled and cut into wedges
- 3 tablespoons olive oil
- 2 tablespoons almonds, chopped
- 2 tablespoons balsamic vinegar
- A pinch of black pepper
- 2 tablespoons parsley, chopped

Directions:

1. In a baking pan, combine the beets with the oil and the other ingredients, toss, introduce in the oven and bake at 400 degrees f for 30 minutes.
2. Divide the mix between plates and serve.

Nutrition: 153 calories, 2.4g protein, 10.8g carbohydrates, 12.2g fat, 2.4g fiber, 0mg cholesterol, 78mg sodium, 343mg potassium

Coconut Kale Sauté

Prep time: 10 minutes | Cooking time: 15 minutes |
Servings: 4

Ingredients:

- 2 tablespoons olive oil
- 3 tablespoons coconut aminos
- 1 pound kale, torn
- 1 red onion, chopped
- 2 garlic cloves, minced
- 1 tablespoon lime juice
- 1 tablespoon cilantro, chopped

Directions:

1. Heat up a pan with the olive oil over medium heat, add the onion and the garlic and sauté for 5 minutes.
2. Add the kale and the other ingredients, toss, cook over medium heat for 10 minutes, divide between plates and serve.

Nutrition: 140 calories, 3.8g protein, 17.2g carbohydrates, 7g fat, 2.3g fiber, 0mg cholesterol, 63mg sodium, 604mg potassium

Allspice Carrots

Prep time: 10 minutes | Cooking time: 20 minutes |
Servings: 4

Ingredients:

- 1 tablespoon lemon juice
- 1 tablespoon olive oil
- ½ teaspoon allspice, ground
- ½ teaspoon cumin, ground
- ½ teaspoon nutmeg, ground
- 1 pound baby carrots, trimmed
- 1 tablespoon rosemary, chopped
- Black pepper to the taste

Directions:

1. In a roasting pan, combine the carrots with the lemon juice, oil and the other ingredients, toss, introduce in the oven and bake at 400 degrees F for 20 minutes.
2. Divide between plates and serve.

Nutrition: 76 calories, 0.9g protein, 10.4g carbohydrates, 4g fat, 3.8g fiber, 0mg cholesterol, 90mg sodium, 290mg potassium

Dill Artichokes

Prep time: 10 minutes | Cooking time: 20 minutes |
Servings: 4

Ingredients:

- 2 tablespoons lemon juice
- 4 artichokes, trimmed and halved
- 1 tablespoon dill, chopped
- 2 tablespoons olive oil
- A pinch of black pepper

Directions:

1. In a roasting pan, combine the artichokes with the lemon juice and the other ingredients, toss gently and bake at 400 degrees F for 20 minutes.
2. Divide between plates and serve.

Nutrition: 140 calories, 5.5g protein, 17.6g carbohydrates, 7.3g fat, 8.9g fiber, 0mg cholesterol, 155mg sodium, 635mg potassium

Rice and Cranberries Mix

Prep time: 10 minutes | Cooking time: 25 minutes | Servings: 4

Ingredients:

- 1 cup cauliflower florets
- 1 cup white rice
- 2 cups low-sodium chicken stock
- 1 tablespoon avocado oil
- 2 shallots, chopped
- ¼ cup cranberries
- ½ cup almonds, sliced

Directions:

1. Heat up a pan with the oil over medium heat, add the shallots, stir and sauté for 5 minutes.
2. Add the cauliflower, the rice and the other ingredients, toss, bring to a simmer and cook over medium heat for 20 minutes.
3. Divide the mix between plates and serve.

Nutrition: 263 calories, 7.5g protein, 43g carbohydrates, 6.7g fat, 3.1g fiber, 0mg cholesterol, 46mg sodium, 255mg potassium

Thyme Black Beans Mix

Prep time: 10 minutes | Cooking time: 30 minutes | Servings: 4

Ingredients:

- 2 tablespoons olive oil
- 1 yellow onion, chopped
- 1 cup canned black beans, no-salt-added, drained and rinsed
- 2 cup black rice
- 4 cups low-sodium chicken stock
- 2 tablespoons thyme, chopped
- Zest of ½ lemon, grated
- A pinch of black pepper

Directions:

1. Heat up a pan with the oil over medium-high heat, add the onion, stir and sauté for 4 minutes.
2. Add the beans, rice and the other ingredients, toss, bring to a boil and cook over medium heat for 25 minutes.
3. Stir the mix, divide between plates and serve.

Nutrition: 591 calories, 19.1g protein, 106.7g carbohydrates, 10.4g fat, 11.9g fiber, 0mg cholesterol, 148mg sodium, 1034mg potassium

Zucchini Salsa

Prep time: 5 minutes | Cooking time: 10 minutes | Servings: 4

Ingredients:

- 2 tablespoons olive oil
- 2 zucchinis, cubed
- 1 avocado, peeled, pitted and cubed
- 2 tomatoes, cubed
- 1 cucumber, cubed
- 1 yellow onion, chopped
- 2 tablespoons fresh lime juice
- 2 tablespoons cilantro, chopped

Directions:

1. Heat up a pan with the oil over medium heat, add the onion and the zucchinis, toss and cook for 5 minutes.
2. Add the rest of the ingredients, toss, cook for 5 minutes more, divide between plates and serve.

Nutrition: 212 calories, 3.5g protein, 15.3g carbohydrates, 17.2g fat, 6.2g fiber, 0mg cholesterol, 19mg sodium, 800mg potassium

Mint Peppers

Prep time: 10 minutes | Cooking time: 30 minutes | Servings: 4

Ingredients:

- 1 pound mixed bell peppers, cut into wedges
- 1 red onion, thinly sliced
- 2 tablespoons olive oil
- Black pepper to the taste
- 1 tablespoon oregano, chopped
- 2 tablespoons mint leaves, chopped

Directions:

1. In a roasting pan, combine the bell peppers with the onion and the other ingredients, toss and bake at 380 degrees F for 30 minutes.
2. Divide the mix between plates and serve.

Nutrition: 85 calories, 0.8g protein, 5.8g carbohydrates, 7.3g fat, 1.7g fiber, 0mg cholesterol, 3mg sodium, 128mg potassium

Chives Cabbage Sauté

Prep time: 5 minutes | Cooking time: 15 minutes | Servings: 4

Ingredients:

- 1 pound red cabbage, shredded
- 8 dates, pitted and sliced
- 2 tablespoons olive oil
- ¼ cup low-sodium vegetable stock
- 2 tablespoons chives, chopped
- 2 tablespoons lemon juice
- Black pepper to the taste

Directions:

1. Heat up a pan with the oil over medium heat, add the cabbage and the dates, toss and cook for 4 minutes.
2. Add the stock and the other ingredients, toss, cook over medium heat for 11 minutes more, divide between plates and serve.

Nutrition: 183 calories, 2g protein, 19.4g carbohydrates, 7.2g fat, 4.2g fiber, 0mg cholesterol, 31mg sodium, 316mg potassium

Avocado Mix

Prep time: 10 minutes | Cooking time: 14 minutes | Servings: 4

Ingredients:

- 1 tablespoon avocado oil
- 1 teaspoon sweet paprika
- 1 pound mixed bell peppers, cut into strips
- 1 avocado, peeled, pitted and halved
- 1 teaspoon garlic powder
- 1 teaspoon rosemary, dried
- ½ cup low-sodium vegetable stock
- Black pepper to the taste

Directions:

1. Heat up a pan with the oil over medium-high heat, add all the bell peppers, stir and sauté for 5 minutes.
2. Add the rest of the ingredients, toss, cook for 9 minutes more over medium heat, divide between plates and serve.

Nutrition: 150 calories, 1.5g protein, 8g carbohydrates, 13.5g fat, 4.3g fiber, 0mg cholesterol, 22mg sodium, 323mg potassium

Roasted Sweet Potato Mix

Prep time: 10 minutes | Cooking time: 1 hour | Servings: 4

Ingredients:

- 3 tablespoons olive oil
- 2 sweet potatoes, peeled and cut into wedges
- 2 beets, peeled, and cut into wedges
- 1 tablespoon oregano, chopped
- 1 tablespoon lime juice
- Black pepper to the taste

Directions:

1. Arrange the sweet potatoes and the beets on a lined baking sheet, add the rest of the ingredients, toss, introduce in the oven and bake at 375 degrees F for 1 hour/
2. Divide between plates and serve as a side dish.

Nutrition: 160 calories, 1.5g protein, 16.2g carbohydrates, 10.8g fat, 3g fiber, 0mg cholesterol, 42mg sodium, 477mg potassium

Oregano Beans Mix

Prep time: 10 minutes | Cooking time: 0 minutes | Servings: 4

Ingredients:

- 2 cups canned black beans, no-salt-added, drained and rinsed
- 2 cups canned white beans, no-salt-added, drained and rinsed
- 2 tablespoons balsamic vinegar
- 2 tablespoons olive oil
- 1 teaspoon oregano, dried
- 1 teaspoon basil, dried
- 1 tablespoon chives, chopped

Directions:

1. In a salad bowl, combine the beans with the vinegar and the other ingredients, toss and serve as a side salad.

Nutrition: 730 calories, 44.6g protein, 121.7g carbohydrates, 9.3g fat, 30.3g fiber, 0mg cholesterol, 21mg sodium, 3266mg potassium

Coconut Beets

Prep time: 5 minutes | Cooking time: 20 minutes | Servings: 4

Ingredients:

- 1 pound beets, peeled and cubed
- 1 red onion, chopped
- 1 tablespoon olive oil
- ½ cup coconut cream
- 4 tablespoons non-fat yogurt
- 1 tablespoon chives, chopped

Directions:

1. Heat up a pan with the oil over medium heat, add the onion, stir and sauté for 4 minutes.
2. Add the beets, cream and the other ingredients, toss, cook over medium heat for 15 minutes more, divide between plates and serve.

Nutrition: 164 calories, 3.1g protein, 16.2g carbohydrates, 10.9g fat, 3.5g fiber, 0mg cholesterol, 96mg sodium, 467mg potassium

Broccoli Rice

Prep time: 10 minutes | Cooking time: 30 minutes | Servings: 4

Ingredients:

- 1 cup broccoli florets, chopped
- 1 cup canned black beans, no-salt-added, drained
- 1 cup white rice
- 2 cups low-sodium chicken stock
- 2 teaspoons sweet paprika
- Black pepper to the taste

Directions:

1. Put the stock in a pot, heat up over medium heat, add the rice and the other ingredients, toss, bring to a boil and cook for 30 minutes stirring from time to time.
2. Divide the mix between plates and serve as a side dish.

Nutrition: 347 calories, 15.1g protein, 69.3g carbohydrates, 1.2g fat, 9g fiber, 0mg cholesterol, 83mg sodium, 869mg potassium

Snacks

Tahini Pumpkin Dip

Prep time: 5 minutes | Cooking time: 0 minutes |
Servings: 4

Ingredients:

- 2 cups pumpkin flesh
- ½ cup pumpkin seeds
- 1 tablespoon lemon juice
- 1 tablespoon sesame seed paste
- 1 tablespoon olive oil

Directions:

1. In a blender, combine the pumpkin with the seeds and the other ingredients, pulse well, divide into bowls and serve a party spread.

Nutrition: 162 calories, 5.5g protein, 9.7g carbohydrates, 12.7g fat, 2.3g fiber, 0mg cholesterol, 5mg sodium, 436mg potassium

Cheesy Spinach Dip

Prep time: 10 minutes | Cooking time: 20 minutes |
Servings: 4

Ingredients:

- 1 pound spinach, chopped
- 1 cup coconut cream
- 1 cup low-fat mozzarella, shredded
- A pinch of black pepper
- 1 tablespoon dill, chopped

Directions:

1. In a baking pan, combine the spinach with the cream and the other ingredients, stir well, introduce in the oven and bake at 400 degrees F for 20 minutes.
2. Divide into bowls and serve.

Nutrition: 206 calories, 12.8g protein, 8.9g carbohydrates, 14.8g fat, 4.9g fiber, 5mg cholesterol, 340mg sodium, 816mg potassium

Olives Salsa

Prep time: 5 minutes | Cooking time: 0 minutes |
Servings: 4

Ingredients:

- 1 red onion, chopped
- 1 cup black olives, pitted and halved
- 1 cucumber, cubed
- ¼ cup cilantro, chopped
- A pinch of black pepper
- 2 tablespoons lime juice

Directions:

1. In a bowl, combine the olives with the cucumber and the rest of the ingredients, toss and serve cold as a snack.

Nutrition: 61 calories, 1.1g protein, 7.5g carbohydrates, 3.7g fat, 2.1g fiber, 0mg cholesterol, 296mg sodium, 159mg potassium

Chives Dip

Prep time: 5 minutes | Cooking time: 25 minutes |
Servings: 4

Ingredients:

- 2 tablespoons olive oil
- 1 red onion, chopped
- 2 tablespoons chives, chopped
- A pinch of black pepper
- 1 beet, peeled and chopped
- 8 ounces low-fat cream cheese
- 1 cup coconut cream

Directions:

1. Heat up a pan with the oil over medium heat, add the onion and sauté for 5 minutes.
2. Add the rest of the ingredients, and cook everything for 20 minutes more stirring often.
3. Transfer the mix to a blender, pulse well, divide into bowls and serve.

Nutrition: 418 calories, 6.4g protein, 10g carbohydrates, 41.2g fat, 2.5g fiber, 62mg cholesterol, 197mg sodium, 346mg potassium

Cucumber Salad

Prep time: 5 minutes | Cooking time: 0 minutes |
Servings: 4

Ingredients:

- 1 pound cucumbers, cubed
- 1 avocado, peeled, pitted and cubed
- 1 tablespoon capers, drained
- 1 tablespoon chives, chopped
- 1 small red onion, cubed
- 1 tablespoon olive oil
- 1 tablespoon balsamic vinegar

Directions:

1. In a bowl, combine the cucumbers with the avocado and the other ingredients, toss, divide into small cups and serve.

Nutrition: 158 calories, 2g protein, 10.2g carbohydrates, 13.5g fat, 4.4g fiber, 0mg cholesterol, 70mg sodium, 442mg potassium

Chickpeas Spread

Prep time: 5 minutes | Cooking time: 0 minutes |
Servings: 4

Ingredients:

- 1 tablespoon olive oil
- 1 tablespoon lemon juice
- 1 tablespoon sesame seeds paste
- 2 tablespoons chives, chopped
- 2 spring onions, chopped
- 2 cups canned chickpeas, no-salt-added, drained and rinsed

Directions:

1. In your blender, combine the chickpeas with the oil and the other ingredients except the chives, pulse well, divide into bowls, sprinkle the chives on top and serve.

Nutrition: 398 calories, 19.5g protein, 61.4g carbohydrates, 9.6g fat, 17.7g fiber, 0mg cholesterol, 26mg sodium, 905mg potassium

Coconut Olives Tapenade

Prep time: 4 minutes | Cooking time: 0 minutes |
Servings: 4

Ingredients:

- 2 cups black olives, pitted and chopped
- 1 cup mint, chopped
- 2 tablespoons avocado oil
- ½ cup coconut cream
- ¼ cup lime juice
- A pinch of black pepper

Directions:

1. In your blender, combine the olives with the mint and the other ingredients, pulse well, divide into bowls and serve.

Nutrition: 166 calories, 2.1g protein, 8.2g carbohydrates, 15.4g fat, 4.7g fiber, 0mg cholesterol, 598mg sodium, 211mg potassium

Coconut Dip

Prep time: 5 minutes | Cooking time: 0 minutes |
Servings: 4

Ingredients:

- 4 spring onions, chopped
- 1 shallot, minced
- 1 tablespoon lime juice
- A pinch of black pepper
- 2 ounces low-fat mozzarella cheese, shredded
- 1 cup coconut cream
- 1 tablespoon parsley, chopped

Directions:

1. In a blender, combine the spring onions with the shallot and the other ingredients, pulse well, divide into bowls and serve as a party dip.

Nutrition: 185 calories, 5.7g protein, 5.4g carbohydrates, 16.8g fat, 1.7g fiber, 8mg cholesterol, 97mg sodium, 213mg potassium

Pine Nuts Dip

Prep time: 5 minutes | Cooking time: 0 minutes | Servings: 4

Ingredients:

- 8 ounces coconut cream
- 1 tablespoon pine nuts, chopped
- 2 tablespoons parsley, chopped
- A pinch of black pepper

Directions:

1. In a bowl, combine the cream with the pine nuts and the rest of the ingredients, whisk well, divide into bowls and serve.

Nutrition: 146 calories, 1.7g protein, 3.5g carbohydrates, 15g fat, 1.4g fiber, 0mg cholesterol, 10mg sodium, 172mg potassium

Cucumbers Salsa Bowls

Prep time: 5 minutes | Cooking time: 0 minutes | Servings: 4

Ingredients:

- 4 scallions, chopped
- 2 tomatoes, cubed
- 4 cucumbers, cubed
- 1 tablespoon balsamic vinegar
- 1 cup baby arugula leaves
- 2 tablespoons lemon juice
- 2 tablespoons olive oil
- A pinch of black pepper

Directions:

1. In a bowl, combine the scallions with the tomatoes and the other ingredients, toss, divide into small bowls and serve as a snack.

Nutrition: 132 calories, 3.6g protein, 15.9g carbohydrates, 7.8g fat, 3.4g fiber, 0mg cholesterol, 23mg sodium, 642mg potassium

Mint Cheesy Dip

Prep time: 5 minutes | Cooking time: 0 minutes | Servings: 6

Ingredients:

- 1 tablespoon mint, chopped
- 1 tablespoon oregano, chopped
- 10 ounces non-fat cream
- cheese
- ½ cup ginger, sliced
- 2 tablespoons coconut aminos

Directions:

1. In your blender, combine the cream cheese with the ginger and the other ingredients, pulse well, divide into small cups and serve.

Nutrition: 78 calories, 7.6g protein, 9.4g carbohydrates, 1.2g fat, 1.3g fiber, 4mg cholesterol, 266mg sodium, 191mg potassium

Dill Dip

Prep time: 5 minutes | Cooking time: 0 minutes | Servings: 4

Ingredients:

- 3 cups non-fat yogurt
- 2 spring onions, chopped
- 1 teaspoon sweet paprika
- ¼ cup almonds, chopped
- ¼ cup dill, chopped

Directions:

1. In a bowl, combine the yogurt with the onions and the other ingredients, whisk, divide into bowls and serve.

Nutrition: 151 calories, 12.6g protein, 19.5g carbohydrates, 3.2g fat, 1.6g fiber, 4mg cholesterol, 173mg sodium, 176mg potassium

Cauliflower and Tomato Salsa

Prep time: 5 minutes | Cooking time: 0 minutes | Servings: 4

Ingredients:

- 1 pound cauliflower florets, blanched
- 1 cup kalamata olives, pitted and halved
- 1 cup cherry tomatoes, halved
- 1 tablespoon olive oil
- 1 tablespoon lime juice
- A pinch of black pepper

Directions:

1. In a bowl, combine the cauliflower with the olives and the other ingredients, toss and serve.

Nutrition: 105 calories, 2.9g protein, 9.9g carbohydrates, 7.3g fat, 4.5g fiber, 0mg cholesterol, 329mg sodium, 453mg potassium

Shrimp Dip

Prep time: 5 minutes | Cooking time: 0 minutes | Servings: 4

Ingredients:

- 8 ounces coconut cream
- 1 pound shrimp, cooked, peeled, deveined and chopped
- 2 tablespoons dill, chopped
- 2 spring onions, chopped
- 1 tablespoon cilantro, chopped
- A pinch of black pepper

Directions:

1. In a bowl, combine the shrimp with the cream and the other ingredients, whisk and serve as a party spread.

Nutrition: 272 calories, 27.6g protein, 6.3g carbohydrates, 15.5g fat, 1.7g fiber, 239mg cholesterol, 290mg sodium, 415mg potassium

Peach and Olives Salsa

Prep time: 4 minutes | Cooking time: 0 minutes | Servings: 4

Ingredients:

- 4 peaches, stones removed and cubed
- 1 cup kalamata olives, pitted and halved
- 1 avocado, pitted, peeled and
- cubed
- 1 cup cherry tomatoes, halved
- 1 tablespoon olive oil
- 1 tablespoon lime juice
- 1 tablespoon cilantro, chopped

Directions:

1. In a bowl, combine the peaches with the olives and the other ingredients, toss well and serve cold.

Nutrition: 238 calories, 3g protein, 6.3g carbohydrates, 22.2g fat, 17.4g fiber, 0mg cholesterol, 298mg sodium, 639mg potassium

Turmeric Carrot Chips

Prep time: 10 minutes | Cooking time: 20 minutes | Servings: 4

Ingredients:

- 4 carrots, thinly sliced
- 2 tablespoons olive oil
- A pinch of black pepper
- 1 teaspoon sweet paprika
- ½ teaspoon turmeric powder
- A pinch of red pepper flakes

Directions:

1. In a bowl, combine the carrot chips with the oil and the other ingredients and toss.
2. Spread the chips on a lined baking sheet, bake at 400 degrees F for 25 minutes, divide into bowls and serve as a snack.

Nutrition: 88 calories, 0.6g protein, 6.5g carbohydrates, 7.1g fat, 1.8g fiber, 0mg cholesterol, 42mg sodium, 214mg potassium

Asparagus Snack Bowls

Prep time: 4 minutes | Cooking time: 20 minutes | Servings: 4

Ingredients:

- 2 tablespoons coconut oil, melted
- 1 pound asparagus, trimmed and halved
- 1 teaspoon garlic powder
- 1 teaspoon rosemary, dried
- 1 teaspoon chili powder

Directions:

1. In a bowl, mix the asparagus with the oil and the other ingredients, toss, spread on a lined baking sheet and bake at 400 degrees F for 20 minutes.
2. Divide into bowls and serve cold as a snack.

Nutrition: 87 calories, 2.7g protein, 5.5g carbohydrates, 7.1g fat, 2.8g fiber, 0mg cholesterol, 9mg sodium, 252mg potassium

Figs Bowls

Prep time: 4 minutes | Cooking time: 12 minutes | Servings: 4

Ingredients:

- 8 figs, halved
- 1 tablespoon avocado oil
- 1 teaspoon nutmeg, ground

Directions:

1. In a roasting pan combine the figs with the oil and the nutmeg, toss, and bake at 400 degrees F for 12 minutes.
2. Divide the figs into small bowls and serve as a snack.

Nutrition: 102 calories, 1.3g protein, 24.7g carbohydrates, 1g fat, 4g fiber, 0mg cholesterol, 4mg sodium, 271mg potassium

Shrimp Salsa

Prep time: 5 minutes | Cooking time: 6 minutes | Servings: 4

Ingredients:

- 2 cups red cabbage, shredded
- 1 pound shrimp, peeled and deveined
- 1 tablespoon olive oil
- A pinch of black pepper
- 2 spring onions, chopped
- 1 cup tomatoes, cubed
- ½ teaspoon garlic powder

Directions:

1. Heat up a pan with the oil over medium heat, add the shrimp, toss and cook for 3 minutes on each side.
2. In a bowl, combine the cabbage with the shrimp and the other ingredients, toss, divide into small bowls and serve.

Nutrition: 185 calories, 26.9g protein, 6.3g carbohydrates, 5.6g fat, 1.7g fiber, 239mg cholesterol, 286mg sodium, 383mg potassium

Avocado Fries

Prep time: 5 minutes | Cooking time: 10 minutes | Servings: 4

Ingredients:

- 2 avocados, peeled, pitted and cut into wedges
- 1 tablespoon avocado oil
- 1 tablespoon lime juice
- 1 teaspoon coriander, ground

Directions:

1. Spread the avocado wedges on a lined baking sheet, add the oil and the other ingredients, toss, and bake at 300 degrees F for 10 minutes.
2. Divide into cups and serve as a snack.

Nutrition: 236 calories, 1.9g protein, 6.3g carbohydrates, 8.6g fat, 23.1g fiber, 0mg cholesterol, 6mg sodium, 488mg potassium

Cilantro Lemon Dip

Prep time: 4 minutes | Cooking time: 0 minutes | Servings: 4

Ingredients:

- 1 cup low-fat cream cheese
- Black pepper to the taste
- ½ cup lemon juice
- 1 tablespoon cilantro, chopped
- 3 garlic cloves, chopped

Directions:

1. In your food processor, mix the cream cheese with the lemon juice and the other ingredients, pulse well, divide into bowls and serve.

Nutrition: 213 calories, 4.8g protein, 2.9g carbohydrates, 20.5g fat, 0.2g fiber, 64mg cholesterol, 178mg sodium, 117mg potassium

Sweet Potatoand and Coconut Dip

Prep time: 10 minutes | Cooking time: 40 minutes | Servings: 4

Ingredients:

- 1 cup sweet potatoes, peeled and cubed
- 1 tablespoon low-sodium vegetable stock
- Cooking spray
- 2 tablespoons coconut cream
- 2 teaspoons rosemary, dried
- Black pepper to the taste

Directions:

1. In a baking pan, combine the potatoes with the stock and the other ingredients, stir, bake at 365 degrees F for 40 minutes, transfer to your blender, pulse well, divide into small bowls and serve

Nutrition: 64 calories, 0.8g protein, 11.3g carbohydrates, 1.9g fat, 2g fiber, 0mg cholesterol, 7mg sodium, 333mg potassium

Beans and Tomato Salsa

Prep time: 5 minutes | Cooking time: 0 minutes | Servings: 4

Ingredients:

- 1 cup canned black beans, no-salt-added, drained
- 1 cup canned red kidney beans, no-salt-added, drained
- 1 teaspoon balsamic vinegar
- 1 cup cherry tomatoes, cubed
- 1 tablespoon olive oil
- 2 shallots, chopped

Directions:

1. In a bowl, combine the beans with the vinegar and the other ingredients, toss and serve as a party snack.

Nutrition: 362 calories, 21.4g protein, 61g carbohydrates, 4.8g fat, 14.9g fiber, 0mg cholesterol, 11mg sodium, 1469mg potassium

Lime Beans Salsa

Prep time: 10 minutes | Cooking time: 10 minutes | Servings: 4

Ingredients:

- 1 pound green beans, trimmed and halved
- 1 tablespoon olive oil
- 2 teaspoons capers, drained
- 6 ounces green olives, pitted and sliced
- 4 garlic cloves, minced
- 1 tablespoon lime juice
- 1 tablespoon oregano, chopped
- Black pepper to the taste

Directions:

1. Heat up a pan with the oil over medium-high heat, add the garlic and the green beans, toss and cook for 3 minutes.
2. Add the rest of the ingredients, toss, cook for another 7 minutes, divide into small cups and serve cold.

Nutrition: 108 calories, 2.8g protein, 12.3g carbohydrates, 6.7g fat, 5.5g fiber, 0mg cholesterol, 432mg sodium, 272mg potassium

Coconut Peppers Dip

Prep time: 4 minutes | Cooking time: 0 minutes | Servings: 4

Ingredients:

- 1 teaspoon turmeric powder
- 1 cup coconut cream
- 14 ounces red peppers, no-
- salt-added, chopped
- Juice of ½ lemon
- 1 tablespoon chives, chopped

Directions:

3. In your blender, combine the peppers with the turmeric and the other ingredients except the chives, pulse well, divide into bowls and serve as a snack with the chives sprinkled on top.

Nutrition: 180 calories, 3.3g protein, 12.5g carbohydrates, 14.8g fat, 3g fiber, 0mg cholesterol, 18mg sodium, 493mg potassium

Lentils Dip

Prep time: 5 minutes | Cooking time: 0 minutes | Servings: 4

Ingredients:

- 14 ounces canned lentils, drained, no-salt-added, rinsed
- Juice of 1 lemon
- 2 garlic cloves, minced
- 2 tablespoons olive oil
- ½ cup cilantro, chopped

Directions:

1. In a blender, combine the lentils with the oil and the other ingredients, pulse well, divide into bowls and serve as a party spread.

Nutrition: 417 calories, 25.9g protein, 60.5g carbohydrates, 8.2g fat, 30.4g fiber, 0mg cholesterol, 10mg sodium, 983mg potassium

Chili Walnuts

Prep time: 5 minutes | Cooking time: 15 minutes | Servings: 8

Ingredients:

- ½ teaspoon smoked paprika
- ½ teaspoon chili powder
- ½ teaspoon garlic powder
- 1 tablespoon avocado oil
- A pinch of cayenne pepper
- 14 ounces walnuts

Directions:

1. Spread the walnuts on a lined baking sheet, add the paprika and the other ingredients, toss and bake at 410 degrees F for 15 minutes.
2. Divide into bowls and serve as a snack.

Nutrition: 310 calories, 12g protein, 5.3g carbohydrates, 29.5g fat, 3.6g fiber, 0mg cholesterol, 3mg sodium, 273mg potassium

Coconut Cranberry Crackers

Prep time: 3 hours and 5 minutes | Cooking time: 0 minutes | Servings: 4

Ingredients:

- 2 ounces coconut cream
- 2 tablespoons rolled oats
- 2 tablespoons coconut,
- shredded
- 1 cup cranberries

Directions:

1. In a blender, combine the oats with the cranberries and the other ingredients, pulse well and spread into a square pan.
2. Cut into squares and keep them in the fridge for 3 hours before serving.

Nutrition: 66 calories, 0.8g protein, 5.4g carbohydrates, 4.4g fat, 1.8g fiber, 0mg cholesterol, 3mg sodium, 102mg potassium

Brussels Sprouts Bowls

Prep time: 10 minutes | Cooking time: 25 minutes | Servings: 4

Ingredients:

- 1 pound Brussels sprouts, trimmed and halved
- 2 tablespoons olive oil
- 1 tablespoon cumin, ground
- 1 cup dill, chopped
- 2 garlic cloves, minced

Directions:

1. In a roasting pan, combine the Brussels sprouts with the oil and the other ingredients, toss and bake at 390 degrees F for 25 minutes.
2. Divide the sprouts into bowls and serve as a snack.

Nutrition: 147 calories, 6.6g protein, 18.2g carbohydrates, 8.3g fat, 6.1g fiber, 0mg cholesterol, 56mg sodium, 871mg potassium

Walnuts Bowls

Prep time: 10 minutes | Cooking time: 15 minutes | Servings: 4

Ingredients:

- 2 cups walnuts
- 3 tablespoons red vinegar
- A drizzle of olive oil
- A pinch of cayenne pepper
- A pinch of red pepper flakes
- Black pepper to the taste

Directions:

1. Spread the walnuts on a lined baking sheet, add the vinegar and the other ingredients, toss, and roast at 400 degrees F for 15 minutes.
2. Divide the walnuts into bowls and serve.

Nutrition: 388 calories, 15g protein, 6.2g carbohydrates, 36.9g fat, 4.3g fiber, 0mg cholesterol, 2mg sodium, 331mg potassium

Turmeric Radish Chips

Prep time: 10 minutes | Cooking time: 20 minutes | Servings: 4

Ingredients:

- 1 pound radishes, thinly sliced
- A pinch of turmeric powder
- Black pepper to the taste
- 2 tablespoons olive oil

Directions:

1. Spread the radish chips on a lined baking sheet, add the oil and the other ingredients, toss and bake at 400 degrees F for 20 minutes.
2. Divide the chips into bowls and serve.

Nutrition: 78 calories, 0.8g protein, 3.9g carbohydrates, 7.1g fat, 1.8g fiber, 0mg cholesterol, 44mg sodium, 266mg potassium

Shrimp Salad

Prep time: 4 minutes | Cooking time: 0 minutes | Servings: 4

Ingredients:

- 2 leeks, sliced
- 1 cup cilantro, chopped
- 1 pound shrimp, peeled, deveined and cooked
- Juice of 1 lime
- 1 tablespoon lime zest, grated
- 1 cup cherry tomatoes, halved
- 2 tablespoons olive oil
- Salt and black pepper to the taste

Directions:

1. In a salad bowl, mix the shrimp with the leeks and the other ingredients, toss, divide into small cups and serve.

Nutrition: 237 calories, 27.1g protein, 11.9g carbohydrates, 9.2g fat, 2.1g fiber, 239mg cholesterol, 290mg sodium, 419mg potassium

Cream Cheese and Leeks Dip

Prep time: 5 minutes | Cooking time: 0 minutes | Servings: 4

Ingredients:

- 1 tablespoon lemon juice
- ½ cup low-fat cream cheese
- 2 tablespoons olive oil
- Black pepper to the taste
- 4 leeks, chopped
- 1 tablespoon cilantro, chopped

Directions:

1. In a blender, combine the cream cheese with the leeks and the other ingredients, pulse well, divide into bowls and serve as a party dip.

Nutrition: 216 calories, 3.6g protein, 13.5g carbohydrates, 17.4g fat, 1.6g fiber, 32mg cholesterol, 105mg sodium, 201mg potassium

Bell Peppers Salsa

Prep time: 5 minutes | Cooking time: 0 minutes | Servings: 4

Ingredients:

- ½ pound red bell pepper, cut into thin strips
- 3 green onions, chopped
- 1 tablespoon olive oil
- 2 teaspoons ginger, grated
- ½ teaspoon rosemary, dried
- 3 tablespoons balsamic vinegar

Directions:

1. In a salad bowl, mix the bell peppers with the onions and the other ingredients, toss, divide into small cups and serve.

Nutrition: 44 calories, 0.5g protein, 2.8g carbohydrates, 3.6g fat, 0.7g fiber, 0mg cholesterol, 3mg sodium, 81mg potassium

Avocado Dip

Prep time: 4 minutes | Cooking time: 0 minutes | Servings: 4

Ingredients:

- 2 tablespoons dill, chopped
- 1 shallot, chopped
- 2 garlic cloves, minced
- 2 avocados, peeled, pitted and chopped
- 1 cup coconut cream
- 2 tablespoons olive oil
- 2 tablespoons lime juice
- Black pepper to the taste

Directions:

1. In a blender, combine the avocados with the shallots, garlic and the other ingredients, pulse well, divide into small bowls and serve as a snack.

Nutrition: 412 calories, 3.8g protein, 14g carbohydrates, 41g fat, 8.3g fiber, 0mg cholesterol, 19mg sodium, 714mg potassium

Corn Spread

Prep time: 30 minutes | Cooking time: 0 minutes | Servings: 4

Ingredients:

- A pinch of cayenne pepper
- A pinch of black pepper
- 2 cups corn
- 1 cup coconut cream
- 2 tablespoons lemon juice
- 2 tablespoon avocado oil

Directions:

1. In a blender, combine the corn with the cream and the other ingredients, pulse well, divide into bowls and serve as a party dip.

Nutrition: 215 calories, 4g protein, 18.4g carbohydrates, 16.2g fat, 3.8g fiber, 0mg cholesterol, 22mg sodium, 397mg potassium

Coconut Beans Bars

Prep time: 2 hours | Cooking time: 0 minutes | Servings: 12

Ingredients:

- 1 cup canned black beans, no-salt-added, drained
- 1 cup coconut flakes, unsweetened
- 1 cup low-fat butter
- ½ cup chia seeds
- ½ cup coconut cream

Directions:

1. In a blender, combine the beans with the coconut flakes and the other ingredients, pulse well, spread this into a square pan, press, keep in the fridge for 2 hours, slice into medium bars and serve.

Nutrition: 158 calories, 6.4g protein, 16.9g carbohydrates, 8g fat, 6.5g fiber, 1mg cholesterol, 19mg sodium, 328mg potassium

Pumpkin Seeds Bowls

Prep time: 10 minutes | Cooking time: 2 hours | Servings: 4

Ingredients:

- Cooking spray
- 2 teaspoons nutmeg, ground
- 1 cup pumpkin seeds
- 2 apples, cored and thinly sliced

Directions:

1. Arrange the pumpkin seeds and the apple chips on a lined baking sheet, sprinkle the nutmeg all over, grease them with the spray, introduce in the oven and bake at 300 degrees F for 2 hours.
2. Divide into bowls and serve as a snack.

Nutrition: 250 calories, 8.8g protein, 22.1g carbohydrates, 16.4g fat, 4.3g fiber, 0mg cholesterol, 7mg sodium, 402mg potassium

Yogurt Dip

Prep time: 5 minutes | Cooking time: 0 minutes | Servings: 4

Ingredients:

- 2 cups fat-free Greek yogurt
- 1 tablespoon parsley, chopped
- ¼ cup canned tomatoes, no-
- salt-added, chopped
- 2 tablespoons chives, chopped
- Black pepper to the taste

Directions:

1. In a bowl, mix the yogurt with the parsley and the other ingredients, whisk well, divide into small bowls and serve as a party dip.

Nutrition: 53 calories, 5.2g protein, 7.6g carbohydrates, 0g fat, 0.2g fiber, 3mg cholesterol, 41mg sodium, 36mg potassium

Rosemary Beet Bites

Prep time: 10 minutes | Cooking time: 35 minutes | Servings: 2

Ingredients:

- 1 teaspoon cayenne pepper
- 2 beets, peeled and cubed
- 1 teaspoon rosemary, dried
- 1 tablespoon olive oil
- 2 teaspoons lime juice

Directions:

1. In a roasting pan, combine the beet bites with the cayenne and the other ingredients, toss, introduce in the oven, roast at 355 degrees F for 35 minutes, divide into small bowls and serve as a snack.

Nutrition: 109 calories, 1.8g protein, 10.9g carbohydrates, 7.4g fat, 2.5g fiber, 0mg cholesterol, 78mg sodium, 329mg potassium

Mushrooms Bowls

Prep time: 10 minutes | Cooking time: 25 minutes | Servings: 4

Ingredients:

- 1 pound small mushroom caps
- 2 tablespoons olive oil
- 1 tablespoon chives, chopped
- 1 tablespoon rosemary, chopped
- Black pepper to the taste

Directions:

1. Put the mushrooms in a roasting pan, add the oil and the rest of the ingredients, toss, bake at 400 degrees F for 25 minutes, divide into bowls and serve as a snack.

Nutrition: 235 calories, 7.3g protein, 9.8g carbohydrates, 19.6g fat, 0.6g fiber, 31mg cholesterol, 310mg sodium, 10mg potassium

Beans Dip

Prep time: 5 minutes | Cooking time: 0 minutes | Servings: 4

Ingredients:

- ½ cup coconut cream
- 1 tablespoon olive oil
- 2 cups canned black beans, no-salt-added, drained and rinsed
- 2 tablespoons green onions, chopped

Directions:

1. In a blender, combine the beans with the cream and the other ingredients, pulse well, divide into bowls and serve.

Nutrition: 431 calories, 21.7g protein, 62.4g carbohydrates, 12g fat, 15.5g fiber, 0mg cholesterol, 10mg sodium, 1526mg potassium

Chili Fennel Salsa

Prep time: 5 minutes | Cooking time: 0 minutes | Servings: 4

Ingredients:

- 2 spring onion, chopped
- 2 fennel bulbs, shredded
- 1 green chili pepper, chopped
- 1 tomato, chopped
- 1 teaspoon turmeric powder
- 1 teaspoon lime juice
- 2 tablespoons coriander, chopped
- Black pepper to the taste

Directions:

1. In a salad bowl, mix the fennel with the onions and the other ingredients, toss, divide into cups and serve.

Nutrition: 44 calories, 1.8g protein, 10.2g carbohydrates, 0.3g fat, 4.2g fiber, 0mg cholesterol, 63mg sodium, 561mg potassium

Pecans Bowls

Prep time: 10 minutes | Cooking time: 10 minutes | Servings: 4

Ingredients:

- 2 cup walnuts
- 1 cup pecans, chopped
- 1 teaspoon avocado oil
- ½ teaspoon sweet paprika

Directions:

1. Spread the grapes and pecans on a lined baking sheet, add the oil and the paprika, toss, and bake at 400 degrees F for 10 minutes.
2. Divide into bowls and serve as a snack.

Nutrition: 584 calories, 18.1g protein, 10.4g carbohydrates, 57.1g fat, 7.4g fiber, 0mg cholesterol, 1mg sodium, 453mg potassium

Almonds Bowls

Prep time: 5 minutes | Cooking time: 10 minutes | Servings: 4

Ingredients:

- 2 cups almonds
- ¼ cup coconut, shredded
- 1 mango, peeled and cubed
- 1 cup sunflower seeds
- Cooking spray

Directions:

1. Spread the almonds, coconut, mango and sunflower seeds on a baking tray, grease with the cooking spray, toss and bake at 400 degrees F for 10 minutes.
2. Divide into bowls and serve as a snack.

Nutrition: 410 calories, 13.3g protein, 25.8g carbohydrates, 31.7g fat, 8.7g fiber, 0mg cholesterol, 3mg sodium, 581mg potassium

Paprika Potato Chips

Prep time: 10 minutes | Cooking time: 20 minutes | Servings: 4

Ingredients:

- 4 gold potatoes, peeled and thinly sliced
- 2 tablespoons olive oil
- 1 tablespoon chili powder
- 1 teaspoon sweet paprika
- 1 tablespoon chives, chopped

Directions:

1. Spread the chips on a lined baking sheet, add the oil and the other ingredients, toss, introduce in the oven and bake at 390 degrees F for 20 minutes.
2. Divide into bowls and serve.

Nutrition: 118 calories, 1.3g protein, 13.4g carbohydrates, 7.4g fat, 2.9g fiber, 0mg cholesterol, 19mg sodium, 361mg potassium

Salmon and Spinach Bowls

Prep time: 10 minutes | Cooking time: 0 minutes | Servings: 6

Ingredients:

- 1 tablespoon avocado oil
- 1 tablespoon balsamic vinegar
- ½ teaspoon oregano, dried
- 1 cup smoked salmon, no-salt-added, boneless, skinless and cubed
- 1 cup salsa
- 4 cups baby spinach

Directions:

1. In a bowl, combine the salmon with the salsa and the other ingredients, toss, divide into small cups and serve.

Nutrition: 48 calories, 5.3g protein, 3.7g carbohydrates, 1.8g fat, 1.3g fiber, 0mg cholesterol, 343mg sodium, 252mg potassium

Corn Salsa

Prep time: 4 minutes | Cooking time: 0 minutes | Servings: 4

Ingredients:

- 3 cups corn
- 2 cups tomatoes, cubed
- 2 green onions, chopped
- 2 tablespoons olive oil
- 1 red chili pepper, chopped
- ½ tablespoon chives, chopped

Directions:

1. In a salad bowl, combine the tomatoes with the corn and the other ingredients, toss and serve cold as a snack.

Nutrition: 178 calories, 4.7g protein, 25.9g carbohydrates, 8.6g fat, 4.5g fiber, 0mg cholesterol, 23mg sodium, 550mg potassium

Seeds Bowls

Prep time: 10 minutes | Cooking time: 20 minutes |
Servings: 4

Ingredients:

- 2 tablespoons olive oil
- 1 teaspoon smoked paprika
- 1 cup sunflower seeds
- 1 cup chia seeds
- 2 apples, cored and cut into wedges
- ½ teaspoon cumin, ground
- A pinch of cayenne pepper

Directions:

1. In a bowl, combine the seeds with the apples and the other ingredients, toss, spread on a lined baking sheet, introduce in the oven and bake at 350 degrees F for 20 minutes.
2. Divide into bowls and serve as a snack.

Nutrition: 291 calories, 6.3g protein, 27.1g carbohydrates, 19.8g fat, 11.2g fiber, 0mg cholesterol, 6mg sodium, 297mg potassium

Coconut Carrot Spread

Prep time: 10 minutes | Cooking time: 30 minutes |
Servings: 4

Ingredients:

- 1 pound carrots, peeled and chopped
- ½ cup walnuts, chopped
- 2 cups low-sodium vegetable stock
- 1 cup coconut cream
- 1 tablespoon rosemary, chopped
- 1 teaspoon garlic powder
- ¼ teaspoon smoked paprika

Directions:

1. In a small pot, mix the carrots with the stock, walnuts and the other ingredients except the cream and the rosemary, stir, bring to a boil over medium heat, cook for 30 minutes, drain and transfer to a blender.
2. Add the cream, blend the mix well, divide into bowls, sprinkle the rosemary on top and serve.

Nutrition: 297 calories, 6.7g protein, 19.1g carbohydrates, 23.7g fat, 6.1g fiber, 0mg cholesterol, 158mg sodium, 686mg potassium

Tomato Spread

Prep time: 10 minutes | Cooking time: 10 minutes |
Servings: 4

Ingredients:

- 1 pound tomatoes, peeled and chopped
- ½ cup garlic, minced
- 2 tablespoons olive oil
- A pinch of black pepper
- 2 shallots, chopped
- 1 teaspoon thyme, dried

Directions:

1. Heat up a pan with the oil over medium-high heat, add the garlic and the shallots, stir and sauté for 2 minutes.
2. Add the tomatoes and the other ingredients, cook for 8 minutes more and transfer to a blender.
3. Pulse well, divide into small cups and serve as a snack.

Nutrition: 110 calories, 2.2g protein, 11g carbohydrates, 7.4g fat, 1.8g fiber, 0mg cholesterol, 9mg sodium, 356mg potassium

Dill Zucchini Spread

Prep time: 5 minutes | Cooking time: 10 minutes |
Servings: 4

Ingredients:

- ½ cup nonfat yogurt
- 2 zucchinis, chopped
- 1 tablespoon olive oil
- 2 spring onions, chopped
- ¼ cup low-sodium vegetable
- stock
- 2 garlic cloves, minced
- 1 tablespoon dill, chopped
- A pinch of nutmeg, ground

Directions:

1. Heat up a pan with the oil over medium heat, add the onions and garlic, stir and sauté for 3 minutes.
2. Add the zucchinis and the other ingredients except the yogurt, toss, cook for 7 minutes more and take off the heat.
3. Add the yogurt, blend using an immersion blender, divide into bowls and serve.

Nutrition: 75 calories, 3.4g protein, 7.2g carbohydrates, 4.1g fat, 1.5g fiber, 2mg cholesterol, 43mg sodium, 389mg potassium

Salmon Muffins

Prep time: 10 minutes | Cooking time: 25 minutes |
Servings: 4

Ingredients:

- 1 cup low-fat mozzarella cheese, shredded
- 8 ounces smoked salmon, skinless, boneless, and chopped
- 1 cup almond flour
- 1 egg, whisked
- 1 teaspoon parsley, dried
- 1 garlic clove, minced
- Black pepper to the taste
- Cooking spray

Directions:

1. In a bowl, combine the salmon with the mozzarella and the other ingredients except the cooking spray and stir well.
2. Divide this mix into a muffin tray greased with the cooking spray, bake in the oven at 375 degrees F for 25 minutes and serve as a snack.

Nutrition: 163 calories, 21.3g protein, 2.9g carbohydrates, 7g fat, 1.8g fiber, 59mg cholesterol, 1392mg sodium, 119mg potassium

Squash Bites

Prep time: 10 minutes | Cooking time: 20 minutes |
Servings: 8

Ingredients:

- A drizzle of olive oil
- 1 big butternut squash, peeled and minced
- 2 tablespoons cilantro, chopped
- 2 eggs, whisked
- ½ cup whole wheat flour
- Black pepper to the taste
- 2 shallots, chopped
- 2 garlic cloves, minced

Directions:

1. In a bowl, mix the squash with the cilantro and the other ingredients except the oil, stir well and shape medium balls out of this mix.
2. Arrange them on a lined baking sheet, grease them with the oil, bake at 400 degrees F for 10 minutes on each side, divide into bowls and serve.

Nutrition: 79 calories, 3g protein, 14.9g carbohydrates, 1.2g fat, 1.6g fiber, 41mg cholesterol, 19mg sodium, 282mg potassium

Almond Bars

Prep time: 10 minutes | Cooking time: 30 minutes |
Servings: 8

Ingredients:

- 2 cups whole wheat flour
- 2 teaspoons baking powder
- A pinch of black pepper
- 2 eggs, whisked
- 1 cup almond milk
- 1 cup cauliflower florets, chopped
- ½ cup low-fat cheddar, shredded

Directions:

1. In a bowl, combine the flour with the cauliflower and the other ingredients and stir well.
2. Spread into a baking tray, introduce in the oven, bake at 400 degrees F for 30 minutes, cut into bars and serve as a snack.

Nutrition: 225 calories, 10.1g protein, 27.4g carbohydrates, 8.6g fat, 1.8g fiber, 43mg cholesterol, 165mg sodium, 291mg potassium

Pearl Onions Snack

Prep time: 10 minutes | Cooking time: 30 minutes |
Servings: 8

Ingredients:

- 20 white pearl onions, peeled
- 3 tablespoons parsley, chopped
- 1 tablespoon chives, chopped
- Black pepper to the taste
- 1 cup low-fat mozzarella, grated
- 1 tablespoon olive oil

Directions:

1. Spread the pearl onions on a lined baking sheet, add the oil, parsley, chives and the black pepper and toss.
2. Sprinkle the mozzarella on top, bake at 390 degrees F for 30 minutes, divide into bowls and serve cold as a snack.

Nutrition: 171 calories, 6.1g protein, 26.2g carbohydrates, 5.5g fat, 6g fiber, 13mg cholesterol, 71mg sodium, 421mg potassium

Oregano Broccoli Bars

Prep time: 10 minutes | Cooking time: 25 minutes |
Servings: 8

Ingredients:

- 1 pound broccoli florets, chopped
- ½ cup low-fat mozzarella cheese, shredded
- 2 eggs, whisked
- 1 teaspoon oregano, dried
- 1 teaspoon basil, dried
- Black pepper to the taste

Directions:

1. In a bowl, mix the broccoli with the cheese and the other ingredients, stir well, spread into a rectangle pan and press well on the bottom.
2. Introduce in the oven at 380 degrees F, bake for 25 minutes, cut into bars and serve cold.

Nutrition: 56 calories, 7g protein, 4.5g carbohydrates, 1.3g fat, 2.1g fiber, 43mg cholesterol, 154mg sodium, 198mg potassium

Pineapple Salsa

Prep time: 10 minutes | Cooking time: 40 minutes |
Servings: 4

Ingredients:

- 20 ounces canned pineapple, drained and cubed
- 1 cup sun-dried tomatoes, cubed
- 1 tablespoon basil, chopped
- 1 tablespoon avocado oil
- 1 teaspoon lime juice
- 1 cup black olives, pitted and sliced
- Black pepper to the taste

Directions:

1. In a bowl, combine the pineapple cubes with the tomatoes and the other ingredients, toss, divide into smaller cups and serve as a snack.

Nutrition: 122 calories, 1.5g protein, 22.7g carbohydrates, 4.3g fat, 3.8g fiber, 0mg cholesterol, 297mg sodium, 277mg potassium

Coconut Kale Spread

Prep time: 10 minutes | Cooking time: 20 minutes |
Servings: 4

Ingredients:

- 1 bunch kale leaves
- 1 cup coconut cream
- 1 shallot, chopped
- 1 tablespoon olive oil
- 1 teaspoon chili powder
- A pinch of black pepper

Directions:

2. Heat up a pan with the oil over medium heat, add the shallots, stir and sauté for 4 minutes.
1. Add the kale and the other ingredients, bring to a simmer and cook over medium heat for 16 minutes.
2. Blend using an immersion blender, divide into bowls and serve as a snack.

Nutrition: 180 calories, 2g protein, 5.9g carbohydrates, 17.9g fat, 1.8g fiber, 0mg cholesterol, 23mg sodium, 261mg potassium

Cumin Beets Chips

Prep time: 10 minutes | Cooking time: 35 minutes |
Servings: 4

Ingredients:

- 2 beets, peeled and thinly sliced
- 1 tablespoon avocado oil
- 1 teaspoon cumin, ground
- 1 teaspoon fennel seeds, crushed
- 2 teaspoons garlic, minced

Directions:

1. Spread the beet chips on a lined baking sheet, add the oil and the other ingredients, toss, introduce in the oven and bake at 400 degrees F for 35 minutes.
2. Divide into bowls and serve as a snack.

Nutrition: 32 calories, 1.1g protein, 6.1g carbohydrates, 0.7g fat, 1.4g fiber, 0mg cholesterol, 40mg sodium, 187mg potassium

Poultry

Creamy Turkey Mix

Prep time: 5 minutes | Cooking time: 25 minutes |
Servings: 4

Ingredients:

- 2 tablespoons olive oil
- 1 turkey breast, skinless, boneless and sliced
- A pinch of black pepper
- 1 tablespoon basil, chopped
- 3 garlic cloves, minced
- 14 ounces canned artichokes, no-salt-added, chopped
- 1 cup coconut cream
- ¾ cup low-fat mozzarella, shredded

Directions:

1. Heat up a pan with the oil over medium-high heat, add the meat, garlic and the black pepper, toss and cook for 5 minutes.
2. Add the rest of the ingredients except the cheese, toss and cook over medium heat for 15 minutes.
3. Sprinkle the cheese, cook everything for 5 minutes more, divide between plates and serve.

Nutrition: 268 calories, 8.8g protein, 15g carbohydrates, 21.5g fat, 7.3g fiber, 3mg cholesterol, 225mg sodium, 537mg potassium

Turkey and Onion Mix

Prep time: 10 minutes | Cooking time: 30 minutes |
Servings: 4

Ingredients:

- 2 tablespoons avocado oil
- 1 red onion, chopped
- 2 garlic cloves, minced
- A pinch of black pepper
- 1 tablespoon oregano, chopped
- 1 big turkey breast, skinless, boneless and cubed
- 1 and ½ cups low-sodium beef stock
- 1 tablespoon chives, chopped

Directions:

1. Heat up a pan with the oil over medium heat, add the onion, stir and sauté for 3 minutes.
2. Add the garlic and the meat, toss and cook for 3 minutes more.
3. Add the rest of the ingredients, toss, simmer everything over medium heat for 25 minutes, divide between plates and serve.

Nutrition: 32 calories, 1.4g protein, 4.6g carbohydrates, 1.1g fat, 1.4g fiber, 0mg cholesterol, 154mg sodium, 90mg potassium

Balsamic Chicken

Prep time: 10 minutes | Cooking time: 35 minutes |
Servings: 4

Ingredients:

- 1 tablespoon avocado oil
- 1 pound chicken breast, skinless, boneless and halved
- 2 garlic cloves, minced
- 2 shallots, chopped
- ½ cup orange juice
- 1 tablespoon orange zest, grated
- 3 tablespoons balsamic vinegar
- 1 teaspoon rosemary, chopped

Directions:

1. Heat up a pan with the oil over medium-high heat, add the shallots and the garlic, toss and sauté for 2 minutes.
2. Add the meat, toss gently and cook for 3 minutes more.
3. Add the rest of the ingredients, toss, introduce the pan in the oven and bake at 340 degrees F for 30 minutes.
4. Divide between plates and serve.

Nutrition: 159 calories, 24.6g protein, 5.4g carbohydrates, 3.4g fat, 0.5g fiber, 73mg cholesterol, 60mg sodium, 530mg potassium

Turkey and Garlic Sauce

Prep time: 10 minutes | Cooking time: 40 minutes |
Servings: 4

Ingredients:

- 1 turkey breast, boneless, skinless and cubed
- ½ pound white mushrooms, halved
- 1/3 cup coconut aminos
- 2 garlic cloves, minced
- 2 tablespoons olive oil
- A pinch of black pepper
- 2 green onion, chopped
- 3 tablespoons garlic sauce
- 1 tablespoon rosemary, chopped

Directions:

1. Heat up a pan with the oil over medium heat, add the green onions, garlic sauce and the garlic and sauté for 5 minutes.
2. Add the meat and brown it for 5 minutes more.
3. Add the rest of the ingredients, introduce in the oven and bake at 390 degrees F for 30 minutes.
4. Divide the mix between plates and serve.

Nutrition: 100 calories, 2.1g protein, 7.5g carbohydrates, 7.3g fat, 1.2g fiber, 0mg cholesterol, 30mg sodium, 216mg potassium

Coconut Chicken and Olives

Prep time: 10 minutes | Cooking time: 25 minutes |
Servings: 4

Ingredients:

- 1 pound chicken breasts, skinless, boneless and roughly cubed
- A pinch of black pepper
- 1 tablespoon avocado oil
- 1 red onion, chopped
- 1 cup coconut milk
- 1 tablespoon lemon juice
- 1 cup kalamata olives, pitted and sliced
- ¼ cup cilantro, chopped

Directions:

1. Heat up a pan with the oil over medium-high heat, add the onion and the meat and brown for 5 minutes.
2. Add the rest of the ingredients, toss, bring to a simmer and cook over medium heat for 20 minutes more.
3. Divide between plates and serve.

Nutrition: 409 calories, 34.9g protein, 8.3g carbohydrates, 26.8g fat, 3.2g fiber, 101mg cholesterol, 402mg sodium, 497mg potassium

Turkey and Peach

Prep time: 10 minutes | Cooking time: 25 minutes |
Servings: 4

Ingredients:

- 1 tablespoon avocado oil
- 1 turkey breast, skinless, boneless and sliced
- A pinch of black pepper
- 1 yellow onion, chopped
- 4 peaches, stones removed and cut into wedges
- ¼ cup balsamic vinegar
- 2 tablespoons chives, chopped

Directions:

1. Heat up a pan with the oil over medium-high heat, add the meat and the onion, toss and brown for 5 minutes.
2. Add the rest of the ingredients except the chives, toss gently and bake at 390 degrees F for 20 minutes.
3. Divide everything between plates and serve with the chives sprinkled on top.

Nutrition: 79 calories, 1.8g protein, 17g carbohydrates, 0.9g fat, 3.1g fiber, 0mg cholesterol, 5mg sodium, 352mg potassium

Paprika Chicken and Spinach

Prep time: 10 minutes | Cooking time: 25 minutes | Servings: 4

Ingredients:

- 1 tablespoon avocado oil
- 1 pound chicken breast, skinless, boneless and cubed
- ½ teaspoon basil, dried
- A pinch of black pepper
- ¼ cup low-sodium vegetable stock.
- 2 cups baby spinach
- 2 shallots, chopped
- 2 garlic cloves, minced
- ½ teaspoon sweet paprika
- 2/3 cup coconut cream
- 2 tablespoons cilantro, chopped

Directions:

1. Heat up a pan with the oil over medium-high heat, add the meat, basil, black pepper and brown for 5 minutes.
2. Add the shallots and the garlic and cook for another 5 minutes.
3. Add the rest of the ingredients, toss, bring to a simmer and cook over medium heat fro 15 minutes more.
4. Divide between plates and serve hot.

Nutrition: 237 calories, 25.8g protein, 4.5g carbohydrates, 12.9g fat, 1.5g fiber, 73mg cholesterol, 81mg sodium, 652mg potassium

Chicken and Tomatoes Mix

Prep time: 10 minutes | Cooking time: 25 minutes | Servings: 4

Ingredients:

- 2 chicken breasts, skinless, boneless and cubed
- 2 tablespoons avocado oil
- 2 spring onions, chopped
- 1 bunch asparagus, trimmed and halved
- ½ teaspoon sweet paprika
- A pinch of black pepper
- 14 ounces canned tomatoes, no-salt-added, drained and chopped

Directions:

1. Heat up a pan with the oil over medium-high heat, add the meat and the spring onions, stir and cook for 5 minutes.
2. Add the asparagus and the other ingredients, toss, cover the pan and cook over medium heat for 20 minutes.
3. Divide everything between plates and serve.

Nutrition: 38 calories, 2g protein, 6.2g carbohydrates, 1.2g fat, 2.5g fiber, 0mg cholesterol, 8mg sodium, 353mg potassium

Basil Turkey and Broccoli

Prep time: 10 minutes | Cooking time: 25 minutes | Servings: 4

Ingredients:

- 1 tablespoon olive oil
- 1 big turkey breast, skinless, boneless and cubed
- 2 cups broccoli florets
- 2 shallots, chopped
- 2 garlic cloves, minced
- 1 tablespoon basil, chopped
- 1 tablespoon cilantro, chopped
- ½ cup coconut cream

Directions:

1. Heat up a pan with the oil over medium-high heat, add the meat, shallots and the garlic, toss and brown for 5 minutes.
2. Add the broccoli and the other ingredients, toss everything, cook for 20 minutes over medium heat, divide between plates and serve.

Nutrition: 121 calories, 2.3g protein, 6.1g carbohydrates, 10.8g fat, 1.9g fiber, 0mg cholesterol, 23mg sodium, 250mg potassium

Chicken with Green Beans and Sauce

Prep time: 10 minutes | Cooking time: 25 minutes | Servings: 4

Ingredients:

- 2 tablespoons olive oil
- 10 ounces green beans, trimmed and halved
- 1 yellow onion, chopped
- 1 tablespoon dill, chopped
- 2 chicken breasts, skinless, boneless and halved
- 2 cups tomato sauce, no-salt-added
- ½ teaspoon red pepper flakes, crushed

Directions:

1. Heat up a pan with the oil over medium-high heat, add the onion and the meat and brown it for 2 minutes on each side.
2. Add the green beans and the other ingredients, toss, introduce in the oven and bake at 380 degrees F for 20 minutes.
3. Divide between plates and serve right away.

Nutrition: 126 calories, 3.5g protein, 14.8g carbohydrates, 7.5g fat, 5g fiber, 0mg cholesterol, 649mg sodium, 625mg potassium

Chicken with Zucchini

Prep time: 5 minutes | Cooking time: 25 minutes | Servings: 4

Ingredients:

- 1 pound chicken breasts, skinless, boneless and cubed
- 1 cup low-sodium chicken stock
- 2 zucchinis, roughly cubed
- 1 tablespoon olive oil
- 1 cup canned tomatoes, no-salt-added, chopped
- 1 yellow onion, chopped
- 1 teaspoon chili powder
- 1 tablespoon cilantro, chopped

Directions:

1. Heat up a pan with the oil over medium-high heat, add the meat and the onion, toss and brown for 5 minutes.
2. Add the zucchinis and the rest of the ingredients, toss gently, reduce the heat to medium and cook for 20 minutes.
3. Divide everything between plates and serve.

Nutrition: 284 calories, 35g protein, 14.8g carbohydrates, 8g fat, 12.3g fiber, 2.4mg cholesterol, 151mg sodium, 693mg potassium

Lemon Chicken Mix

Prep time: 10 minutes | Cooking time: 20 minutes | Servings: 4

Ingredients:

- 2 chicken breasts, skinless, boneless and halved
- Juice of ½ lemon
- 2 tablespoons olive oil
- 2 garlic cloves, minced
- ½ cup low-sodium vegetable stock
- 1 avocado, peeled, pitted and cut into wedges
- A pinch of black pepper

Directions:

1. Heat up a pan with the oil over medium heat, add the garlic and the meat and brown for 2 minutes on each side.
2. Add the lemon juice and the other ingredients, bring to a simmer and cook over medium heat for 15 minutes.
3. Divide the whole mix between plates and serve.

Nutrition: 170 calories, 1.4g protein, 6g carbohydrates, 16.9g fat, 3.7g fiber, 0mg cholesterol, 21mg sodium, 277mg potassium

Ginger Turkey Mix

Prep time: 10 minutes | Cooking time: 20 minutes |
Servings: 4

Ingredients:

- 1 turkey breast, boneless, skinless and roughly cubed
- 2 scallions, chopped
- 1 pound bok choy, torn
- 2 tablespoons olive oil
- ½ teaspoon ginger, grated
- A pinch of black pepper
- ½ cup low-sodium vegetable stock

Directions:

1. Heat up a pot with the oil over medium-high heat, add the scallions and the ginger and sauté for 2 minutes.
2. Add the meat and brown for 5 minutes more.
3. Add the rest of the ingredients, toss, simmer for 13 minutes more, divide between plates and serve.

Nutrition: 81 calories, 2g protein, 3.7g carbohydrates, 7.3g fat, 1.5g fiber, 0mg cholesterol, 95mg sodium, 327mg potassium

Chives Chicken

Prep time: 10 minutes | Cooking time: 25 minutes |
Servings: 4

Ingredients:

- 2 chicken breasts, skinless, boneless and roughly cubed
- 3 red onions, sliced
- 2 tablespoons olive oil
- 1 cup low-sodium vegetable
- stock
- A pinch of black pepper
- 1 tablespoon cilantro, chopped
- 1 tablespoon chives, chopped

Directions:

1. Heat up a pan with the oil over medium heat, add the onions and a pinch of black pepper, and sauté for 10 minutes stirring often.
2. Add the chicken and cook for 3 minutes more.
3. Add the rest of the ingredients, bring to a simmer and cook over medium heat for 12 minutes more.
4. Divide the chicken and onions mix between plates and serve.

Nutrition: 99 calories, 1.3g protein, 8.8g carbohydrates, 7.1g fat, 2.1g fiber, 0mg cholesterol, 39mg sodium, 158mg potassium

Turkey with Pepper and Rice

Prep time: 10 minutes | Cooking time: 42 minutes |
Servings: 4

Ingredients:

- 1 turkey breast, skinless, boneless and cubed
- 1 cup white rice
- 2 cups low-sodium vegetable stock
- 1 teaspoon hot paprika
- 2 small Serrano peppers, chopped
- 2 garlic cloves, minced
- 2 tablespoons olive oil
- ½ red bell pepper chopped
- A pinch of black pepper

Directions:

1. Heat up a pan with the oil over medium heat, add the Serrano peppers and garlic and sauté for 2 minutes.
2. Add the meat and brown it for 5 minutes.
3. Add the rice and the other ingredients, bring to a simmer and cook over medium heat for 35 minutes.
4. Stir, divide between plates and serve.

Nutrition: 245 calories, 4g protein, 40.2g carbohydrates, 7.3g fat, 1.3g fiber, 0mg cholesterol, 76mg sodium, 134mg potassium

Chicken and Leeks

Prep time: 10 minutes | Cooking time: 40 minutes |
Servings: 4

Ingredients:

- 1 pound chicken breast, skinless, boneless and cubed
- A pinch of black pepper
- 2 tablespoons avocado oil
- 1 tablespoon tomato sauce,
- no-salt-added
- 1 cup low-sodium vegetable stock
- 4 leek, roughly chopped
- ½ cup lemon juice

Directions:

1. Heat up a pan with the oil over medium heat, add the leeks, toss and sauté for 10 minutes.
2. Add the chicken and the other ingredients, toss, cook over medium heat for 20 minutes more, divide between plates and serve.

Nutrition: 214 calories, 25.9g protein, 14.7g carbohydrates, 5.1g fat, 2.1g fiber, 73mg cholesterol, 172mg sodium, 652mg potassium

Turkey and Cabbage Mix

Prep time: 10 minutes | Cooking time: 35 minutes |
Servings: 4

Ingredients:

- 1 big turkey breast, skinless, boneless and cubed
- 1 cup low-sodium chicken stock
- 1 tablespoon coconut oil, melted
- 1 Savoy cabbage, shredded
- 1 teaspoon chili powder
- 1 teaspoon sweet paprika
- 1 garlic clove, minced
- 1 yellow onion, chopped
- A pinch of salt and black pepper

Directions:

1. Heat up a pan with the oil over medium heat, add the meat and brown for 5 minutes.
2. Add the garlic and the onion, toss and sauté for 5 minutes more.
3. Add the cabbage and the other ingredients, toss, bring to a simmer and cook over medium heat for 25 minutes.
4. Divide everything between plates and serve.

Nutrition: 91 calories, 3.1g protein, 13.8g carbohydrates, 3.8g fat, 5.5g fiber, 0mg cholesterol, 76mg sodium, 372mg potassium

Spiced Chicken Mix

Prep time: 10 minutes | Cooking time: 30 minutes |
Servings: 4

Ingredients:

- 1 pound chicken breast, skinless, boneless and sliced
- 4 scallions, chopped
- 1 tablespoon olive oil
- 1 tablespoon sweet paprika
- 1 cup low-sodium chicken stock
- 1 tablespoon ginger, grated
- 1 teaspoon oregano, dried
- 1 teaspoon cumin, ground
- 1 teaspoon allspice, ground
- ½ cup cilantro, chopped
- A pinch of black pepper

Directions:

1. Heat up a pan with the oil over medium heat, add the scallions and the meat and brown for 5 minutes.
2. Add the rest of the ingredients, toss, introduce in the oven and bake at 390 degrees F for 25 minutes.
3. Divide the chicken and scallions mix between plates and serve.

Nutrition: 180 calories, 25.1g protein, 3.9g carbohydrates, 6.9g fat, 1.6g fiber, 73mg cholesterol, 97mg sodium, 551mg potassium

Mustard Chicken

Prep time: 10 minutes | Cooking time: 35 minutes | Servings: 4

Ingredients:

- 1 pound chicken thighs, boneless and skinless
- 1 tablespoon avocado oil
- 2 tablespoons mustard
- 1 shallot, chopped
- 1 cup low-sodium chicken stock
- A pinch of salt and black pepper
- 3 garlic cloves, minced
- ½ teaspoon basil, dried

Directions:

1. Heat up a pan with the oil over medium heat, add the shallot, garlic and the chicken and brown everything for 5 minutes.
2. Add the mustard and the rest of the ingredients, toss gently, bring to a simmer and cook over medium heat for 30 minutes.
3. Divide everything between plates and serve hot.

Nutrition: 253 calories, 34.7g protein, 3.3g carbohydrates, 10.5g fat, 1g fiber, 101mg cholesterol, 132mg sodium, 343mg potassium

Chili Chicken Mix

Prep time: 10 minutes | Cooking time: 35 minutes | Servings: 4

Ingredients:

- A pinch of black pepper
- 2 pounds chicken breast, skinless, boneless and cubed
- 2 tablespoons olive oil
- 1 cup celery, chopped
- 3 garlic cloves, minced
- 1 poblano pepper, chopped
- 1 cup low-sodium vegetable stock
- 1 teaspoon chili powder
- 2 tablespoons chives, chopped

Directions:

1. Heat up a pan with the oil over medium heat, add the garlic, celery and poblano pepper, toss and cook for 5 minutes.
2. Add the meat, toss and cook for another 5 minutes.
3. Add the rest of the ingredients except the chives, bring to a simmer and cook over medium heat for 25 minutes more.
4. Divide the whole mix between plates and serve with the chives sprinkled on top.

Nutrition: 338 calories, 49g protein, 4g carbohydrates, 12.9g fat, 1.1g fiber, 145mg cholesterol, 179mg sodium, 1001mg potassium

Turkey and Potatoes

Prep time: 10 minutes | Cooking time: 40 minutes | Servings: 4

Ingredients:

- 1 turkey breast, skinless, boneless and sliced
- 2 tablespoons olive oil
- 1 pound baby potatoes, peeled and halved
- 1 tablespoon sweet paprika
- 1 yellow onion, chopped
- 1 teaspoon chili powder
- 1 teaspoon rosemary, dried
- 2 cups low-sodium chicken stock
- A pinch of black pepper
- Zest of 1 lime, grated
- 1 tablespoon lime juice
- 1 tablespoon cilantro, chopped

Directions:

1. Heat up a pan with the oil over medium heat, add the onion, chili powder and the rosemary, toss and sauté for 5 minutes.
2. Add the meat, and brown for 5 minutes more.
3. Add the potatoes and the rest of the ingredients except the cilantro, toss gently, bring to a simmer and cook over medium heat for 30 minutes.
4. Divide the mix between plates and serve with the cilantro sprinkled on top.

Nutrition: 149 calories, 4.2g protein, 18.5g carbohydrates, 7.5g fat, 4.5g fiber, 0mg cholesterol, 90mg sodium, 571mg potassium

Chicken and Greens

Prep time: 10 minutes | Cooking time: 25 minutes | Servings: 4

Ingredients:

- 2 chicken breasts, skinless, boneless and cubed
- 3 cups mustard greens
- 1 cup canned tomatoes, no-salt-added, chopped
- 1 red onion, chopped
- 2 tablespoons avocado oil
- 1 teaspoon oregano, dried
- 2 garlic cloves, minced
- 1 tablespoon chives, chopped
- 1 tablespoon balsamic vinegar
- A pinch of black pepper

Directions:

1. Heat up a pan with the oil over medium-high heat, add the onion and the garlic and sauté for 5 minutes.
2. Add the meat and brown it for 5 minutes more.
3. Add the greens, tomatoes and the other ingredients, toss, cook for 20 minutes over medium heat, divide between plates and serve.

Nutrition: 281 calories, 38.2g protein, 7.6g carbohydrates, 10.4g fat, 3g fiber, 111mg cholesterol, 132mg sodium, 639mg potassium

Herbed Chicken Mix

Prep time: 10 minutes | Cooking time: 50 minutes | Servings: 4

Ingredients:

- 2 pounds chicken thighs, boneless and skinless
- 2 tablespoons olive oil
- 2 red onions, sliced
- A pinch of black pepper
- 1 teaspoon thyme, dried
- 1 teaspoon basil, dried
- 1 cup green apples, cored and
- roughly cubed
- 2 garlic cloves, minced
- 2 cups low-sodium chicken stock
- 1 tablespoon lemon juice
- 1 cup tomatoes, cubed
- 1 tablespoon cilantro, chopped

Directions:

1. Heat up a pan with the oil over medium-high heat, add the onions and garlic, and sauté for 5 minutes.
2. Add the chicken and brown for another 5 minutes.
3. Add the thyme, basil and the other ingredients, toss gently, introduce in the oven and bake at 390 degrees F for 40 minutes.
4. Divide the chicken and apples mix between plates and serve.

Nutrition: 557 calories, 67.4g protein, 15.4g carbohydrates, 24.1g fat, 3.2g fiber, 202mg cholesterol, 269mg sodium, 813mg potassium

Cumin Chicken

Prep time: 10 minutes | Cooking time: 1 hour | Servings: 6

Ingredients:

- 2 pounds chicken thighs, boneless and skinless
- 1 yellow onion, chopped
- 2 tablespoons olive oil
- 3 garlic cloves, minced
- 1 tablespoon coriander seeds, ground
- 1 teaspoon cumin, ground
- 1 cup low-sodium chicken stock
- 4 tablespoons chipotle chili paste
- A pinch of black pepper
- 1 tablespoon coriander, chopped

Directions:

1. Heat up a pan with the oil over medium heat, add the onion and the garlic and sauté for 5 minutes.
2. Add the meat and brown for 5 minutes more.
3. Add the rest of the ingredients, toss, introduce everything in the oven and bake at 390 degrees F for 50 minutes.
4. Divide the whole mix between plates and serve.

Nutrition: 372 calories, 44.9g protein, 6.4g carbohydrates, 17.6g fat, 0.5g fiber, 138mg cholesterol, 274mg sodium, 407mg potassium

Oregano Turkey and Tomato Mix

Prep time: 10 minutes | Cooking time: 35 minutes | Servings: 4

Ingredients:

- 1 big turkey breast, boneless, skinless and sliced
- 1 tablespoon chives, chopped
- 1 tablespoon oregano, chopped
- 1 tablespoon basil, chopped
- 1 tablespoon coriander, chopped
- 2 shallots, chopped
- 2 tablespoons olive oil
- 1 cup low-sodium chicken stock
- 1 cup tomatoes, cubed
- Salt and black pepper to the taste

Directions:

1. Heat up a pan with the oil over medium heat, add the shallots and the meat and brown for 5 minutes.
2. Add the chives and the other ingredients, toss, bring to a simmer and cook over medium heat for 30 minutes.
3. Divide the mix between plates and serve.

Nutrition: 189 calories, 14.5g protein, 11.1g carbohydrates, 10.2g fat, 1.5g fiber, 55mg cholesterol, 1237mg sodium, 497mg potassium

Ginger Chicken

Prep time: 10 minutes | Cooking time: 35 minutes | Servings: 4

Ingredients:

- 1 pound chicken breast, skinless, boneless and cubed
- 1 tablespoon ginger, grated
- 1 tablespoon olive oil
- 2 shallots, chopped
- 1 tablespoon balsamic vinegar
- A pinch of black pepper
- ¾ cup low-sodium chicken stock
- 1 tablespoon basil, chopped

Directions:

1. Heat up a pan with the oil over medium heat, add the shallots and the ginger, stir and sauté for 5 minutes.
2. Add the rest of the ingredients except the chicken, toss, bring to a simmer and cook for 5 minutes more.
3. Add the chicken, toss, simmer the whole mix for 25 minutes, divide between plates and serve.

Nutrition: 169 calories, 24.5g protein, 1.9g carbohydrates, 6.4g fat, 0.2g fiber, 73mg cholesterol, 84mg sodium, 459mg potassium

Chicken and Green Onions

Prep time: 10 minutes | Cooking time: 35 minutes | Servings: 4

Ingredients:

- 2 pounds chicken breast, skinless, boneless and halved
- 2 cups corn
- 2 tablespoons avocado oil
- A pinch of black pepper
- 1 teaspoon smoked paprika
- 1 bunch green onions, chopped
- 1 cup low-sodium chicken stock

Directions:

1. Heat up a pan with the oil over medium-high heat, add the green onions, stir and sauté them for 5 minutes.
2. Add the chicken and brown it for 5 minutes more.
3. Add the corn and the other ingredients, toss, introduce the pan in the oven and cook at 390 degrees F for 25 minutes.
4. Divide the mix between plates and serve.

Nutrition: 338 calories, 51.1g protein, 15.5g carbohydrates, 7.5g fat, 2.7g fiber, 145mg cholesterol, 162mg sodium, 1092mg potassium

Parsley Turkey and Quinoa

Prep time: 10 minutes | Cooking time: 40 minutes | Servings: 4

Ingredients:

- 1 pound turkey breast, skinless, boneless and cubed
- 1 tablespoon olive oil
- 1 cup quinoa
- 2 cups low-sodium chicken
- stock
- 1 tablespoon lime juice
- 1 tablespoon parsley, chopped
- A pinch of black pepper
- 1 tablespoon red curry paste

Directions:

1. Heat up a pan with the oil over medium-high heat, add the meat and brown it for 5 minutes.
2. Add the quinoa and the rest of the ingredients, toss, bring to a simmer and cook over medium heat for 35 minutes.
3. Divide everything between plates and serve.

Nutrition: 322 calories, 25.9g protein, 32.9g carbohydrates, 9.1g fat, 3.6g fiber, 49mg cholesterol, 1416mg sodium, 587mg potassium

Turkey and Parsnips

Prep time: 10 minutes | Cooking time: 40 minutes | Servings: 4

Ingredients:

- 1 pound turkey breast, skinless, boneless and cubed
- 2 parsnips, peeled and cubed
- 2 teaspoons cumin, ground
- 1 tablespoon parsley, chopped
- 2 tablespoons avocado oil
- 2 shallots, chopped
- 1 cup low-sodium chicken stock
- 4 garlic cloves, minced
- A pinch of black pepper

Directions:

1. Heat up a pan with the oil over medium heat, add the shallots and the garlic and sauté for 5 minutes.
2. Add the turkey, toss and cook for 5 minutes more.
3. Add the parsnips and the other ingredients, toss, simmer over medium heat for 30 minutes more, divide between plates and serve.

Nutrition: 166 calories, 20.6g protein, 13.5g carbohydrates, 3.1g fat, 2.7g fiber, 49mg cholesterol, 1192mg sodium, 542mg potassium

Turkey and Chickpeas

Prep time: 10 minutes | Cooking time: 40 minutes | Servings: 4

Ingredients:

- 1 cup canned chickpeas, no-salt-added, drained
- 1 cup low-sodium chicken stock
- 1 pound turkey breast, skinless, boneless and cubed
- A pinch of black pepper
- 1 teaspoon oregano, dried
- 1 teaspoon nutmeg, ground
- 2 tablespoons olive oil
- 1 yellow onion, chopped
- 1 green bell pepper, chopped
- 1 cup cilantro, chopped

Directions:

1. Heat up a pan with the oil over medium heat, add the onion, bell pepper and the meat and cook for 10 minutes stirring often.
2. Add the rest of the ingredients, toss, bring to a simmer and cook over medium heat for 30 minutes.
3. Divide the mix between plates and serve.

Nutrition: 387 calories, 30g protein, 40.6g carbohydrates, 12.3g fat, 10.6g fiber, 49mg cholesterol, 1201mg sodium, 905mg potassium

Buttery Cashew Turkey

Prep time: 10 minutes | Cooking time: 40 minutes | Servings: 4

Ingredients:

- 1 pound turkey breast, skinless, boneless and cubed
- 1 cup cashews, chopped
- 1 yellow onion, chopped
- ½ tablespoon olive oil
- Black pepper to the taste
- ½ teaspoon sweet paprika
- 2 and ½ tablespoons cashew butter
- ¼ cup low-sodium chicken stock
- 1 tablespoon cilantro, chopped

Directions:

1. Heat up a pan with the oil over medium-high heat, add the onion, stir and sauté for 5 minutes.
2. Add the meat and brown it for 5 minutes more.
3. Add the rest of the ingredients, toss, bring to a simmer and cook over medium heat for 30 minutes.
4. Divide the whole mix between plates and serve.

Nutrition: 401 calories, 26.8g protein, 21.5g carbohydrates, 24.5g fat, 2.5g fiber, 49mg cholesterol, 1168mg sodium, 638mg potassium

Turkey and Cranberries Mix

Prep time: 10 minutes | Cooking time: 35 minutes | Servings: 6

Ingredients:

- 2 pounds turkey breasts, skinless, boneless and cubed
- 1 tablespoon olive oil
- 1 red onion, chopped
- 1 cup dried cranberries
- 1 cup low-sodium chicken stock
- ¼ cup cilantro, chopped
- Black pepper to the taste

Directions:

1. Heat up a pot with the oil over medium-high heat, add the onion, stir and sauté for 5 minutes.
2. Add the meat, berries and the other ingredients, bring to a simmer and cook over medium heat for 30 minutes more.
3. Divide the mix between plates and serve.

Nutrition: 272 calories, 26.2g protein, 30.8g carbohydrates, 4.9g fat, 2.5g fiber, 65mg cholesterol, 1558mg sodium, 487mg potassium

Chicken Breast and Tomatoes

Prep time: 5 minutes | Cooking time: 35 minutes | Servings: 4

Ingredients:

- 1 cup tomatoes, crushed
- 1 teaspoon five spice
- 2 chicken breast halves, skinless, boneless and halved
- 1 tablespoon avocado oil
- 2 tablespoons coconut aminos
- Black pepper to the taste
- 1 tablespoons hot pepper
- 1 tablespoon cilantro, chopped

Directions:

1. Heat up a pan with the oil over medium heat, add the meat and brown it for 2 minutes on each side.
2. Add the tomatoes, five spice and the other ingredients, bring to a simmer and cook over medium heat for 30 minutes.
3. Divide the whole mix between plates and serve.

Nutrition: 167 calories, 22g protein, 4.8g carbohydrates, 6g fat, 1.7g fiber, 65mg cholesterol, 74mg sodium, 317mg potassium

Turkey and Greens

Prep time: 10 minutes | Cooking time: 17 minutes | Servings: 4

Ingredients:

- 1 pound turkey breast, boneless, skinless and cubed
- 1 cup mustard greens
- 1 teaspoon nutmeg, ground
- 1 teaspoon allspice, ground
- 1 yellow onion, chopped
- Black pepper to the taste
- 1 tablespoon olive oil

Directions:

1. Heat up a pan with the oil over medium-high heat, add the onion and the meat and brown for 5 minutes.
2. Add the rest of the ingredients, toss, cook over medium heat for 12 minutes more, divide between plates and serve.

Nutrition: 167 calories, 20.1g protein, 49g carbohydrates, 5.7g fat, 1.8g fiber, 49mg cholesterol, 1156mg sodium, 439mg potassium

Chicken and Almond Mushrooms

Prep time: 10 minutes | Cooking time: 20 minutes | Servings: 4

Ingredients:

- 2 chicken breasts, skinless, boneless and halved
- ½ pound white mushrooms, halved
- 1 tablespoon olive oil
- 1 cup canned tomatoes, no-
- salt-added, chopped
- 2 tablespoons almonds, chopped
- 2 tablespoons olive oil
- ½ teaspoon chili flakes
- Black pepper to the taste

Directions:

1. Heat up a pan with the oil over medium-high heat, add the mushrooms, toss and sauté for 5 minutes.
2. Add the meat, toss and cook for 5 minutes more.
3. Add the tomatoes and the other ingredients, bring to a simmer and cook over medium heat for 10 minutes.
4. Divide the mix between plates and serve.

Nutrition: 206 calories, 23.9g protein, 4.3g carbohydrates, 10.7g fat, 1.5g fiber, 65mg cholesterol, 68mg sodium, 487mg potassium

Chili Chicken

Prep time: 10 minutes | Cooking time: 20 minutes | Servings: 4

Ingredients:

- 2 red chilies, chopped
- 1 tablespoon olive oil
- 1 yellow onion, chopped
- 1 pound chicken breasts, skinless, boneless and cubed
- 1 cup tomatoes, crushed
- 10 ounces canned artichoke hearts, drained and quartered
- Black pepper to the taste
- ½ cup low-sodium chicken stock
- 2 tablespoons lime juice

Directions:

1. Heat up a pan with the oil over medium heat, add the onion and the chilies, stir and sauté for 5 minutes.
2. Add the meat, toss and brown for 5 minutes more.
3. Add the rest of the ingredients, bring to a simmer over medium heat and cook for 10 minutes.
4. Divide the mix between plates and serve.

Nutrition: 299 calories, 36g protein, 11.9g carbohydrates, 12.1g fat, 5g fiber, 101mg cholesterol, 185mg sodium, 689mg potassium

Parsley Chicken and Peas

Prep time: 10 minutes | Cooking time: 30 minutes | Servings: 4

Ingredients:

- 2 pounds chicken breasts, skinless, boneless and cubed
- 2 cups snow peas
- 2 tablespoons olive oil
- 1 red onion, chopped
- 1 cup canned tomato sauce, no-salt-added
- 2 tablespoons parsley, chopped
- A pinch of black pepper

Directions:

1. Heat up a pan with the oil over medium heat, add the onion and the meat and brown for 5 minutes.
2. Add the peas and the rest of the ingredients, bring to a simmer and cook over medium heat for 25 minutes.
3. Divide the mix between plates and serve.

Nutrition: 551 calories, 69.4g protein, 2.4g carbohydrates, 11.6g fat, 24.2g fiber, 202mg cholesterol, 521mg sodium, 997mg potassium

Turkey and Broccoli

Prep time: 10 minutes | Cooking time: 30 minutes | Servings: 4

Ingredients:

- 1 red onion, chopped
- 1 pound turkey breast, skinless, boneless and cubed
- 2 cups broccoli florets
- 1 teaspoon cumin, ground
- 3 garlic cloves, minced
- 2 tablespoons olive oil
- 14 ounces coconut milk
- A pinch of black pepper
- ¼ cup cilantro, chopped

Directions:

1. Heat up a pot with the oil over medium heat, add the onion and the garlic, stir and sauté for 5 minutes.
2. Add the turkey, toss and brown for 5 minutes.
3. Add the broccoli and the rest of the ingredients, bring to a simmer over medium heat and cook for 20 minutes.
4. Divide the mix between plates and serve.

Nutrition: 438 calories, 23.5g protein, 16.9g carbohydrates, 32.9g fat, 4.7g fiber, 49mg cholesterol, 1184mg sodium, 811mg potassium

Paprika Chicken

Prep time: 10 minutes | Cooking time: 30 minutes | Servings: 4

Ingredients:

- 1 pound chicken breast, skinless, boneless and cubed
- 1 cup low-sodium chicken stock
- 1 tablespoons avocado oil
- 2 teaspoons cloves, ground
- 1 yellow onion, chopped
- 2 teaspoons sweet paprika
- 3 tomatoes, cubed
- A pinch of salt and black pepper
- ½ cup parsley, chopped

Directions:

1. Heat up a pan with the oil over medium heat, add the onion and sauté for 5 minutes.
2. Add the chicken and brown for 5 minutes more.
3. Add the stock and the rest of the ingredients, bring to a simmer and cook over medium heat for 20 minutes more.
4. Divide the mix between plates and serve.

Nutrition: 172 calories, 25.9g protein, 8.1g carbohydrates, 3.9g fat, 2.9g fiber, 73mg cholesterol, 104mg sodium, 767mg potassium

Chicken and Artichokes

Prep time: 10 minutes | Cooking time: 30 minutes | Servings: 4

Ingredients:

- 2 chicken breasts, skinless, boneless and halved
- 1 tablespoon ginger, grated
- 1 cup canned tomatoes, no-salt-added, chopped
- 10 ounces canned artichokes, no-salt-added, drained and quartered
- 2 tablespoons lemon juice
- 2 tablespoons olive oil
- A pinch of black pepper

Directions:

1. Heat up a pan with the oil over medium heat, add the ginger and the artichokes, toss and cook for 5 minutes.
2. Add the chicken and cook for 5 minutes more.
3. Add the rest of the ingredients, bring to a simmer and cook for 20 minutes more.
4. Divide everything between plates and serve.

Nutrition: 247 calories, 24g protein, 10.3g carbohydrates, 12.8g fat, 4.6g fiber, 65mg cholesterol, 134mg sodium, 574mg potassium

Peppercorn Turkey

Prep time: 10 minutes | Cooking time: 30 minutes | Servings: 4

Ingredients:

- ½ tablespoon black peppercorns
- 1 tablespoon olive oil
- 1 pound turkey breast, skinless, boneless and cubed
- 1 cup low-sodium chicken stock
- 3 garlic cloves, minced
- 2 tomatoes, cubed
- A pinch of black pepper
- 2 tablespoons spring onions, chopped

Directions:

1. Heat up a pan with the oil over medium heat, add the garlic and the turkey and brown for 5 minutes.
2. Add the peppercorns and the rest of the ingredients, bring to a simmer and cook over medium heat for 25 minutes.
3. Divide the mix between plates and serve.

Nutrition: 167 calories, 20.4g protein, 8.6g carbohydrates, 5.6g fat, 1.7g fiber, 49mg cholesterol, 1189mg sodium, 516mg potassium

Chicken and Veggies

Prep time: 10 minutes | Cooking time: 40 minutes | Servings: 4

Ingredients:

- 2 pounds chicken breasts, skinless, boneless and cubed
- 1 carrot, cubed
- 1 celery stalk, chopped
- 1 tomato, cubed
- 2 small red onions, sliced
- 1 zucchini, cubed
- 2 garlic cloves, minced
- 1 tablespoon rosemary, chopped
- 2 tablespoons olive oil
- Black pepper to the taste
- ½ cup low-sodium vegetable stock

Directions:

1. Heat up a pan with the oil over medium heat, add the onions and the garlic, stir and sauté for 5 minutes.
2. Add the chicken, toss and brown it for 5 minutes more.
3. Add the carrot and the other ingredients, toss, bring to a simmer and cook over medium heat for 30 minutes.
4. Divide the mix between plates and serve.

Nutrition: 530 calories, 67.2g protein, 8.7g carbohydrates, 24.1g fat, 2.4g fiber, 202mg cholesterol, 234mg sodium, 857mg potassium

Garlic Chicken Wings

Prep time: 10 minutes | Cooking time: 20 minutes |
Servings: 4

Ingredients:

- 2 pounds chicken wings
- 2 teaspoons allspice, ground
- 2 tablespoons avocado oil
- 5 garlic cloves, minced
- Black pepper to the taste
- 2 tablespoons chives, chopped

Directions:

1. In a bowl, combine the chicken wings with the allspice and the other ingredients and toss well.
2. Arrange the chicken wings in a roasting pan and bake at 400 degrees F for 20 minutes.
3. Divide the chicken wings between plates and serve.

Nutrition: 449 calories, 66.1g protein, 2.4g carbohydrates, 17.8g fat, 0.6g fiber, 202mg cholesterol, 197mg sodium, 603mg potassium

Chicken and Cabbage

Prep time: 10 minutes | Cooking time: 25 minutes |
Servings: 4

Ingredients:

- 1 pound chicken breast, skinless, boneless and cubed
- 2 tablespoons olive oil
- 2 carrots, peeled and grated
- 1 teaspoon sweet paprika
- ½ cup low-sodium vegetable stock
- 1 red cabbage head, shredded
- 1 yellow onion, chopped
- Black pepper to the taste

Directions:

1. Heat up a pan with the oil over medium heat, add the onion, stir and sauté for 5 minutes.
2. Add the meat, and brown it for 5 minutes more.
3. Add the carrots and the other ingredients, toss, bring to a simmer and cook over medium heat for 15 minutes.
4. Divide everything between plates and serve.

Nutrition: 261 calories, 27.1g protein, 16.7g carbohydrates, 10.1g fat, 6.1g fiber, 73mg cholesterol, 130mg sodium, 889mg potassium

Turkey Sandwich

Prep time: 10 minutes | Cooking time: 25 minutes |
Servings: 4

Ingredients:

- 1 turkey breast, skinless, boneless and sliced into 4 pieces
- 1 eggplant, sliced into 4 slices
- Black pepper to the taste
- 1 tablespoon olive oil
- 1 tablespoon oregano, chopped
- ½ cup low sodium tomato sauce
- ½ cup low-fat cheddar cheese, shredded
- 4 whole wheat bread slices

Directions:

1. Heat up a grill over medium-high heat, add the turkey slices, drizzle half of the oil over them, sprinkle the black pepper, cook for 8 minutes on each side and transfer to a plate.
2. Arrange the eggplant slices on the heated grill, drizzle the rest of the oil over them, season with black pepper as well, cook them for 4 minutes on each side and transfer to the plate with the turkey slices as well.
3. Arrange 2 bread slices on a working surface, divide the cheese on each, divide the eggplant slices and turkey ones on each, sprinkle the oregano, drizzle the sauce all over and top with the other 2 bread slices.
4. Divide the sandwiches between plates and serve.

Nutrition: 265 calories, 21.2g protein, 22.1g carbohydrates, 10.6g fat, 6.3g fiber, 47mg cholesterol, 985mg sodium, 572mg potassium

Turkey and Lentils

Prep time: 10 minutes | Cooking time: 40 minutes |
Servings: 4

Ingredients:

- 2 pounds turkey breast, skinless, boneless and cubed
- 1 cup canned lentils, no-salt-added, drained and rinsed
- 1 tablespoon green curry paste
- 1 teaspoon garam masala
- 2 tablespoons olive oil
- 1 yellow onion, chopped
- 1 garlic clove, minced
- A pinch of black pepper
- 1 tablespoon cilantro, chopped

Directions:

1. Heat up a pan with the oil over medium heat, add the onion, garlic and the meat and brown for 5 minutes stirring often.
2. Add the lentils and the other ingredients, bring to a simmer and cook over medium heat for 35 minutes.
3. Divide the mix between plates and serve.

Nutrition: 224 calories, 19.8g protein, 16.9g carbohydrates, 8.9g fat, 5g fiber, 38mg cholesterol, 941mg sodium, 491mg potassium

Turkey and Barley

Prep time: 5 minutes | Cooking time: 55 minutes |
Servings: 4

Ingredients:

- 1 tablespoon olive oil
- 1 turkey breast, skinless, boneless and sliced
- Black pepper to the taste
- 2 celery stalks, chopped
- 1 red onion, chopped
- 2 cups low-sodium chicken stock
- ½ cup barley
- 1 teaspoon lemon zest, grated
- 1 tablespoon lemon juice
- 1 tablespoon chives, chopped

Directions:

1. Heat up a pot with the oil over medium-high heat, add the meat and the onion, toss and brown for 5 minutes.
2. Add the celery and the other ingredients, toss, bring to a simmer, reduce heat to medium, simmer for 50 minutes, divide into bowls and serve.

Nutrition: 194 calories, 15.5g protein, 23.3g carbohydrates, 4.1g fat, 4.8g fiber, 25mg cholesterol, 796mg sodium, 195mg potassium

Turkey with Radishes

Prep time: 10 minutes | Cooking time: 35 minutes |
Servings: 4

Ingredients:

- 1 turkey breast, skinless, boneless and cubed
- 2 red beets, peeled and cubed
- 1 cup radishes, cubed
- 1 red onion, chopped
- ¼ cup low-sodium chicken stock
- Black pepper to the taste
- 1 tablespoon olive oil
- 2 tablespoon chives, chopped

Directions:

1. Heat up a pan with the oil over medium-high heat, add the meat and the onion, toss and brown for 5 minutes.
2. Add the beets, radishes and the other ingredients, bring to a simmer and cook over medium heat for 30 minutes more.
3. Divide the mix between plates and serve.

Nutrition: 124 calories, 10.6g protein, 10.9g carbohydrates, 4.6g fat, 2.4g fiber, 23mg cholesterol, 605mg sodium, 427mg potassium

Rosemary Chicken and Quinoa

Prep time: 10 minutes | Cooking time: 35 minutes |
Servings: 8

Ingredients:

- 1 tablespoon olive oil
- 2 pounds chicken breasts, skinless, boneless and halved
- 1 teaspoon rosemary, ground
- A pinch of salt and black pepper
- 2 shallots, chopped
- 3 tablespoons low-sodium tomato sauce
- 2 cups quinoa, already cooked

Directions:

1. Heat up a pan with the oil over medium-high heat, add the meat and shallots and brown for 2 minutes on each side.
2. Add the rosemary and the other ingredients, toss, introduce in the oven and cook at 370 degrees F for 30 minutes.
3. Divide the mix between plates and serve.

Nutrition: 39 calories, 39g protein, 28.1g carbohydrates, 12.8g fat, 3.1g fiber, 101mg cholesterol, 130mg sodium, 544mg potassium

Turkey Tortillas

Prep time: 10 minutes | Cooking time: 20 minutes |
Servings: 4

Ingredients:

- 4 whole wheat tortillas
- ½ cup fat-free yogurt
- 1 pound turkey, breast, skinless, boneless and cut into strips
- 1 tablespoon olive oil
- 1 red onion, sliced
- 1 zucchini, cubed
- 2 tomatoes, cubed
- Black pepper to the taste

Directions:

1. Heat up a pan with the oil over medium heat, add the onion, stir and sauté for 5 minutes.
2. Add the zucchini and tomatoes, toss and cook for 2 minutes more.
3. Add the turkey meat, toss and cook for 13 minutes more.
4. Spread the yogurt on each tortilla, add divide the turkey and zucchini mix, roll, divide between plates and serve.

Nutrition: 380 calories, 40.4g protein, 31g carbohydrates, 10.5g fat, 4.9g fiber, 86mg cholesterol, 242mg sodium, 730mg potassium

Chicken with Peppers

Prep time: 10 minutes | Cooking time: 25 minutes |
Servings: 4

Ingredients:

- 2 chicken breasts, skinless, boneless and cubed
- 1 red onion, chopped
- 2 tablespoons olive oil
- 1 eggplant, cubed
- 1 red bell pepper, cubed
- 1 yellow bell pepper, cubed
- Black pepper to the taste
- 2 cups coconut milk

Directions:

1. Heat up a pan with the oil over medium-high heat, add the onion, stir and cook for 3 minutes.
2. Add the bell peppers, toss and cook for 2 minutes more.
3. Add the chicken and the other ingredients, toss, bring to a simmer and cook over medium heat for 20 minutes more.
4. Divide everything between plates and serve.

Nutrition: 524 calories, 25.6g protein, 18.2g carbohydrates, 41.3g fat, 7.7g fiber, 65mg cholesterol, 85mg sodium, 851mg potassium

Coconut Turkey

Prep time: 10 minutes | Cooking time: 23 minutes |
Servings: 4

Ingredients:

- 1 pound turkey breast, skinless, boneless and cubed
- 1 tablespoon olive oil
- ½ cup low-fat parmesan, grated
- 2 shallots, chopped
- 1 cup coconut milk
- Black pepper to the taste

Directions:

1. Heat up a pan with the oil over medium-high heat, add the shallots, toss and cook for 5 minutes.
2. Add the meat, coconut milk, and black pepper, toss and cook over medium heat for 15 minutes more.
3. Add the parmesan, cook for 2-3 minutes, divide everything between plates and serve.

Nutrition: 323 calories, 23.4g protein, 9.1g carbohydrates, 22.2g fat, 1.9g fiber, 60mg cholesterol, 1352mg sodium, 533mg potassium

Chicken and Shrimp

Prep time: 10 minutes | Cooking time: 14 minutes |
Servings: 4

Ingredients:

- 1 tablespoon olive oil
- 1 pound chicken breast, skinless, boneless and cubed
- ¼ cup low-sodium chicken stock
- 1 pound shrimp, peeled and deveined
- ½ cup coconut cream
- 1 tablespoon cilantro, chopped

Directions:

1. Heat up a pan with the oil over medium heat, add the chicken, toss and cook for 8 minutes.
2. Add the shrimp and the other ingredients, toss, cook everything for 6 minutes more, divide into bowls and serve.

Nutrition: 363 calories, 50.6g protein, 3.4g carbohydrates, 15.4g fat, 0.7g fiber, 311mg cholesterol, 348mg sodium, 692mg potassium

Turkey and Asparagus

Prep time: 10 minutes | Cooking time: 40 minutes |
Servings: 4

Ingredients:

- 1 pound turkey breast, skinless, and cut into strips
- 1 cup coconut cream
- 1 cup low-sodium chicken stock
- 2 tablespoons parsley, chopped
- 1 bunch asparagus, trimmed and halved
- 1 teaspoon chili powder
- 2 tablespoons olive oil
- A pinch of sea salt and black pepper

Directions:

1. Heat up a pan with the oil over medium-high heat, add the turkey and some black pepper, toss and cook for 5 minutes.
2. Add the asparagus, chili powder and the other ingredients, toss, bring to a simmer and cook over medium heat for 30 minutes more.
3. Divide everything between plates and serve.

Nutrition: 327 calories, 21.9g protein, 9.9g carbohydrates, 23.4g fat, 2.9g fiber, 49mg cholesterol, 1202mg sodium, 591mg potassium

Chicken with Tomatoes and Grapes

Prep time: 10 minutes | Cooking time: 40 minutes | Servings: 4

Ingredients:

- 1 carrot, cubed
- 1 yellow onion, sliced
- 1 tablespoon olive oil
- 1 cup tomatoes, cubed
- ¼ cup low-sodium chicken stock
- 2 garlic cloves, chopped
- 1 pound chicken thighs, skinless and boneless
- 1 cup green grapes
- Black pepper to the taste

Directions:

1. Grease a baking pan with the oil, arrange the chicken thighs inside and add the other ingredients on top.
2. Bake at 390 degrees F for 40 minutes, divide between plates and serve.

Nutrition: 289 calories, 33.9g protein, 10.3g carbohydrates, 12.1g fat, 1.7g fiber, 101mg cholesterol, 120mg sodium, 521mg potassium

Turkey and Olives

Prep time: 10 minutes | Cooking time: 35 minutes | Servings: 4

Ingredients:

- 1 cup black beans, no-salt-added and drained
- 1 cup green olives, pitted and halved
- 1 pound turkey breast, skinless, boneless and sliced
- 1 tablespoon cilantro, chopped
- 1 cup tomato sauce, no-salt-added
- 1 tablespoon olive oil

Directions:

1. Grease a baking dish with the oil, arrange the turkey slices inside, add the other ingredients as well, introduce in the oven and bake at 380 degrees F for 35 minutes.
2. Divide between plates and serve.

Nutrition: 291 calories, 25.6g protein, 24g carbohydrates, 10.1g fat, 6.8g fiber, 49mg cholesterol, 1405mg sodium, 546mg potassium

Balsamic Turkey

Prep time: 10 minutes | Cooking time: 40 minutes | Servings: 4

Ingredients:

- 1 big turkey breast, skinless, boneless and sliced
- 2 tablespoons balsamic vinegar
- 1 tablespoon olive oil
- 2 garlic cloves, minced
- 1 tablespoon Italian seasoning
- Black pepper to the taste
- 1 tablespoon cilantro, chopped

Directions:

1. In a baking dish, mix the turkey with the vinegar, the oil and the other ingredients, toss, introduce in the oven at 400 degrees F and bake for 40 minutes.
2. Divide everything between plates and serve with a side salad.

Nutrition: 149 calories, 17.2g protein, 5.2g carbohydrates, 6.2g fat, 0.5g fiber, 45mg cholesterol, 1017mg sodium, 317mg potassiumя

Cheesy Turkey

Prep time: 10 minutes | Cooking time: 1 hour | Servings: 4

Ingredients:

- 1 pound turkey breast, skinless, boneless and sliced
- 2 tablespoons olive oil
- 1 cup canned tomatoes, no-salt-added, chopped
- Black pepper to the taste
- 1 cup fat-free cheddar cheese, shredded
- 2 tablespoons parsley, chopped

Directions:

1. Grease a baking dish with the oil, arrange the turkey slices into the pan, spread the tomatoes over them, season with black pepper, sprinkle the cheese and parsley on top, introduce in the oven at 400 degrees F and bake for 1 hour.
2. Divide everything between plates and serve.

Nutrition: 301 calories, 26.9g protein, 7g carbohydrates, 18.4g fat, 1.2g fiber, 78mg cholesterol, 1330mg sodium, 487mg potassium

Chives Chicken and Beets

Prep time: 10 minutes | Cooking time: 0 minutes | Servings: 4

Ingredients:

- 1 carrot, shredded
- 2 beets, peeled and shredded
- ½ cup avocado mayonnaise
- 1 cup smoked chicken breast, skinless, boneless, cooked and shredded
- 1 teaspoon chives, chopped

Directions:

1. In a bowl, combine the chicken with the beets and the other ingredients, toss and serve right away.

Nutrition: 348 calories, 27g protein, 6.5g carbohydrates, 25.6g fat, 1.4g fiber, 105mg cholesterol, 354mg sodium, 202mg potassium

Turkey Salad

Prep time: 4 minutes | Cooking time: 0 minutes | Servings: 4

Ingredients:

- 2 cups turkey breast, skinless, boneless, cooked and shredded
- 1 cup celery stalks, chopped
- 2 spring onions, chopped
- 1 cup black olives, pitted and halved
- 1 tablespoon olive oil
- 1 teaspoon lime juice
- 1 cup fat-free yogurt

Directions:

1. In a bowl, combine the turkey with the celery and the other ingredients, toss and serve cold.

Nutrition: 187 calories, 17.7g protein, 12g carbohydrates, 7.3g fat, 1.7g fiber, 30mg cholesterol, 1198mg sodium, 245mg potassium

Meat

Paprika Pork Mix

Prep time: 10 minutes | Cooking time: 45 minutes |
Servings: 8

Ingredients:

- 2 pounds pork meat, boneless and cubed
- 1 red onion, chopped
- 1 tablespoon olive oil
- 3 garlic cloves, minced
- 1 cup low-sodium beef stock
- 2 tablespoons sweet paprika
- Black pepper to the taste
- 1 tablespoon chives, chopped

Directions:

1. Heat up a pan with the oil over medium heat, add the onion and the meat, toss and brown for 5 minutes.
2. Add the rest of the ingredients, toss, reduce heat to medium, cover and cook for 40 minutes.
3. Divide the mix between plates and serve.

Nutrition: 199 calories, 22.8g protein, 2.6g carbohydrates, 10g fat, 1g fiber, 75mg cholesterol, 104mg sodium, 66mg potassium

Pork and Carrots

Prep time: 10 minutes | Cooking time: 30 minutes |
Servings: 4

Ingredients:

- 1 pound pork stew meat, cubed
- ¼ cup low-sodium vegetable stock
- 2 carrots, peeled and sliced
- 2 tablespoons olive oil
- 1 red onion, sliced
- 2 teaspoons sweet paprika
- Black pepper to the taste

Directions:

1. Heat up a pan with the oil over medium heat, add the onion, stir and sauté for 5 minutes.
2. Add the meat, toss and brown for 5 minutes more.
3. Add the rest of the ingredients, bring to a simmer and cook over medium heat for 20 minutes.
4. Divide the mix between plates and serve.

Nutrition: 328 calories, 34g protein, 6.4g carbohydrates, 18.1g fat, 1.8g fiber, 98mg cholesterol, 98mg sodium, 596mg potassium

Cilantro Pork

Prep time: 10 minutes | Cooking time: 35 minutes |Servings: 4

Ingredients:

- 2 red onions, sliced
- 2 green onions, chopped
- 1 tablespoon olive oil
- 2 teaspoons ginger, grated
- 4 pork chops
- 3 garlic cloves, chopped
- Black pepper to the taste
- 1 carrot, chopped
- 1 cup low sodium beef stock
- 2 tablespoons tomato paste
- 1 tablespoon cilantro, chopped

Directions:

1. Heat up a pan with the oil over medium heat, add the green and red onions, toss and sauté them for 3 minutes.
2. Add the garlic and the ginger, toss and cook for 2 minutes more.
3. Add the pork chops and cook them for 2 minutes on each side.
4. Add the rest of the ingredients, bring to a simmer and cook over medium heat for 25 minutes more.
5. Divide the mix between plates and serve.

Nutrition: 332 calories, 19.9g protein, 10.1g carbohydrates, 23.6g fat, 2.3g fiber, 69mg cholesterol, 11mg sodium, 528mg potassium

Coriander Pork

Prep time: 10 minutes | Cooking time: 45 minutes |
Servings: 4

Ingredients:

- ½ cup low-sodium beef stock
- 2 tablespoons olive oil
- 2 pounds pork stew meat, cubed
- 1 teaspoon coriander, ground
- 2 teaspoons cumin, ground
- Black pepper to the taste
- 1 cup cherry tomatoes, halved
- 4 garlic cloves, minced
- 1 tablespoon cilantro, chopped

Directions:

1. Heat up a pan with the oil over medium heat, add the garlic and the meat, toss and brown for 5 minutes.
2. Add the stock and the other ingredients, bring to a simmer and cook over medium heat for 40 minutes.
3. Divide everything between plates and serve.

Nutrition: 559 calories, 67.4g protein, 10.1g carbohydrates, 3.2g fat, 29.3g fiber, 195mg cholesterol, 156mg sodium, 988mg potassium

Balsamic Pork

Prep time: 10 minutes | Cooking time: 20 minutes |
Servings: 4

Ingredients:

- 2 tablespoons balsamic vinegar
- 1/3 cup coconut aminos
- 1 tablespoon olive oil
- 4 ounces mixed salad greens
- 1 cup cherry tomatoes, halved
- 4 ounces pork stew meat, cut into strips
- 1 tablespoon chives, chopped

Directions:

1. Heat up a pan with the oil over medium heat, add the pork, coconut aminos and the vinegar, toss and cook for 15 minutes.
2. Add the salad greens and the other ingredients, toss, cook for 5 minutes more, divide between plates and serve.

Nutrition: 125 calories, 9.1g protein, 6.8g carbohydrates, 6.4g fat, 0.6g fiber, 24mg cholesterol, 49mg sodium, 269mg potassium

Cilantro Pork Skillet

Prep time: 10 minutes | Cooking time: 25 minutes |
Servings: 4

Ingredients:

- 1 pound pork butt, trimmed and cubed
- 1 tablespoon olive oil
- 1 yellow onion, chopped
- 3 garlic cloves, minced
- 1 tablespoon thyme, dried
- 1 cup low-sodium chicken stock
- 2 tablespoons low-sodium tomato paste
- 1 tablespoon cilantro, chopped

Directions:

1. Heat up a pan with the oil over medium-high heat, add the onion and the garlic, toss and cook for 5 minutes.
2. Add the meat, toss and cook for 5 more minutes.
3. Add the rest of the ingredients, toss, bring to a simmer, reduce heat to medium and cook the mix for 15 minutes more.
4. Divide the mix between plates and serve right away.

Nutrition: 274 calories, 36.6g protein, 5.3g carbohydrates, 11.2g fat, 1.2g fiber, 104mg cholesterol, 104mg sodium, 484mg potassium

Pork and Zucchinis

Prep time: 10 minutes | Cooking time: 30 minutes | Servings: 4

Ingredients:

- 2 pounds pork loin boneless, trimmed and cubed
- 2 tablespoons avocado oil
- ¾ cup low-sodium vegetable stock
- ½ tablespoon garlic powder
- 1 tablespoon marjoram, chopped
- 2 zucchinis, roughly cubed
- 1 teaspoon sweet paprika
- Black pepper to the taste

Directions:

1. Heat up a pan with the oil over medium-high heat, add the meat, garlic powder and the marjoram, toss and cook for 10 minutes.
2. Add the zucchinis and the other ingredients, toss, bring to a simmer, reduce heat to medium and cook the mix for 20 minutes more.
3. Divide everything between plates and serve.

Nutrition: 359 calories, 61.1g protein, 5.7g carbohydrates, 9.1g fat, 2.1g fiber, 166mg cholesterol, 166mg sodium, 1289mg potassium

Nutmeg Pork

Prep time: 10 minutes | Cooking time: 8 hours | Servings: 4

Ingredients:

- 3 tablespoons olive oil
- 2 pounds pork shoulder roast
- 2 teaspoons sweet paprika
- 1 teaspoon garlic powder
- 1 teaspoon onion powder
- 1 teaspoon nutmeg, ground
- 1 teaspoon allspice, ground
- Black pepper to the taste
- 1 cup low-sodium vegetable stock

Directions:

1. In your slow cooker, combine the roast with the oil and the other ingredients, toss, put the lid on and cook on Low for 8 hours.
2. Slice the roast, divide it between plates and serve with the cooking juices drizzled on top.

Nutrition: 689 calories, 38.8g protein, 3.2g carbohydrates, 57.1g fat, 1g fiber, 161mg cholesterol, 187mg sodium, 77mg potassium

Peppercorn Pork

Prep time: 10 minutes | Cooking time: 35 minutes | Servings: 4

Ingredients:

- 2 pounds pork stew meat, cubed
- 2 tablespoons olive oil
- 1 cup low-sodium vegetable stock
- 1 celery stalk, chopped
- 1 teaspoon black peppercorns
- 2 shallots, chopped
- 1 tablespoon chives, chopped
- 1 cup coconut cream
- Black pepper to the taste

Directions:

1. Heat up a pan with the oil over medium heat, add the shallots and the meat, toss and brown for 5 minutes.
2. Add the celery and the other ingredients, toss, bring to a simmer and cook over medium heat for 30 minutes more.
3. Divide everything between plates and serve right away.

Nutrition: 690 calories, 68.2g protein, 5.7g carbohydrates, 43.3g fat, 1.8g fiber, 195mg cholesterol, 182mg sodium, 1077mg potassium

Parsley Pork and Tomatoes

Prep time: 10 minutes | Cooking time: 30 minutes | Servings: 4

Ingredients:

- 2 garlic cloves, minced
- 2 pounds pork stew meat, ground
- 2 cups cherry tomatoes, halved
- 1 tablespoon olive oil
- Black pepper to the taste
- 1 red onion, chopped
- ½ cup low-sodium vegetable stock
- 2 tablespoons low-sodium tomato paste
- 1 tablespoon parsley, chopped

Directions:

1. Heat up a pan with the oil over medium heat, add the onion and the garlic, toss and sauté for 5 minutes.
2. Add the meat and brown it for 5 minutes more.
3. Add the rest of the ingredients, toss, bring to a simmer, cook over medium heat for 20 minutes more, divide into bowls and serve.

Nutrition: 551 calories, 68.2g protein, 8.6g carbohydrates, 25.6g fat, 2.1g fiber, 195mg cholesterol, 163mg sodium, 1131mg potassium

Lemon Pork Chops

Prep time: 10 minutes | Cooking time: 35 minutes | Servings: 4

Ingredients:

- 4 pork chops
- 2 tablespoons olive oil
- 1 teaspoon smoked paprika
- 1 tablespoon sage, chopped
- 2 garlic cloves, minced
- 1 tablespoon lemon juice
- Black pepper to the taste

Directions:

1. In a baking dish, combine the pork chops with the oil and the other ingredients, toss, introduce in the oven and bake at 400 degrees F for 35 minutes.
2. Divide the pork chops between plates and serve with a side salad.

Nutrition: 322 calories, 18.2g protein, 1.2g carbohydrates, 27.1g fat, 0.5g fiber, 69mg cholesterol, 57mg sodium, 304mg potassium

Coconut Pork Mix

Prep time: 10 minutes | Cooking time: 30 minutes | Servings: 4

Ingredients:

- 1 pound pork stew meat, cubed
- 1 eggplant, cubed
- 1 tablespoon coconut aminos
- 1 teaspoon five spice
- 2 garlic cloves, minced
- 2 Thai chilies, chopped
- 2 tablespoons olive oil
- 2 tablespoons low-sodium tomato paste
- 1 tablespoon cilantro, chopped
- ½ cup low-sodium vegetable stock

Directions:

1. Heat up a pan with the oil over medium-high heat, add the garlic, chilies and the meat and brown for 6 minutes.
2. Add the eggplant and the other ingredients, bring to a simmer and cook over medium heat for 24 minutes.
3. Divide the mix between plates and serve.

Nutrition: 348 calories, 35.1g protein, 10.5g carbohydrates, 18.2g fat, 4.5g fiber, 98mg cholesterol, 134mg sodium, 711mg potassium

Lime Pork

Prep time: 10 minutes | Cooking time: 30 minutes |
Servings: 4

Ingredients:

- 2 tablespoons lime juice
- 4 scallions, chopped
- 1 pound pork stew meat, cubed
- 2 garlic cloves, minced
- 2 tablespoons olive oil
- Black pepper to the taste
- ½ cup low-sodium vegetable stock
- 1 tablespoon cilantro, chopped

Directions:

1. Heat up a pan with the oil over medium heat, add the scallions and the garlic, toss and cook for 5 minutes.
2. Add the meat, toss and cook for 5 minutes more.
3. Add the rest of the ingredients, bring to a simmer and cook over medium heat for 20 minutes.
4. Divide the mix between plates and serve.

Nutrition: 310 calories, 33.7g protein, 2.1g carbohydrates, 18g fat, 0.6g fiber, 98mg cholesterol, 87mg sodium, 490mg potassium

Coriander Pork

Prep time: 10 minutes | Cooking time: 30 minutes |
Servings: 4

Ingredients:

- 1 red onion, sliced
- 1 pound pork stew meat, cubed
- 2 red chilies, chopped
- 2 tablespoons balsamic vinegar
- ½ cup coriander leaves, chopped
- Black pepper to the taste
- 2 tablespoons olive oil
- 1 tablespoon low-sodium tomato sauce

Directions:

1. Heat up a pan with the oil over medium heat, add the onion and the chilies, toss and cook for 5 minutes.
2. Add the meat, toss and cook for 5 minutes more.
3. Add the rest of the ingredients, toss, bring to a simmer and cook over medium heat for 20 minutes more.
4. Divide everything between plates and serve right away.

Nutrition: 323 calories, 34g protein, 4.9g carbohydrates, 18.1g fat, 1.1g fiber, 98mg cholesterol, 91mg sodium, 566mg potassium

Basil Pork Mix

Prep time: 10 minutes | Cooking time: 36 minutes |
Servings: 4

Ingredients:

- 2 tablespoons olive oil
- 2 spring onions, chopped
- 1 pound pork chops
- 2 tablespoons basil pesto
- 1 cup cherry tomatoes, cubed
- 2 tablespoons low-sodium tomato paste
- ½ cup parsley, chopped
- ½ cup low-sodium vegetable stock
- Black pepper to the taste

Directions:

1. Heat up a pan with the olive oil over medium-high heat, add the spring onions and the pork chops, and brown for 3 minutes on each side.
2. Add the pesto and the other ingredients, toss gently, bring to a simmer and cook over medium heat for 30 minutes more.
3. Divide everything between plates and serve.

Nutrition: 446 calories, 26.9g protein, 4.8g carbohydrates, 35.4g fat, 1.4g fiber, 98mg cholesterol, 110mg sodium, 579mg potassium

Pork and Tomatoes

Prep time: 10 minutes | Cooking time: 1 hour |
Servings: 4

Ingredients:

- 1 green bell pepper, chopped
- 1 red bell pepper, chopped
- 1 yellow bell pepper, chopped
- 1 red onion, chopped
- 1 pound pork chops
- 1 tablespoon olive oil
- Black pepper to the taste
- 26 ounces canned tomatoes, no-salt-added and chopped
- 2 tablespoons parsley, chopped

Directions:

1. Grease a roasting pan with the oil, arrange the pork chops inside and add the other ingredients on top.
2. Bake at 390 degrees F for 1 hour, divide everything between plates and serve.

Nutrition: 459 calories, 28.3g protein, 14.9g carbohydrates, 32.3g fat, 4.3g fiber, 98mg cholesterol, 93mg sodium, 1038mg potassium

Lamb and Cherry Tomatoes Mix

Prep time: 10 minutes | Cooking time: 25 minutes |
Servings: 4

Ingredients:

- 1 tablespoon olive oil
- 1 red onion, chopped
- 1 cup cherry tomatoes, halved
- 1 pound lamb stew meat, ground
- 1 tablespoon chili powder
- Black pepper to the taste
- 2 teaspoons cumin, ground
- 1 cup low-sodium vegetable stock
- 2 tablespoons cilantro, chopped

Directions:

1. Heat up the a pan with the oil over medium-high heat, add the onion, lamb and chili powder, toss and cook for 10 minutes.
2. Add the rest of the ingredients, toss, cook over medium heat for 15 minutes more.
3. Divide into bowls and serve.

Nutrition: 275 calories, 33.2g protein, 6.8g carbohydrates, 12.5g fat, 2.1g fiber, 102mg cholesterol, 145mg sodium, 617mg potassium

Pork with Green Beans

Prep time: 10 minutes | Cooking time: 35 minutes |
Servings: 4

Ingredients:

- 1 pound pork stew meat, cubed
- 1 cup radishes, cubed
- ½ pound green beans, trimmed and halved
- 1 yellow onion, chopped
- 1 tablespoon olive oil
- 2 garlic cloves, minced
- 1 cup canned tomatoes, no-salt-added and chopped
- 2 teaspoons oregano, dried
- Black pepper to the taste

Directions:

1. Heat up a pan with the oil over medium-high heat, add the onion and the garlic, toss and cook for 5 minutes.
2. Add the meat, toss and cook for 5 minutes more.
3. Add the rest of the ingredients, bring to a simmer and cook over medium heat for 25 minutes.
4. Divide everything into bowls and serve.

Nutrition: 316 calories, 35.3g protein, 10.3g carbohydrates, 14.8g fat, 3.9g fiber, 98mg cholesterol, 85mg sodium, 777mg potassium

Lamb with Scallions and Mushrooms

Prep time: 10 minutes | Cooking time: 40 minutes |
Servings: 4

Ingredients:

- 1 pound lamb shoulder, boneless and cubed
- 8 white mushrooms, halved
- 2 tablespoons olive oil
- 1 yellow onion, chopped
- 2 garlic cloves, minced
- 1 an ½ tablespoons fennel powder
- Black pepper to the taste
- A bunch of scallions, chopped
- 1 cup low-sodium vegetable stock

Directions:

1. Heat up a pan with the oil over medium heat, add the onion and the garlic, toss and cook for 5 minutes.
2. Add the meat and the mushrooms, toss and cook for 5 minutes more.
3. Add the other ingredients, toss, bring to a simmer and cook over medium heat for 30 minutes.
4. Divide the mix into bowls and serve.

Nutrition: 298 calories, 33.7g protein, 5.4g carbohydrates, 15.5g fat, 1.3g fiber, 102mg cholesterol, 126mg sodium, 581mg potassium

Pork with Tomatoes and Spinach

Prep time: 10 minutes | Cooking time: 30 minutes |
Servings: 4

Ingredients:

- 1 pound pork, ground
- 2 tablespoons olive oil
- 1 red onion, chopped
- ½ pound baby spinach
- 4 garlic cloves, minced
- ½ cup low-sodium vegetable
- stock
- ½ cup canned tomatoes, no-salt-added, chopped
- Black pepper to the taste
- 1 tablespoon chives, chopped

Directions:

1. Heat up a pan with the oil over medium-high heat, add the onion and the garlic, toss and cook for 5 minutes.
2. Add the meat, toss and brown for 5 minutes more.
3. Add the rest of the ingredients except the spinach, toss, bring to a simmer, reduce heat to medium and cook for 15 minutes.
4. Add the spinach, toss, cook the mix for another 5 minutes, divide everything into bowls and serve.

Nutrition: 257 calories, 32.1g protein, 7g carbohydrates, 11.3g fat, 2.3g fiber, 83mg cholesterol, 130mg sodium, 918mg potassium

Warm Pork Salad

Prep time: 10 minutes | Cooking time: 15 minutes |
Servings: 4

Ingredients:

- 2 cups baby spinach
- 1 pound pork steak, cut into strips
- 1 tablespoon olive oil
- 1 cup cherry tomatoes, halved
- 2 avocados, peeled, pitted and cut into wedges
- 1 tablespoon balsamic vinegar
- ½ cup low-sodium vegetable stock

Directions:

1. Heat up a pan with the oil over medium-high heat, add the meat, toss and cook for 10 minutes.
2. Add the spinach and the other ingredients, toss, cook for 5 minutes more, divide into bowls and serve.

Nutrition: 544calories, 31.9g protein, 11.5g carbohydrates, 42.1g fat, 7.7g fiber, 108mg cholesterol, 116mg sodium, 1066mg potassium

Chili Pork and Apples

Prep time: 10 minutes | Cooking time: 40 minutes |
Servings: 4

Ingredients:

- 2 pounds pork stew meat, cut into strips
- 2 green apples, cored and cut into wedges
- 2 garlic cloves, minced
- 2 shallots, chopped
- 1 tablespoon sweet paprika
- ½ teaspoon chili powder
- 2 tablespoons avocado oil
- 1 cup low-sodium chicken stock
- Black pepper to the taste
- A pinch of red chili pepper flakes

Directions:

1. Heat up a pan with the oil over medium heat, add the shallots and the garlic, toss and sauté for 5 minutes.
2. Add the meat and brown for another 5 minutes.
3. Add the apples and the other ingredients, toss, bring to a simmer and cook over medium heat for 30 minutes more.
4. Divide everything between plates and serve.

Nutrition: 561calories, 67.6g protein, 18.3g carbohydrates, 23.3g fat, 3.8g fiber, 195mg cholesterol, 174mg sodium, 1062mg potassium

Hot Pork Chops

Prep time: 10 minutes | Cooking: 1 hour and 10 minutes |
Servings: 4

Ingredients:

- 4 pork chops
- 2 tablespoons olive oil
- 2 garlic cloves, minced
- ¼ cup low-sodium vegetable stock
- 1 tablespoon cinnamon powder
- Black pepper to the taste
- 1 teaspoon chili powder
- ½ teaspoon onion powder

Directions:

1. In a roasting pan, combine the pork chops with the oil and the other ingredients, toss, introduce in the oven and bake at 390 degrees F for 1 hour and 10 minutes.
2. Divide the pork chops between plates and serve with a side salad.

Nutrition: 323calories, 18.3g protein, 1.4g carbohydrates, 27g fat, 0.3g fiber, 69mg cholesterol, 72mg sodium, 35mg potassium

Creamy Pork Chops

Prep time: 10 minutes | Cooking time: 20 minutes |
Servings: 4

Ingredients:

- 2 tablespoons olive oil
- 4 pork chops
- 1 yellow onion, chopped
- 1 tablespoon chili powder
- 1 cup coconut milk
- ¼ cup cilantro, chopped

Directions:

1. Heat up a pan with the oil over medium-high heat, add the onion and the chili powder, toss and sauté for 5 minutes.
2. Add the pork chops and brown them for 2 minutes on each side.
3. Add the coconut milk, toss, bring to a simmer and cook over medium heat for 11 minutes more.
4. Add the cilantro, toss, divide everything into bowls and serve.

Nutrition: 471calories, 19.9g protein, 7g carbohydrates, 41.5g fat, 2.6g fiber, 69mg cholesterol, 86mg sodium, 514mg potassium

Pork with Paprika Peaches

Prep time: 10 minutes | Cooking time: 25 minutes |
Servings: 4

Ingredients:

- 2 pounds pork tenderloin, roughly cubed
- 2 peaches, stones removed and cut into quarters
- ¼ teaspoon onion powder
- 2 tablespoons olive oil
- ¼ teaspoon smoked paprika
- ¼ cup low-sodium vegetable stock
- Black pepper to the taste

Directions:

1. Heat up a pan with the oil over medium heat, add the meat, toss and cook for 10 minutes.
2. Add the peaches and the other ingredients, toss, bring to a simmer and cook over medium heat for 15 minutes more.
3. Divide the whole mix between plates and serve.

Nutrition: 416calories, 60.2g protein, 7.4g carbohydrates, 15.2g fat, 1.3g fiber, 166mg cholesterol, 138mg sodium, 1110mg potassium

Lamb and Radish Skillet

Prep time: 10 minutes | Cooking time: 35 minutes |
Servings: 4

Ingredients:

- ½ cup low-sodium vegetable stock
- 1 pound lamb stew meat, cubed
- 1 cup radishes, cubed
- 1 tablespoon cocoa powder
- Black pepper to the taste
- 1 yellow onion, chopped
- 1 tablespoon olive oil
- 2 garlic cloves, minced
- 1 tablespoon parsley, chopped

Directions:

1. Heat up a pan with the oil over medium-high heat, add the onion and the garlic, toss and sauté for 5 minutes.
2. Add the meat, toss and brown for 2 minutes on each side.
3. Add the stock and the other ingredients, toss, bring to a simmer and cook over medium heat for 25 minutes more.
4. Divide everything between plates and serve.

Nutrition: 265calories, 32.8g protein, 5.4g carbohydrates, 12.1g fat, 1.6g fiber, 102mg cholesterol, 117mg sodium, 549mg potassium

Pork and Lemon Artichokes Mix

Prep time: 10 minutes | Cooking time: 25 minutes |
Servings: 4

Ingredients:

- 2 pounds pork stew meat, cut into strips
- 2 tablespoons avocado oil
- 1 tablespoon lemon juice
- 1 tablespoon lemon zest, grated
- 1 cup canned artichokes, drained and cut into quarters
- 1 red onion, chopped
- 2 garlic cloves, minced
- ½ teaspoon chili powder
- Black pepper to the taste
- 1 teaspoon sweet paprika
- 1 jalapeno, chopped
- ¼ cup low-sodium vegetable stock
- ¼ cup rosemary, chopped

Directions:

1. Heat up a pan with the oil over medium-high heat, add the onion and the garlic, toss and sauté for 4 minutes.
2. Add the meat, artichokes, chili powder, the jalapeno and the paprika, toss and cook for 6 minutes more.
3. Add the rest of the ingredients, toss, bring to a simmer and cook over medium heat for 15 minutes more.
4. Divide the whole mix into bowls and serve.

Nutrition: 544calories, 68.6g protein, 12.1g carbohydrates, 23.7g fat, 6.7g fiber, 195mg cholesterol, 176mg sodium, 1117mg potassium

Parmesan Pork and Sauce

Prep time: 10 minutes | Cooking time: 20 minutes |
Servings: 4

Ingredients:

- 2 pounds pork stew meat, roughly cubed
- 1 cup cilantro leaves
- 4 tablespoons olive oil
- 1 tablespoon pine nuts
- 1 tablespoon fat-free parmesan, grated
- 1 tablespoon lemon juice
- 1 teaspoon chili powder
- Black pepper to the taste

Directions:

1. In a blender, combine the cilantro with the pine nuts, 3 tablespoons oil, parmesan and lemon juice and pulse well.
2. Heat up a pan with the remaining oil over medium heat, add the meat, chili powder and the black pepper, toss and brown for 5 minutes.
3. Add the cilantro sauce, and cook over medium heat for 15 minutes more, stirring from time to time.
4. Divide the pork between plates and serve right away.

Nutrition: 622calories, 67.1g protein, 0.9g carbohydrates, 37.8g fat, 0.4g fiber, 196mg cholesterol, 162mg sodium, 903mg potassium

Pork with Mango and Tomatoes

Prep time: 10 minutes | Cooking time: 25 minutes |
Servings: 4

Ingredients:

- 2 shallots, chopped
- 2 tablespoons avocado oil
- 1 pound pork stew meat, cubed
- 1 mango, peeled and roughly
- cubed
- 2 garlic cloves, minced
- 1 cup tomatoes, and chopped
- Black pepper to the taste
- ½ cup basil, chopped

Directions:

1. Heat up a pan with the oil over medium heat, add the shallots and the garlic, toss and cook for 5 minutes.
2. Add the meat, toss and cook for 5 minutes more.
3. Add the rest of the ingredients, toss, bring to a simmer and cook over medium heat for 15 minutes more.
4. Divide the mix into bowls and serve.

Nutrition: 315calories, 34.7g protein, 16.1g carbohydrates, 12.3g fat, 2.3g fiber, 98mg cholesterol, 71mg sodium, 727mg potassium

Pork and Sweet Potatoes

Prep time: 10 minutes | Cooking time: 35 minutes |
Servings: 4

Ingredients:

- 1 red onion, cut into wedges
- 2 sweet potatoes, peeled and cut into wedges
- 4 pork chops
- 1 tablespoon rosemary, chopped
- 1 tablespoon lemon juice
- 2 teaspoons olive oil
- Black pepper to the taste
- 2 teaspoons thyme, chopped
- ½ cup low-sodium vegetable stock

Directions:

1. In a roasting pan, combine the pork chops with the potatoes, onion and the other ingredients and toss gently.
2. Bake at 400 degrees F for 35 minutes, divide everything between plates and serve.

Nutrition: 335calories, 18.9g protein, 13.7g carbohydrates, 22.5g fat, 2.5g fiber, 69mg cholesterol, 63mg sodium, 635mg potassium

Cilantro Pork and Chickpeas

Prep time: 10 minutes | Cooking time: 25 minutes | Servings: 4

Ingredients:

- 1 pound pork stew meat, cubed
- 1 cup canned chickpeas, no-salt-added, drained
- 1 yellow onion, chopped
- 1 tablespoon olive oil
- Black pepper to the taste
- 10 ounces canned tomatoes, no-salt-added and chopped
- 2 tablespoons cilantro, chopped

Directions:

1. Heat up a pan with the oil over medium-high heat, add the onion, toss and sauté for 5 minutes.
2. Add the meat, toss and cook for 5 minutes more.
3. Add the rest of the ingredients, toss, simmer over medium heat for 15 minutes, divide everything into bowls and serve.

Nutrition: 476calories, 43.8g protein, 35.7g carbohydrates, 17.6g fat, 10.2g fiber, 98mg cholesterol, 84mg sodium, 1073mg potassium

Lamb Chops and Greens

Prep time: 10 minutes | Cooking time: 35 minutes | Servings: 4

Ingredients:

- 1 cup kale, torn
- 1 pound lamb chops
- ½ cup low-sodium vegetable stock
- 2 tablespoons low-sodium
- tomato paste
- 1 yellow onion, sliced
- 1 tablespoon olive oil
- A pinch of black pepper

Directions:

1. Grease a roasting pan with the oil, arrange the lamb chops inside, also add the kale and the other ingredients and toss gently.
2. Bake everything at 390 degrees F for 35 minutes, divide between plates and serve.

Nutrition: 270calories, 33.3g protein, 6.3g carbohydrates, 11.8g fat, 1.2g fiber, 102mg cholesterol, 117mg sodium, 519mg potassium

Lamb and Red Onions Mix

Prep time: 10 minutes | Cooking time: 45 minutes | Servings: 4

Ingredients:

- 2 pounds lamb stew meat, cubed
- 1 tablespoon avocado oil
- 1 teaspoon chili powder
- 1 teaspoon hot paprika
- 2 red onions, roughly chopped
- 1 cup low-sodium vegetable stock
- ½ cup low-sodium tomato sauce
- 1 tablespoon cilantro, chopped

Directions:

1. Heat up a pot with the oil over medium heat, add the onion and the meat and brown for 10 minutes.
2. Add the chili powder and the other ingredients except the cilantro, toss, bring to a simmer and cook over medium heat for 35 minutes more.
3. Divide the mix into bowls and serve with the cilantro sprinkled on top.

Nutrition: 463calories, 65.1g protein, 8.4g carbohydrates, 17.3g fat, 2.3g fiber, 204mg cholesterol, 377mg sodium, 999mg potassium

Meatballs and Spinach

Prep time: 10 minutes | Cooking time: 25 minutes | Servings: 4

Ingredients:

- 1 pound pork stew meat, ground
- 1 yellow onion, chopped
- 1 egg, whisked
- 1 tablespoon mint, chopped
- Black pepper to the taste
- 2 garlic cloves, minced
- 2 tablespoons olive oil
- 1 cup cherry tomatoes, halved
- 1 cup baby spinach
- ½ cup low-sodium vegetable stock

Directions:

1. In a bowl, combine the meat with the onion and the other ingredients except the oil, cherry tomatoes and the spinach, stir well and shape medium meatballs out of this mix.
2. Heat up a pan with the olive oil over medium-high heat, add the meatballs and cook them for 5 minutes on each side.
3. Add the spinach, tomatoes and the stock, toss, simmer everything for 15 minutes.
4. Divide everything into bowls and serve.

Nutrition: 342calories, 35.8g protein, 5.8g carbohydrates, 19.2g fat, 1.6g fiber, 138mg cholesterol, 110mg sodium, 657mg potassium

Creamy Meatballs Mix

Prep time: 10 minutes | Cooking time: 20 minutes | Servings: 4

Ingredients:

- 2 pounds pork, ground
- Black pepper to the taste
- ¾ cup almond flour
- 2 eggs, whisked
- 1 tablespoon parsley, chopped
- 2 red onions, chopped
- 2 tablespoons olive oil
- ½ cup coconut cream
- Black pepper to the taste

Directions:

1. In a bowl, mix the pork with the almond flour and the other ingredients except the onions, oil and the cream, stir well and shape medium meatballs out of this mix.
2. Heat up a pan with the oil over medium heat, add the onions, stir and sauté for 5 minutes.
3. Add the meatballs, and cook for 5 minutes more.
4. Add coconut cream, bring to a simmer, cook everything for 10 minutes more, divide into bowls and serve.

Nutrition: 537calories, 64.6g protein, 8.2g carbohydrates, 27g fat, 2.4g fiber, 247g cholesterol, 169mg sodium, 1149mg potassium

Turmeric Pork Mix

Prep time: 10 minutes | Cooking time: 25 minutes | Servings: 4

Ingredients:

- 1 pound pork stew meat, cubed
- ½ cup tomato sauce, no-salt-added
- 1 yellow onion, chopped
- 2 tablespoons olive oil
- 1 cup canned lentils, no-salt-added, drained
- 1 teaspoon curry powder
- 1 teaspoon turmeric powder
- Black pepper to the taste

Directions:

1. Heat a pan with the oil over medium-high heat, add the onion and the meat, and brown for 5 minutes.
2. Add the sauce and the other ingredients, toss, cook over medium heat for 20 minutes, divide everything into bowls and serve.

Nutrition: 492calories, 46.4g protein, 33.7g carbohydrates, 18.7g fat, 16g fiber, 98g cholesterol, 232mg sodium, 1047mg potassium

Lamb with Veggies Mix

Prep time: 10 minutes | Cooking time: 25 minutes |
Servings: 4

Ingredients:

- 1 pound lamb meat, ground
- 1 tablespoon avocado oil
- 1 red bell pepper, cut into strips
- 1 red onion, sliced
- 2 tomatoes, cubed
- 1 carrot, cubed
- 2 fennel bulbs, sliced
- Black pepper to the taste
- 2 tablespoons balsamic vinegar
- 1 tablespoon cilantro, chopped

Directions:

1. Heat a pan with the oil over medium-high heat, add the onion and the meat, and brown for 5 minutes.
2. Add the bell pepper and the other ingredients, toss, cook over medium heat for 20 minutes more, divide into bowls, and serve right away.

Nutrition: 293calories, 20.3g protein, 27.6g carbohydrates, 11g fat, 8g fiber, 61g cholesterol, 728mg sodium, 793mg potassium

Coconut Pork with Beets

Prep time: 10 minutes | Cooking time: 30 minutes |
Servings: 4

Ingredients:

- 1 pound pork meat, cubed
- 2 small beets, peeled and cubed
- 2 tablespoons olive oil
- 1 yellow onion, chopped
- 2 garlic cloves, minced
- Salt and black pepper to the taste
- ½ cup coconut cream

Directions:

1. Heat a pan with the oil over medium-high heat, add the onion and the garlic, stir and cook for 5 minutes.
2. Add the meat and brown for 5 minutes more.
3. Add the rest of the ingredients, bring to a simmer and cook over medium heat for 20 minutes.
4. Divide the mix between plates and serve.

Nutrition: 355calories, 25g protein, 9.7g carbohydrates, 24.3g fat, 2.3g fiber, 80g cholesterol, 110mg sodium, 278mg potassium

Thyme Lamb and Cabbage Stew

Prep time: 10 minutes | Cooking time: 35 minutes |
Servings: 4

Ingredients:

- 2 tablespoons avocado oil
- 1 pound lamb stew meat, roughly cubed
- 1 green cabbage head, shredded
- 1 cup canned tomatoes, no-salt-added, chopped
- 1 yellow onion, chopped
- 1 teaspoon thyme, dried
- Black pepper to the taste
- 2 garlic cloves, minced

Directions:

1. Heat a pan with the oil over medium-high heat, add the onion and garlic and sauté for 5 minutes.
2. Add the meat and brown for another 5 minutes.
3. Add the rest of the ingredients, toss, bring to a simmer and cook over medium heat for 25 minutes more.
4. Divide everything between plates and serve.

Nutrition: 287calories, 35g protein, 15.7g carbohydrates, 9.5g fat, 6g fiber, 102g cholesterol, 122mg sodium, 866mg potassium

Lamb with Carrot and Bok Choy

Prep time: 10 minutes | Cooking time: 30 minutes |
Servings: 4

Ingredients:

- 1 cup low-sodium chicken stock
- 1 cup bok choy, torn
- 1 pound lamb stew meat, roughly cubed
- 2 tablespoons avocado oil
- 1 yellow onion, chopped
- 1 carrot, chopped
- Black pepper to the taste

Directions:

1. Heat a pan with the oil over medium-high heat, add the onion and the carrot and sauté for 5 minutes.
2. Add the meat and brown for 5 minutes more.
3. Add the rest of the ingredients, bring to a simmer and cook over medium heat for 20 minutes.
4. Divide everything between plates and serve.

Nutrition: 241calories, 32.9g protein, 4.8g carbohydrates, 9.3g fat, 1.5g fiber, 102g cholesterol, 143mg sodium, 535mg potassium

Pork with Olives

Prep time: 10 minutes | Cooking time: 35 minutes |
Servings: 4

Ingredients:

- ½ cup low-sodium vegetable stock
- 1 cup okra, trimmed
- 1 cup black olives, pitted and halved
- 2 tablespoons olive oil
- 4 pork chops
- 1 red onion, cut into wedges
- Black pepper to the taste
- ½ tablespoon red pepper flakes
- 3 tablespoons coconut aminos

Directions:

1. Grease a roasting pan with the oil and arrange the pork chops inside.
2. Add the rest of the ingredients, toss gently, and bake at 390 degrees F for 35 minutes.
3. Divide everything between plates and serve.

Nutrition: 391calories, 19.3g protein, 9.7g carbohydrates, 30.7g fat, 2.8g fiber, 69g cholesterol, 382mg sodium, 422mg potassium

Chives Pork and Barley

Prep time: 10 minutes | Cooking time: 35 minutes |
Servings: 4

Ingredients:

- 1 cup barley
- 2 cups low-sodium chicken stock
- 1 pound pork stew meat, cubed
- 1 red onion, sliced
- 1 tablespoon olive oil
- Black pepper to the taste
- 1 teaspoon fenugreek powder
- 1 tablespoon chives, chopped
- 1 tablespoon capers, drained

Directions:

1. Heat a pan with the oil over medium-high heat, add the onion and the meat, and brown for 5 minutes.
2. Add the barley and the other ingredients, toss, bring to a simmer cook over medium heat for 30 minutes.
3. Divide everything into bowls and serve.

Nutrition: 447calories, 39.8g protein, 36.5g carbohydrates, 15.6g fat, 8.6g fiber, 98g cholesterol, 205mg sodium, 676mg potassium

Simple Pork and Leeks

Prep time: 10 minutes | Cooking time: 45 minutes |
Servings: 4

Ingredients:

- 2 pounds pork stew meat, roughly cubed
- 2 leeks, sliced
- 2 tablespoons olive oil
- 2 garlic cloves, minced
- 1 teaspoon sweet paprika
- 1 tablespoon parsley, chopped
- 1 cup low-sodium vegetable stock
- Black pepper to the taste

Directions:

1. Heat up a pan with the oil over medium heat, add the leeks, garlic and the paprika, toss and cook for 10 minutes.
2. Add the meat and brown it for 5 minutes more.
3. Add the remaining ingredients, toss, simmer over medium heat for 30 minutes, divide everything into bowls and serve.

Nutrition: 577calories, 67.5g protein, 8.2g carbohydrates, 29.1g fat, 1.3g fiber, 195mg cholesterol, 179mg sodium, 987mg potassium

Pork with Parsley Peas

Prep time: 10 minutes | Cooking time: 25 minutes |
Servings: 4

Ingredients:

- 4 pork chops
- 2 tablespoons olive oil
- 2 shallots, chopped
- 1 cup snow peas
- 1 cup low-sodium vegetable
- stock
- 2 tablespoons no-salt-added tomato paste
- 1 tablespoon parsley, chopped

Directions:

1. Heat up a pan with the oil over medium heat, add the shallots, toss and sauté for 5 minutes.
2. Add the pork chops and brown for 2 minutes on each side.
3. Add the rest of the ingredients, bring to a simmer and cook over medium heat for 15 minutes.
4. Divide the mix between plates and serve.

Nutrition: 357calories, 20.7g protein, 7.7g carbohydrates, 27g fat, 1.9g fiber, 69mg cholesterol, 104mg sodium, 426mg potassium

Oregano Lamb Chops

Prep time: 10 minutes | Cooking time: 30 minutes |
Servings: 4

Ingredients:

- 4 lamb chops
- 1 tablespoon oregano, chopped
- 1 tablespoon olive oil
- 1 yellow onion, chopped
- 2 tablespoons low-fat
- parmesan, grated
- 1/3 cup low sodium veggie stock
- Black pepper to the taste
- 1 teaspoon Italian seasoning

Directions:

1. Heat up a pan with the oil over medium-high heat, add the lamb chops and the onion and brown for 4 minutes on each side.
2. Add the rest of the ingredients except the cheese and toss.
3. Sprinkle the cheese on top, introduce the pan in the oven and bake at 350 degrees F for 20 minutes.
4. Divide everything between plates and serve.

Nutrition: 214calories, 24.9g protein, 3.8g carbohydrates, 10.7g fat, 1.2g fiber, 80mg cholesterol, 116mg sodium, 358mg potassium

Pork Meatballs and Sauce

Prep time: 10 minutes | Cooking time: 30 minutes |
Servings: 4

Ingredients:

- 3 tablespoons almond flour
- 2 tablespoons avocado oil
- 2 egg, whisked
- Black pepper to the taste
- 2 pounds pork, ground
- 1 tablespoon cilantro, chopped
- 10 ounces canned tomato sauce, no-salt-added

Directions:

1. In a bowl, combine the pork with the flour and the other ingredients except the sauce and the oil, stir well and shape medium meatballs out of this mix.
2. Heat up a pan with the oil over medium heat, add the meatballs and brown for 3 minutes on each side.
3. Add the sauce, toss gently, bring to a simmer and cook over medium heat for 20 minutes more.
4. Divide everything into bowls and serve.

Nutrition: 502calories, 67.7g protein, 8.9g carbohydrates, 21.7g fat, 3.6g fiber, 247mg cholesterol, 539mg sodium, 1242mg potassium

Pork with Chili Endives

Prep time: 10 minutes | Cooking time: 35 minutes |
Servings: 4

Ingredients:

- 1 pound pork stew meat, cubed
- 2 endives, trimmed and shredded
- 1 cup low-sodium beef stock
- 1 teaspoon chili powder
- A pinch of black pepper
- 1 red onion, chopped
- 1 tablespoon olive oil

Directions:

1. Heat up a pan with the oil over medium heat, add the onion and the endives, toss and cook for 5 minutes.
2. Add the meat, toss and cook for 5 minutes more.
3. Add the rest of the ingredients, bring to a simmer and cook over medium heat for 25 minutes more.
4. Divide everything between plates and serve.

Nutrition: 288calories, 34.2g protein, 3.4g carbohydrates, 11.6g fat, 1.2g fiber, 98mg cholesterol, 112mg sodium, 517mg potassium

Pork and Radish Hash

Prep time: 10 minutes | Cooking time: 35 minutes |
Servings: 4

Ingredients:

- 1 cup radishes, cubed
- 1 pound pork stew meat, cubed
- 1 tablespoon olive oil
- 1 red onion, chopped
- 1 cup canned tomatoes, no-
- salt-added, crushed
- 1 tablespoon chives, chopped
- 2 garlic cloves, minced
- Black pepper to the taste
- 1 teaspoon balsamic vinegar

Directions:

1. Heat up a pan with the oil over medium heat, add the onion and the garlic, stir and cook for 5 minutes.
2. Add the meat and brown for 5 minutes more.
3. Add the radishes and the other ingredients, bring to a simmer and cook over medium heat for 25 minutes more.
4. Divide everything into bowls and serve.

Nutrition: 297calories, 34.2g protein, 5.9g carbohydrates, 14.6g fat, 1.6g fiber, 98mg cholesterol, 82mg sodium, 649mg potassium

Pork and Green Beans

Prep time: 10 minutes | Cooking time: 20 minutes |
Servings: 4

Ingredients:

- 1 yellow onion, chopped
- 2 pounds pork meat, cut into strips
- ½ pound green beans, trimmed and halved
- 1 red bell pepper, chopped
- Black pepper to the taste
- 1 tablespoon olive oil
- ¼ cup red hot chili pepper, chopped
- 1 cup low-sodium vegetable stock

Directions:

1. Heat a pan with the oil over medium-high heat, add the onion and sauté for 5 minutes.
2. Add the meat and brown for 5 minutes more.
3. Add the rest of the ingredients, toss, cook for 10 minutes over medium heat, divide between plates and serve.

Nutrition: 489calories, 72.8g protein, 11.7g carbohydrates, 15.4g fat, 3.9g fiber, 209g cholesterol, 170mg sodium, 1153mg potassium

Coconut Lamb and Quinoa

Prep time: 10 minutes | Cooking time: 30 minutes |
Servings: 5

Ingredients:

- 1 cup quinoa
- 2 cups low-sodium chicken stock
- 1 tablespoon olive oil
- 1 cup coconut cream
- 2 pounds lamb stew meat,
- cubed
- 2 shallots, chopped
- 2 garlic cloves, minced
- Black pepper to the taste
- A pinch of red pepper flakes, crushed

Directions:

1. Heat a pot with the oil over medium-high heat, add the shallots and the garlic, stir and sauté for 5 minutes.
2. Add the meat and brown for 5 minutes more.
3. Add the rest of the ingredients, stir, bring to a simmer, reduce heat to medium, and cook for 20 minutes.
4. Divide the mix bowls and serve.

Nutrition: 604calories, 57.4g protein, 25.6g carbohydrates, 29.6g fat, 3.5g fiber, 163g cholesterol, 202mg sodium, 944mg potassium

Pork and Onions Bowls

Prep time: 10 minutes | Cooking time: 40 minutes |
Servings: 5

Ingredients:

- 1 pound pork meat, cubed
- 1 tablespoon avocado oil
- 1 yellow onion, chopped
- 1 bunch green onion, chopped
- 4 garlic cloves, minced
- 1 cup low-sodium tomato sauce
- Black pepper to the taste

Directions:

1. Heat a pan with the oil over medium-high heat, add the onion and green onions, stir and cook for 5 minutes.
2. Add the meat, stir, and cook for 5 minutes more.
3. Add the rest of the ingredients, toss and cook over medium heat for 30 minutes more.
4. Divide everything into bowls and serve.

Nutrition: 165calories, 18.8g protein, 5.6g carbohydrates, 6.9g fat, 1.5g fiber, 60g cholesterol, 327mg sodium, 221mg potassium

Lamb with Okra

Prep time: 10 minutes | Cooking time: 30 minutes |
Servings: 4

Ingredients:

- 1 pound lamb stew meat, roughly cubed
- 1 yellow onion, chopped
- 2 garlic cloves, minced
- 2 tablespoons avocado oil
- 1 cup okra, chopped
- 1 cup of corn
- 1 cup low-sodium vegetable stock
- 1 tablespoon parsley, chopped

Directions:

1. Heat a pan with the oil over medium-high heat, add the onion and the garlic, stir and sauté for 5 minutes.
2. Add the meat, toss and cook for 5 minutes more.
3. Add the rest of the ingredients, toss, bring to a simmer and cook over medium heat for 20 minutes.
4. Divide everything into bowls and serve.

Nutrition: 282calories, 34.2g protein, 13.6g carbohydrates, 9.8g fat, 3.1g fiber, 102g cholesterol, 131mg sodium, 665mg potassium

Pork with Spring Onions and Sprouts

Prep time: 10 minutes | Cooking time: 35 minutes |
Servings: 4

Ingredients:

- 2 pounds pork stew meat, cubed
- ¼ cup low-sodium tomato sauce
- Black pepper to the taste
- ½ pound Brussels sprouts, halved
- 1 tablespoon olive oil
- 2 spring onions, chopped
- 1 tablespoon cilantro, chopped

Directions:

1. Heat a pan with the oil over medium-high heat, add the onions and the sprouts and brown for 5 minutes.
2. Add the meat and the other ingredients, bring to a simmer, and cook over medium heat for 30 minutes more.
3. Divide everything between plates and serve.

Nutrition: 541calories, 68.7g protein, 6.5g carbohydrates, 25.6g fat, 2.6g fiber, 195g cholesterol, 230mg sodium, 1144mg potassium

Pork with Beans

Prep time: 5 minutes | Cooking time: 40 minutes |
Servings: 8

Ingredients:

- 2 tablespoons olive oil
- 1 cup canned black beans, no-salt-added, drained
- 1 yellow onion, chopped
- 1 cup canned tomatoes, no-salt-added, chopped
- 2 pounds pork stew meat, cubed
- 2 garlic cloves, minced
- Black pepper to the taste
- ½ teaspoon nutmeg, ground

Directions:

1. Heat a pan with the oil over medium heat, add the onion and the garlic and sauté for 5 minutes.
2. Add the meat, toss and cook for 5 minutes more.
3. Add the rest of the ingredients, toss, bring to a simmer and cook over medium heat for 30 minutes.
4. Divide the mix into bowls and serve.

Nutrition: 365calories, 38.8g protein, 17.6g carbohydrates, 14.9g fat, 4.3g fiber, 98g cholesterol, 70mg sodium, 862mg potassium

Pork with Capers

Prep time: 10 minutes | Cooking time: 35 minutes |
Servings: 4

Ingredients:

- 2 tablespoons olive oil
- 1 cup low-sodium vegetable stock
- 2 tablespoons capers, drained
- 1 pound pork chops
- 1 cup bean sprouts
- 1 yellow onion, cut into wedges
- Black pepper to the taste

Directions:

1. Heat a pan with the oil over medium-high heat, add the onion and the meat, and brown for 5 minutes.
2. Add the rest of the ingredients, introduce the pan in the oven, and bake at 390 degrees F for 30 minutes.
3. Divide everything between plates and serve.

Nutrition: 453calories, 28.1g protein, 5.7g carbohydrates, 35.5g fat, 1g fiber, 98g cholesterol, 246mg sodium, 550mg potassium

Pork and Olives

Prep time: 10 minutes | Cooking time: 35 minutes |
Servings: 4

Ingredients:

- 4 pork chops
- 2 tablespoons olive oil
- 1 cup kalamata olives, pitted and halved
- 1 teaspoon allspice, ground
- ¼ cup coconut milk
- 1 yellow onion, chopped
- 1 tablespoon chives, chopped

Directions:

1. Heat up a pan with the oil over medium heat, add the onion and the meat and brown for 4 minutes on each side.
2. Add the rest of the ingredients, toss gently, introduce in the oven and bake at 390 degrees F for 25 minutes more.
3. Divide everything between plates and serve.

Nutrition: 396calories, 18.9g protein, 5.6g carbohydrates, 33.6g fat, 2g fiber, 69mg cholesterol, 307mg sodium, 364mg potassium

Pork and Cilantro Rice

Prep time: 10 minutes | Cooking time: 35 minutes |
Servings: 4

Ingredients:

- 1 tablespoon olive oil
- 1 pound pork stew meat, cubed
- 1 tablespoon oregano, chopped
- 1 cup white rice
- 2 cups low-sodium chicken stock
- Black pepper to the taste
- 2 garlic cloves, minced
- Juice of ½ lemon
- 1 tablespoon cilantro, chopped

Directions:

1. Heat up a pot with the oil over medium heat, add the meat and the garlic and brown for 5 minutes.
2. Add the rice, the stock and the other ingredients, bring to a simmer and cook over medium heat for 30 minutes.
3. Divide everything between plates and serve.

Nutrition: 449calories, 37.3g protein, 38.8g carbohydrates, 14.9g fat, 1.1g fiber, 98mg cholesterol, 137mg sodium, 512mg potassium

Lime Lamb

Prep time: 10 minutes | Cooking time: 25 minutes |
Servings: 4

Ingredients:

- Juice of 2 limes
- 1 tablespoon lime zest, grated
- 1 tablespoon dill, chopped
- 2 garlic cloves, minced
- 2 tablespoons olive oil
- 2 pounds lamb meat, cubed
- 1 cup cilantro, chopped
- Black pepper to the taste

Directions:

1. Heat up a pan with the oil over medium-high heat, add the garlic and the meat and brown for 4 minutes on each side.
2. Add the lime juice and the other ingredients and cook for 15 minutes more stirring often.
3. Divide everything between plates and serve.

Nutrition: 497calories, 35.6g protein, 23.4g carbohydrates, 27.3g fat, 4.8g fiber, 121mg cholesterol, 1307mg sodium, 81mg potassium

Minty Pork

Prep time: 10 minutes | Cooking time: 1 hour |
Servings: 4

Ingredients:

- 4 pork chops
- 1 cup low-sodium vegetable stock
- 1 cup corn
- 1 tablespoon mint, chopped
- 1 teaspoon sweet paprika
- Black pepper to the taste
- 1 tablespoon olive oil

Directions:

1. Put the pork chops in a roasting pan, add the rest of the ingredients, toss, introduce in the oven and bake at 380 degrees F for 1 hour.
2. Divide everything between plates and serve.

Nutrition: 326calories, 19.6g protein, 8.7g carbohydrates, 23.9g fat, 1.6g fiber, 69mg cholesterol, 97mg sodium, 431mg potassium

Tarragon Pork Roast

Prep time: 10 minutes | Cooking time: 8 hours |
Servings: 4

Ingredients:

- 2 pounds pork roast, sliced
- 2 tablespoons olive oil
- Black pepper to the taste
- 1 tablespoon tarragon, chopped
- 2 shallots, chopped
- 1 cup low-sodium vegetable stock
- 1 tablespoon thyme, chopped
- 1 tablespoon mustard

Directions:

1. In a slow cooker, combine the roast with the black pepper and the other ingredients, put the lid on, and cook on Low for 8 hours.
2. Divide the pork roast between plates, drizzle the mustard sauce all over and serve.

Nutrition: 554calories, 65.9g protein, 3.5g carbohydrates, 29.3g fat, 0.9g fiber, 195g cholesterol, 163mg sodium, 999mg potassium

Fish and Seafood

Coconut Flounder

Prep time: 10 minutes | Cooking time: 20 minutes |
Servings: 4

Ingredients:

- 2 tablespoons olive oil
- 1 red onion, chopped
- Black pepper to the taste
- ½ cup low-sodium vegetable
- stock
- 4 flounder fillets, boneless
- ½ cup coconut cream
- 1 tablespoon dill, chopped

Directions:

1. Heat a pan with the oil over medium heat, add the onion, stir and sauté for 5 minutes.
2. Add the fish and cook it for 4 minutes on each side.
3. Add the rest of the ingredients, cook for 7 minutes more, divide between plates and serve.

Nutrition: 293calories, 32g protein, 5.2g carbohydrates, 16.2g fat, 1.5g fiber, 86g cholesterol, 158mg sodium, 598mg potassium

Lime Salmon and Mango

Prep time: 5 minutes |Cooking time: 0 minutes |
Servings: 4

Ingredients:

- 1-pound salmon, boneless, skinless and flaked
- Black pepper to the taste
- 1 red onion, chopped
- 1 mango, peeled, seedless and
- chopped
- 2 jalapeno peppers, chopped
- ¼ cup parsley, chopped
- 3 tablespoons lime juice
- 1 tablespoon olive oil

Directions:

1. In a bowl, mix the salmon with the black pepper and the other ingredients, toss and serve.

Nutrition: 302calories, 30.1g protein, 16g carbohydrates, 13.2g fat, 2.4g fiber, 81g cholesterol, 251mg sodium, 937mg potassium

Shrimp and Radish Mix

Prep time: 5 minutes | Cooking time: 0 minutes |
Servings: 4

Ingredients:

- 2 teaspoons lemon juice
- 1 tablespoon olive oil
- 1 tablespoon dill, chopped
- 1-pound shrimp, cooked,
- peeled and deveined
- Black pepper to the taste
- 1 cup radishes, cubed

Directions:

1. In a bowl, combine the shrimp with the lemon juice and the other ingredients, toss and serve.

Nutrition: 172calories, 26.2g protein, 3.2g carbohydrates, 5.5g fat, 0.6g fiber, 239g cholesterol, 290mg sodium, 289mg potassium

Salmon Spread

Prep time: 4 minutes | Cooking time: 0 minutes |
Servings: 6

Ingredients:

- 6 ounces salmon, boneless, skinless and shredded, cooked
- 2 tablespoons non-fat yogurt
- 3 teaspoons lemon juice
- 2 spring onions, chopped
- 8 ounces low-fat cream cheese
- ¼ cup cilantro, chopped

Directions:

1. In a bowl, mix the salmon with the yogurt and the other ingredients, whisk and serve cold.

Nutrition: 175calories, 8.6g protein, 2.1g carbohydrates, 15g fat, 0.2g fiber, 54g cholesterol, 129mg sodium, 174mg potassium

Salmon Soup

Prep time: 5 minutes | Cooking time: 20 minutes |
Servings: 4

Ingredients:

- 1 pound salmon fillets, boneless, skinless and cubed
- 1 cup yellow onion, chopped
- 2 tablespoons olive oil
- Black pepper to the taste
- 2 cups low-sodium vegetable stock
- 1 and ½ cups tomatoes, chopped
- 1 tablespoon basil, chopped

Directions:

1. Heat a pot with the oil over medium heat, add the onion, stir and sauté for 5 minutes.
2. Add the salmon and the other ingredients, bring to a simmer, and cook over medium heat for 15 minutes.
3. Divide the chowder into bowls and serve.

Nutrition: 244calories, 23.4g protein, 7.3g carbohydrates, 14.2g fat, 1.9g fiber, 50g cholesterol, 124mg sodium, 704mg potassium

Cilantro and Nutmeg Shrimp

Prep time: 3 minutes | Cooking time: 6 minutes |
Servings: 4

Ingredients:

- 1 pound shrimp, peeled and deveined
- 2 tablespoons olive oil
- 1 tablespoon lemon juice
- 1 tablespoon nutmeg, ground
- Black pepper to the taste
- 1 tablespoon cilantro, chopped

Directions:

1. Heat a pan with the oil over medium heat, add the shrimp, lemon juice and the other ingredients, toss, cook for 6 minutes, divide into bowls and serve.

Nutrition: 205calories, 26g protein, 2.7g carbohydrates, 9.6g fat, 0.4g fiber, 239g cholesterol, 278mg sodium, 204mg potassium

Shrimp and Strawberries

Prep time: 4 minutes | Cooking time: 6 minutes |
Servings: 4

Ingredients:

- 1 pound shrimp, peeled and deveined
- ½ cup tomatoes, cubed
- 2 tablespoons olive oil
- 1 tablespoon balsamic vinegar
- ½ cup strawberries, chopped
- Black pepper to the taste

Directions:

1. Heat a pan with the oil over medium heat, add the shrimp, toss and cook for 3 minutes.
2. Add the rest of the ingredients, toss, cook for 3-4 minutes more, divide into bowls and serve.

Nutrition: 205calories, 26.2g protein, 4g carbohydrates, 9g fat, 0.6g fiber, 239g cholesterol, 278mg sodium, 276mg potassium

Baked Trout

Prep time: 10 minutes | Cooking time: 30 minutes |
Servings: 4

Ingredients:

- 4 trout
- 1 tablespoon lemon zest, grated
- 2 tablespoons olive oil
- 2 tablespoons lemon juice
- A pinch of black pepper
- 2 tablespoons cilantro, chopped

Directions:

1. In a baking dish, combine the fish with the lemon zest and the other ingredients and rub.
2. Bake at 370 degrees F for 30 minutes, divide between plates and serve.

Nutrition: 181calories, 16.6g protein, 0.5g carbohydrates, 12.3g fat, 0.1g fiber, 46g cholesterol, 43mg sodium, 304mg potassium

Salmon Salad

Prep time: 10 minutes | Cooking time: 0 minutes |
Servings: 4

Ingredients:

- 2 smoked salmon fillets, boneless, skinless and cubed
- 2 peaches, stones removed and cubed
- 1 teaspoon olive oil
- A pinch of black pepper
- 2 cups baby spinach
- ½ tablespoon balsamic vinegar
- 1 tablespoon lemon juice
- 1 tablespoon cilantro, chopped

Directions:

3. In a salad bowl, combine the salmon with the peaches and the other ingredients, toss, and serve cold.

Nutrition: 162calories, 18.4g protein, 7.7g carbohydrates, 7g fat, 1.5g fiber, 39g cholesterol, 52mg sodium, 575mg potassium

Dill Salmon

Prep time: 10 minutes | Cooking time: 15 minutes |
Servings: 4

Ingredients:

- 2 tablespoons olive oil
- 4 salmon fillets, boneless
- 1 tablespoon capers, drained
- 1 tablespoon dill, chopped
- 1 shallot, chopped
- ½ cup coconut cream
- A pinch of black pepper

Directions:

1. Heat a pan with the oil over medium-high heat, add the shallot and the capers, toss and sauté for 4 minutes.
2. Add the salmon and cook it for 3 minutes on each side.
3. Add the rest of the ingredients, cook everything for 5 minutes more, divide between plates and serve.

Nutrition: 369calories, 35.5g protein, 2.6g carbohydrates, 25.2g fat, 0.8g fiber, 78g cholesterol, 149mg sodium, 797mg potassium

Chives Salmon Salad

Prep time: 10 minutes | Cooking time: 0 minutes |
Servings: 4

Ingredients:

- 2 tablespoons olive oil
- ½ teaspoon lemon juice
- ½ teaspoon lemon zest, grated
- A pinch of black pepper
- 1 cup black olives, pitted and halved
- 1 cup cucumber, cubed
- ½ pound smoked salmon, boneless and cubed
- 1 tablespoon chives, chopped

Directions:

1. In a salad bowl, combine the salmon with the olives and the other ingredients, toss and serve.

Nutrition: 169calories, 10.9g protein, 3.1g carbohydrates, 13.1g fat, 1.3g fiber, 13g cholesterol, 1428mg sodium, 144mg potassium

Chili Tuna

Prep time: 4 minutes | Cooking time: 10 minutes |
Servings: 4

Ingredients:

- 2 tablespoons olive oil
- 4 tuna steaks, boneless
- 2 teaspoons sweet paprika
- ½ teaspoon chili powder
- A pinch of black pepper

Directions:

1. Heat a pan with the oil over medium-high heat, add the tuna steaks, season with paprika, black pepper, and chili powder, cook for 5 minutes on each side, divide between plates and serve with a side salad.

Nutrition: 220calories, 25.6g protein, 42g carbohydrates, 12.5g fat, 0.5g fiber, 42g cholesterol, 46mg sodium, 305mg potassium

Lime Tuna

Prep time: 10 minutes | Cooking time: 15 minutes |
Servings: 4

Ingredients:

- 4 tuna fillets, boneless and skinless
- 1 tablespoon olive oil
- 2 shallots, chopped
- 2 tablespoons lime juice
- A pinch of black pepper
- 1 teaspoon sweet paprika
- ½ cup low-sodium chicken stock

Directions:

1. Heat a pan with the oil over medium-high heat, add shallots and sauté for 3 minutes.
2. Add the fish and cook it for 4 minutes on each side.
3. Add the rest of the ingredients, cook everything for 3 minutes more, divide between plates and serve.

Nutrition: 399calories, 21.4g protein, 1.4g carbohydrates, 34.6g fat, 0.2g fiber, 0g cholesterol, 18mg sodium, 32mg potassium

Citrus Cod

Prep time: 5 minutes | Cooking time: 12 minutes |
Servings: 4

Ingredients:

- 1 tablespoon parsley, chopped
- 4 cod fillets, boneless
- 1 cup of orange juice
- 2 spring onions, chopped
- 1 teaspoon orange zest, grated
- 1 tablespoon olive oil
- 1 teaspoon balsamic vinegar
- A pinch of black pepper

Directions:

1. Heat a pan with the oil over medium heat, add the spring onions, and sauté for 2 minutes.
2. Add the fish and the other ingredients, cook for 5 minutes on each side, divide everything between plates and serve.

Nutrition: 151calories, 20.6g protein, 7.2g carbohydrates, 4.7g fat, 0.4g fiber, 40g cholesterol, 82mg sodium, 152mg potassium

Cod and Coconut Asparagus

Prep time: 10 minutes | Cooking time: 14 minutes |
Servings: 4

Ingredients:

- 1 tablespoon olive oil
- 1 red onion, chopped
- 1 pound cod fillets, boneless
- 1 bunch asparagus, trimmed
- Black pepper to the taste
- 1 cup coconut cream
- 1 tablespoon chives, chopped

Directions:

1. Heat a pan with the oil over medium heat, add the onion and the cod and cook it for 3 minutes on each side.
2. Add the rest of the ingredients, cook everything for 8 minutes more, divide between plates and serve.

Nutrition: 298calories, 27.4g protein, 7.2g carbohydrates, 19.1g fat, 2.6g fiber, 50g cholesterol, 111mg sodium, 268mg potassium

Trout and Avocado Salad

Prep time: 6 minutes | Cooking time: 0 minutes |
Servings: 4

Ingredients:

- 4 ounces smoked trout, skinless, boneless and cubed
- 1 tablespoon lime juice
- 1/3 cup non-fat yogurt
- 2 avocados, peeled, pitted and cubed
- 3 tablespoons chives, chopped
- Black pepper to the taste
- 1 tablespoon olive oil

Directions:

1. In a bowl, combine the trout with the avocados and the other ingredients, toss, and serve.

Nutrition: 298calories, 10g protein, 10.3g carbohydrates, 25.5g fat, 6.8g fiber, 21g cholesterol, 35mg sodium, 650mg potassium

Thyme Shrimp

Prep time: 10 minutes | Cooking time: 10 minutes | Servings: 4

Ingredients:

- 1 pound shrimp, peeled and deveined
- 2 tablespoons pine nuts
- 1 tablespoon lime juice
- 2 tablespoons olive oil
- 3 garlic cloves, minced
- Black pepper to the taste
- 1 tablespoon thyme, chopped
- 2 tablespoons chives, finely chopped

Directions:

1. Heat a pan with the oil over medium-high heat, add the garlic, thyme, pine nuts, and lime juice, toss and cook for 3 minutes.
2. Add the shrimp, black pepper and the chives, toss, cook for 7 minutes more, divide between plates and serve.

Nutrition: 229calories, 26.7g protein, 3.5g carbohydrates, 11.9g fat, 0.5g fiber, 239g cholesterol, 278mg sodium, 237mg potassium

Hot Cod

Prep time: 10 minutes | Cooking time: 14 minutes | Servings: 4

Ingredients:

- 4 cod fillets, boneless
- ½ pound green beans, trimmed and halved
- 1 tablespoon lime juice
- 1 tablespoon lime zest, grated
- 1 yellow onion, chopped
- 2 tablespoons olive oil
- 1 teaspoon cumin, ground
- 1 teaspoon chili powder
- ½ cup low-sodium vegetable stock
- A pinch of salt and black pepper

Directions:

1. Heat a pan with the oil over medium-high heat, add the onion, toss and cook for 2 minutes.
2. Add the fish and cook it for 3 minutes on each side.
3. Add the green beans and the rest of the ingredients, toss gently, cook for 7 minutes more, divide between plates and serve.

Nutrition: 187calories, 21.7g protein, 8.3g carbohydrates, 8.3g fat, 3.2g fiber, 40g cholesterol, 121mg sodium, 210mg potassium

Salmon with Scallions and Green Beans

Prep time: 10 minutes | Cooking time: 20 minutes | Servings: 4

Ingredients:

- 2 tablespoons olive oil
- 1 cup low-sodium chicken stock
- 4 salmon fillets, boneless
- 2 garlic cloves, minced
- 1 tablespoon ginger, grated
- ½ pound green beans, trimmed and halved
- 2 teaspoons balsamic vinegar
- ¼ cup scallions, chopped

Directions:

1. Heat a pan with the oil over medium heat, add the scallion, and the garlic and sauté for 5 minutes.
2. Add the salmon and cook it for 5 minutes on each side.
3. Add the rest of the ingredients, cook everything for 5 minutes more, divide between plates and serve.

Nutrition: 324calories, 36.1g protein, 6g carbohydrates, 18.2g fat, 2.3g fiber, 78g cholesterol, 117mg sodium, 845mg potassium

Tuna and Chives Meatballs

Prep time: 10 minutes | Cooking time: 30 minutes | Servings: 4

Ingredients:

- 2 tablespoons olive oil
- 1 pound tuna, skinless, boneless and minced
- 1 yellow onion, chopped
- ¼ cup chives, chopped
- 1 egg, whisked
- 1 tablespoon coconut flour
- A pinch of salt and black pepper

Directions:

1. In a bowl, mix the tuna with the onion and the other ingredients except for the oil, stir well and shape medium meatballs out of this mix.
2. Arrange the meatballs on a baking sheet, grease them with the oil, introduce in the oven at 350 degrees F, cook for 30 minutes, divide between plates and serve.

Nutrition: 306calories, 32.1g protein, 4g carbohydrates, 17.5g fat, 1.4g fiber, 76g cholesterol, 73mg sodium, 441mg potassium

Salmon with Zucchini and Eggplant

Prep time: 10 minutes | Cooking time: 12 minutes | Servings: 4

Ingredients:

- 4 salmon fillets, boneless and roughly cubed
- 2 tablespoons olive oil
- 1 red bell pepper, cut into strips
- 1 zucchini, roughly cubed
- 1 eggplant, roughly cubed
- 1 tablespoon lemon juice
- 1 tablespoon dill, chopped
- ¼ cup low-sodium vegetable stock
- 1 teaspoon garlic powder
- A pinch of black pepper

Directions:

1. Heat a pan with oil over medium-high heat, add the bell pepper, zucchini, and the eggplant, toss and sauté for 3 minutes.
2. Add the salmon and the other ingredients, toss gently, cook everything for 9 minutes more, divide between plates and serve.

Nutrition: 348calories, 36.9g protein, 11.9g carbohydrates, 18.4g fat, 5.2g fiber, 78g cholesterol, 48mg sodium, 1176mg potassium

Turmeric Cod Mix

Prep time: 10 minutes | Cooking time: 25 minutes | Servings: 4

Ingredients:

- 4 cod fillets, skinless and boneless
- A pinch of black pepper
- 1 teaspoon ginger, grated
- 1 tablespoon mustard
- 2 tablespoons olive oil
- 1 teaspoon thyme, dried
- ¼ teaspoon cumin, ground
- 1 teaspoon turmeric powder
- ¼ cup cilantro, chopped
- 1 cup low-sodium vegetable stock
- 3 garlic cloves, minced

Directions:

1. In a roasting pan, combine the cod with the black pepper, ginger, and the other ingredients, toss gently, and bake at 380 degrees F for 25 minutes.
2. Divide the mix between plates and serve.

Nutrition: 176calories, 21.2g protein, 3.7g carbohydrates, 9g fat, 1g fiber, 55g cholesterol, 107mg sodium, 90mg potassium

Balsamic Salmon

Prep time: 5 minutes | Cooking time: 14 minutes |
Servings: 4

Ingredients:

- 2 tablespoons olive oil
- 4 salmon fillets, skinless
- 2 garlic cloves, minced
- A pinch of black pepper
- 2 tablespoons balsamic vinegar
- 2 tablespoons basil, chopped

Directions:

1. Heat a pan with the olive oil, add the fish and cook for 4 minutes on each side.
2. Add the rest of the ingredients, cook everything for 6 minutes more.
3. Divide everything between plates and serve.

Nutrition: 300calories, 34.7g protein, 0.6g carbohydrates, 18g fat, 0.1g fiber, 78g cholesterol, 79mg sodium, 699mg potassium

Cod and Coconut Sauce

Prep time: 10 minutes | Cooking time: 15 minutes |
Servings: 4

Ingredients:

- 2 tablespoons olive oil
- 4 cod fillets, boneless and skinless
- 1 shallot, chopped
- ½ cup coconut cream
- 3 tablespoons non-fat yogurt
- 2 tablespoons dill, chopped
- A pinch of black pepper
- 1 garlic clove minced

Directions:

1. Heat a pan with the oil over medium heat, add the shallots and sauté for 5 minutes.
2. Add the fish and the other ingredients, and cook for 10 minutes more.
3. Divide everything between plates and serve.

Nutrition: 230calories, 21.2g protein, 3.4g carbohydrates, 15.2g fat, 0.9g fiber, 40g cholesterol, 108mg sodium, 139mg potassium

Cilantro Halibut and Radishes

Prep time: 10 minutes | Cooking time: 15 minutes |
Servings: 4

Ingredients:

- 2 shallots, chopped
- 4 halibut fillets, boneless
- 1 cup radishes, halved
- 1 cup tomatoes, cubed
- 1 tablespoon olive oil
- 1 tablespoon cilantro, chopped
- 2 teaspoons lemon juice
- A pinch of black pepper

Directions:

1. Grease a roasting pan with the oil and arrange the fish inside.
2. Add the rest of the ingredients, introduce in the oven, and bake at 400 degrees F for 15 minutes.
3. Divide everything between plates and serve.

Nutrition: 365calories, 61.3g protein, 3.6g carbohydrates, 10.4g fat, 1g fiber, 93g cholesterol, 171mg sodium, 1502mg potassium

Balsamic Scallops

Prep time: 5 minutes | Cooking time: 8 minutes |
Servings: 4

Ingredients:

- 12 scallops
- 1 red onion, sliced
- 2 tablespoons olive oil
- ½ teaspoon garlic, minced
- 2 tablespoons lemon juice
- Black pepper to the taste
- 1 teaspoon balsamic vinegar

Directions:

1. Heat a pan with the oil over medium heat, add the onion and the garlic and sauté for 2 minutes.
2. Add the scallops and the other ingredients, cook over medium heat for 6 minutes more, divide between plates and serve hot.

Nutrition: 153calories, 15.5g protein, 5g carbohydrates, 7.8g fat, 0.6g fiber, 30g cholesterol, 148mg sodium, 342mg potassium

Citrus Tuna

Prep time: 5 minutes | Cooking time: 12 minutes |
Servings: 4

Ingredients:

- 4 tuna fillets, boneless
- Black pepper to the taste
- 2 tablespoons olive oil
- 2 shallots, chopped
- 3 tablespoons orange juice
- 1 orange, peeled and cut into segments
- 1 tablespoon oregano, chopped

Directions:

1. Heat a pan with the oil over medium-high heat, add the shallots, stir and sauté for 2 minutes.
2. Add the tuna and the other ingredients, cook everything for 10 minutes more, divide between plates and serve.

Nutrition: 457calories, 21.8g protein, 8.2g carbohydrates, 38.2g fat, 1.6g fiber, 0g cholesterol, 1mg sodium, 142mg potassium

Creamy Salmon Curry

Prep time: 10 minutes | Cooking time: 20 minutes |
Servings: 4

Ingredients:

- 1 pound salmon fillet, boneless and cubed
- 3 tablespoons red curry paste
- 1 red onion, chopped
- 1 teaspoon sweet paprika
- 1 cup coconut cream
- 1 tablespoon olive oil
- Black pepper to the taste
- ½ cup low-sodium chicken stock
- 3 tablespoons basil, chopped

Directions:

1. Heat a pan with the oil over medium-high heat, add the onion, paprika, and the curry paste, toss and cook for 5 minutes.
2. Add the salmon and the other ingredients, toss gently, cook over medium heat for 15 minutes, divide into bowls and serve.

Nutrition: 377calories, 23.9g protein, 8.5g carbohydrates, 28.3g fat, 2.1g fiber, 50g cholesterol, 662mg sodium, 652mg potassium

Chives Salmon and Olives

Prep time: 10 minutes | Cooking time: 20 minutes | Servings: 4

Ingredients:

- 1 yellow onion, chopped
- 1 cup green olives, pitted and halved
- 1 teaspoon chili powder
- Black pepper to the taste
- 2 tablespoons olive oil
- ¼ cup low-sodium vegetable stock
- 4 salmon fillets, skinless and boneless
- 2 tablespoons chives, chopped

Directions:

1. Heat a pan with the oil over medium-high heat, add the onion and sauté for 3 minutes.
2. Add the salmon and cook for 5 minutes on each side. Add the rest of the ingredients, cook the mix for 5 minutes more, divide between plates and serve.

Nutrition: 317calories, 35.1g protein, 3.7g carbohydrates, 18.7g fat, 1.1g fiber, 78g cholesterol, 169mg sodium, 749mg potassium

Lemon Fennel and Salmon

Prep time: 5 minutes | Cooking time: 15 minutes | Servings: 4

Ingredients:

- 4 medium salmon fillets, skinless and boneless
- 1 fennel bulb, chopped
- ½ cup low-sodium vegetable stock
- 2 tablespoons olive oil
- Black pepper to the taste
- ¼ cup low-sodium vegetable stock
- 1 tablespoon lemon juice
- 1 tablespoon cilantro, chopped

Directions:

1. Heat a pan with the oil over medium heat, add the fennel and cook for 3 minutes.
2. Add the fish and brown it for 4 minutes on each side.
3. Add the rest of the ingredients, cook everything for 4 minutes more, divide between plates and serve.

Nutrition: 317calories, 35.4g protein, 4.9g carbohydrates, 18.1g fat, 2g fiber, 78g cholesterol, 127mg sodium, 948mg potassium

Chives Sea Bass

Prep time: 10 minutes | Cooking time: 30 minutes | Servings: 4

Ingredients:

- 2 tablespoons olive oil
- 2 pounds sea bass fillets, skinless and boneless
- Black pepper to the taste
- 2 cups cherry tomatoes,
- halved
- 1 tablespoon chives, chopped
- 1 tablespoon lemon zest, grated
- ¼ cup lemon juice

Directions:

1. Grease a roasting pan with the oil and arrange the fish inside.
2. Add the tomatoes and the other ingredients, introduce the pan in the oven and bake at 380 degrees F for 30 minutes.
3. Divide everything between plates and serve.

Nutrition: 362calories, 54.6g protein, 4.2g carbohydrates, 13.1g fat, 1.3g fiber, 120g cholesterol, 205mg sodium, 983mg potassium

Shrimp and Black Beans

Prep time: 10 minutes | Cooking time: 12 minutes | Servings: 4

Ingredients:

- 1 pound shrimp, deveined and peeled
- 1 tablespoon olive oil
- Juice of 1 lime
- 1 cup canned black beans, no-salt-added, drained
- 1 shallot, chopped
- 1 tablespoon oregano, chopped
- 2 garlic cloves, chopped
- Black pepper to the taste

Directions:

1. Heat a pan with the oil over medium-high heat, add the shallot and the garlic, stir and cook for 3 minutes.
2. Add the shrimp and cook for 2 minutes on each side.
3. Add the beans and the other ingredients, cook everything over medium heat for 5 minutes more, divide into bowls and serve.

Nutrition: 340calories, 36.6g protein, 34.5g carbohydrates, 6.3g fat, 7.9g fiber, 239g cholesterol, 280mg sodium, 957mg potassium

Shrimp with Artichokes and Tomatoes

Prep time: 4 minutes | Cooking time: 8 minutes | Servings: 4

Ingredients:

- 2 green onions, chopped
- 1 cup canned artichokes, no-salt-added, drained and quartered
- 2 tablespoons cilantro, chopped
- 1 pound shrimp, peeled and
- deveined
- 1 cup cherry tomatoes, cubed
- 1 tablespoon olive oil
- 1 tablespoon balsamic vinegar
- A pinch of salt and black pepper

Directions:

1. Heat a pan with the oil over medium heat, add the onions and the artichokes, toss and cook for 2 minutes.
2. Add the shrimp, toss and cook over medium heat for 6 minutes.
3. Divide everything into bowls and serve.

Nutrition: 191calories, 27.4g protein, 7.3g carbohydrates, 5.6g fat, 2.5g fiber, 23g cholesterol, 311mg sodium, 443mg potassium

Salmon and Veggies Mix

Prep time: 10 minutes | Cooking time: 15 minutes | Servings: 4

Ingredients:

- 4 salmon fillets, boneless
- 1 red onion, chopped
- 2 carrots, sliced
- 2 tablespoons olive oil
- 2 tablespoons balsamic
- vinegar
- Black pepper to the taste
- 2 tablespoons chives, chopped
- ¼ cup low-sodium vegetable stock

Directions:

1. Heat a pan with the oil over medium heat, add the onion and the carrots, toss and sauté for 5 minutes.
2. Add the salmon and the other ingredients, cook everything for 10 minutes more, divide between plates and serve.

Nutrition: 322calories, 35.2g protein, 6g carbohydrates, 18g fat, 1.4g fiber, 78g cholesterol, 110mg sodium, 839mg potassium

Balsamic Scallops and Scallions

Prep time: 4 minutes | Cooking time: 6 minutes |
Servings: 4

Ingredients:

- 12 ounces sea scallops
- 2 tablespoons olive oil
- 2 garlic cloves, minced
- 1 tablespoon balsamic vinegar
- 1 cup scallions, sliced
- 2 tablespoons cilantro, chopped

Directions:

1. Heat a pan with the oil over medium heat, add the scallions and the garlic and sauté for 2 minutes.
2. Add the scallops and the other ingredients, cook them for 2 minutes on each side, divide between plates and serve.

Nutrition: 146calories, 14.8g protein, 4.4g carbohydrates, 7.7g fat, 0.7g fiber, 28g cholesterol, 142mg sodium, 354mg potassium

Garlic Cod and Tomatoes

Prep time: 10 minutes | Cooking time: 16 minutes |
Servings: 4

Ingredients:

- 2 tablespoons olive oil
- 2 garlic cloves, minced
- ½ cup low-sodium vegetable stock
- 4 cod fillets, boneless
- 1 cup cherry tomatoes, halved
- 2 tablespoons lime juice
- A pinch of black pepper
- 1 tablespoon chives, chopped

Directions:

1. Heat a pan with the oil over medium-high heat, add the garlic and the fish and cook for 3 minutes on each side.
2. Add the rest of the ingredients, bring to a simmer and cook over medium heat for 10 minutes more.
3. Divide everything between plates and serve.

Nutrition: 164calories, 20.7g protein, 3g carbohydrates, 8.1g fat, 0.7g fiber, 40g cholesterol, 100mg sodium, 134mg potassium

Coconut Sea Bass Mix

Prep time: 10 minutes | Cooking time: 14 minutes |
Servings: 4

Ingredients:

- 4 sea bass fillets, boneless
- 1 cup coconut cream
- 1 yellow onion, chopped
- 1 tablespoon lime juice
- 2 tablespoons avocado oil
- 1 tablespoon parsley, chopped
- A pinch of black pepper

Directions:

1. Heat a pan with the oil over medium heat, add the onion, toss and sauté for 2 minutes.
2. Add the fish and cook it for 4 minutes on each side.
3. Add the rest of the ingredients, cook everything for 4 minutes more, divide between plates and serve.

Nutrition: 284calories, 25.7g protein, 6.3g carbohydrates, 17.8g fat, 2.3g fiber, 54g cholesterol, 99mg sodium, 557mg potassium

Garlic Trout

Prep time: 5 minutes | Cooking time: 15 minutes |
Servings: 4

Ingredients:

- 3 tablespoons balsamic vinegar
- 2 tablespoons olive oil
- 4 trout fillets, boneless
- 3 tablespoons parsley, finely chopped
- 2 garlic cloves, minced

Directions:

1. Heat a pan with the oil over medium heat, add the trout and cook for 6 minutes on each side.
2. Add the rest of the ingredients, cook for 3 minutes more, divide between plates and serve with a side salad.

Nutrition: 183calories, 16.7g protein, 0.8g carbohydrates, 12.3g fat, 0.1g fiber, 46g cholesterol, 44mg sodium, 317mg potassium

Shrimp and Quinoa Bowls

Prep time: 5 minutes | Cooking time: 8 minutes |
Servings: 4

Ingredients:

- 1 pound shrimp, peeled and deveined
- 1 cup quinoa, cooked
- Black pepper to the taste
- 1 tablespoon olive oil
- 1 tablespoon oregano, chopped
- 1 red onion, chopped
- Juice of 1 lemon

Directions:

1. Heat a pan with the oil over medium-high heat, add the onion, stir and sauté for 2 minutes.
2. Add the shrimp, toss and cook for 5 minutes.
3. Add the rest of the ingredients, toss, divide everything into bowls, and serve.

Nutrition: 339calories, 32.3g protein, 33.3g carbohydrates, 8.2g fat, 4.1g fiber, 239g cholesterol, 280mg sodium, 506mg potassium

Lemon and Mint Cod

Prep time: 10 minutes | Cooking time: 17 minutes |
Servings: 4

Ingredients:

- 2 tablespoons olive oil
- 1 tablespoon lemon juice
- 1 tablespoon mint, chopped
- 4 cod fillets, boneless
- 1 teaspoons lemon zest, grated
- A pinch of black pepper
- ¼ cup shallot, chopped
- ½ cup low-sodium chicken stock

Directions:

1. Heat a pan with the oil over medium heat, add the shallots, stir and sauté for 5 minutes.
2. Add the cod, the lemon juice and the other ingredients, bring to a simmer and cook over medium heat for 12 minutes.
3. Divide everything between plates and serve.

Nutrition: 160calories, 20.5g protein, 2g carbohydrates, 8.1g fat, 0.2g fiber, 40g cholesterol, 99mg sodium, 46mg potassium

Salmon and Spring Onions

Prep time: 5 minutes | Cooking time: 12 minutes | Servings: 4

Ingredients:

- 2 spring onions, chopped
- 2 teaspoons lime juice
- 1 tablespoon chives, minced
- 1 tablespoon olive oil
- 4 salmon fillets, boneless
- Black pepper to the taste
- 2 tablespoons parsley, chopped

Directions:

1. Heat a pan with the oil over medium heat, add the spring onions, stir and sauté for 2 minutes.
2. Add the salmon and the other ingredients, cook for 5 minutes on each side, divide between plates and serve.

Nutrition: 269calories, 34.8g protein, 0.7g carbohydrates, 14.5g fat, 0.3g fiber, 78g cholesterol, 81mg sodium, 717mg potassium

Trout and Arugula Salad

Prep time: 5 minutes | Cooking time: 0 minutes | Servings: 4

Ingredients:

- 2 tablespoons olive oil
- ½ cup kalamata olives, pitted and minced
- Black pepper to the taste
- 1 pound smoked trout, boneless, skinless and cubed
- ½ teaspoon lemon zest, grated
- 1 tablespoon lemon juice
- 1 cup cherry tomatoes, halved
- ½ red onion, sliced
- 2 cups baby arugula

Directions:

1. In a bowl, combine smoked trout with the olives, black pepper, and the other ingredients, toss and serve.

Nutrition: 325calories, 31.3g protein, 5.3g carbohydrates, 19.8g fat, 1.9g fiber, 84g cholesterol, 329mg sodium, 696mg potassium

Saffron Salmon and Onion

Prep time: 10 minutes | Cooking time: 12 minutes | Servings: 4

Ingredients:

- Black pepper to the taste
- ½ teaspoon sweet paprika
- 4 salmon fillets, boneless
- 3 tablespoons olive oil
- 1 yellow onion, chopped
- 2 garlic cloves, minced
- ¼ teaspoon saffron powder

Directions:

1. Heat a pan with the oil over medium-high heat, add the onion and the garlic, toss and sauté for 2 minutes.
2. Add the salmon and the other ingredients, cook for 5 minutes on each side, divide between plates and serve.

Nutrition: 340calories, 35g protein, 3.2g carbohydrates, 21.6g fat, 0.7g fiber, 78g cholesterol, 80mg sodium, 736mg potassium

Shrimp and Basil Salad

Prep time: 10 minutes | Cooking time: 0 minutes | Servings: 4

Ingredients:

- ¼ cup basil, chopped
- 2 cups watermelon, peeled and cubed
- 2 tablespoons balsamic vinegar
- 2 tablespoons olive oil
- 1 pound shrimp, peeled, deveined and cooked
- Black pepper to the taste
- 1 tablespoon parsley, chopped

Directions:

1. In a bowl, combine the shrimp with the watermelon and the other ingredients, toss and serve.

Nutrition: 220calories, 26.4g protein, 7.6g carbohydrates, 9g fat, 0.4g fiber, 239g cholesterol, 279mg sodium, 292mg potassium

Crab and Tomatoes Salad

Prep time: 10 minutes | Cooking time: 0 minutes | Servings: 4

Ingredients:

- 1 tablespoon olive oil
- 2 cups crab meat
- Black pepper to the taste
- 1 cup cherry tomatoes, halved
- 1 shallot, chopped
- 1 tablespoon lemon juice
- 1/3 cup cilantro, chopped

Directions:

1. In a bowl, combine the crab with the tomatoes and the other ingredients, toss and serve.

Nutrition: 54calories, 2.3g protein, 2.6g carbohydrates, 3.9g fat, 0.6g fiber, 8g cholesterol, 91mg sodium, 127mg potassium

Allspice Shrimp

Prep time: 5 minutes | Cooking time: 8 minutes | Servings: 4

Ingredients:

- 1 teaspoon garlic powder
- 1 teaspoon smoked paprika
- 1 teaspoon cumin, ground
- 1 teaspoon allspice, ground
- 2 tablespoons olive oil
- 2 pounds shrimp, peeled and deveined
- 1 tablespoon chives, chopped

Directions:

1. Heat a pan with the oil over medium heat, add the shrimp, garlic powder and the other ingredients, cook for 4 minutes on each side, divide into bowls and serve.

Nutrition: 337calories, 52g protein, 4.9g carbohydrates, 11.1g fat, 0.5g fiber, 478g cholesterol, 555mg sodium, 421mg potassium

Shrimp and Sauce

Prep time: 5 minutes | Cooking time: 8 minutes | Servings: 4

Ingredients:

- 1 pound shrimp, peeled and deveined
- 2 tablespoons olive oil
- Zest of 1 lemon, grated
- Juice of ½ lemon
- 1 tablespoon chives, chopped

Directions:

1. Heat a pan with the oil over medium-high heat, add the lemon zest, lemon juice, and the cilantro, toss and cook for 2 minutes.
2. Add the shrimp, cook everything for 6 minutes more, divide between plates and serve.

Nutrition: 195calories, 25.9g protein, 1.8g carbohydrates, 89g fat, 0g fiber, 239g cholesterol, 277mg sodium, 194mg potassium

Parsley Salmon Mix

Prep time: 10 minutes | Cooking time: 15 minutes | Servings: 4

Ingredients:

- 2 tablespoons olive oil
- ½ cup almonds, chopped
- 4 salmon fillets, boneless
- 1 shallot, chopped
- ½ cup low-sodium vegetable
- stock
- 2 tablespoons parsley, chopped
- Black pepper to the taste

Directions:

1. Heat a pan with the oil over medium heat, add the shallot and sauté for 4 minutes.
2. Add the salmon and the other ingredients, cook for 5 minutes on each side, divide everything between plates and serve.

Nutrition: 369calories, 37.3g protein, 3.6g carbohydrates, 24g fat, 1.7g fiber, 78g cholesterol, 97mg sodium, 806mg potassium

Coconut Cod and Broccoli

Prep time: 10 minutes | Cooking time: 20 minutes | Servings: 4

Ingredients:

- 2 tablespoons coconut aminos
- 1 pound broccoli florets
- 4 cod fillets, boneless
- 1 red onion, chopped
- 2 tablespoons olive oil
- ¼ cup low-sodium chicken stock
- Black pepper to the taste

Directions:

1. Heat a pan with the oil over medium heat, add the onion and the broccoli and cook for 5 minutes.
2. Add the fish and the other ingredients, cook for 20 minutes more, divide everything between plates and serve.

Nutrition: 207calories, 23.5g protein, 11.6g carbohydrates, 8.4g fat, 3.5g fiber, 40g cholesterol, 135mg sodium, 399mg potassium

Seafood and Tomato Bowls

Prep time: 5 minutes | Cooking time: 12 minutes | Servings: 4

Ingredients:

- 1 pound mussels, scrubbed
- ½ cup low-sodium chicken stock
- 1 pound shrimp, peeled and deveined
- 2 shallots, minced
- 1 cup cherry tomatoes, cubed
- 2 garlic cloves, minced
- 1 tablespoon olive oil
- Juice of 1 lemon

Directions:

1. Heat a pan with the oil over medium heat, add the shallots and the garlic and sauté for 2 minutes.
2. Add the shrimp, mussels and the other ingredients, cook everything over medium heat for 10 minutes, divide into bowls and serve.

Nutrition: 280calories, 40.1g protein, 10g carbohydrates, 8.1g fat, 0.6g fiber, 271g cholesterol, 621mg sodium, 700mg potassium

Cod and Green Onions Mix

Prep time: 10 minutes | Cooking time: 20 minutes | Servings: 4

Ingredients:

- 4 cod fillets, boneless
- ½ cup low-fat parmesan cheese, shredded
- 3 garlic cloves, minced
- 1 tablespoon olive oil
- 1 tablespoon lemon juice
- ½ cup green onion, chopped

Directions:

1. Heat a pan with the oil over medium heat, add the garlic and the green onions, toss and sauté for 5 minutes.
2. Add the fish and cook it for 4 minutes on each side.
3. Add the lemon juice, sprinkle the parmesan on top, cook everything for 2 minutes more, divide between plates and serve.

Nutrition: 195calories, 25.4g protein, 2.1g carbohydrates, 9.6g fat, 0.4g fiber, 62g cholesterol, 465mg sodium, 79mg potassium

Ginger Sea Bass

Prep time: 10 minutes | Cooking time: 15 minutes | Servings: 4

Ingredients:

- 1 tablespoon balsamic vinegar
- 1 tablespoon ginger, grated
- 2 tablespoons olive oil
- Black pepper to the taste
- 4 sea bass fillets, boneless
- 1 tablespoon cilantro, chopped

Directions:

1. Heat a pan with the oil over medium heat, add the fish and cook for 5 minutes on each side.
2. Add the rest of the ingredients, cook everything for 5 minutes more, divide everything between plates, and serve.

Nutrition: 191calories, 24g protein, 1g carbohydrates, 9.7g fat, 0.2g fiber, 54g cholesterol, 89mg sodium, 353mg potassium

Parsley Shrimp and Pineapple Bowls

Prep time: 10 minutes | Cooking time: 10 minutes | Servings: 4

Ingredients:

- 1 tablespoon olive oil
- 1 pound shrimp, peeled and deveined
- 1 cup pineapple, peeled and
- cubed
- Juice of 1 lemon
- A bunch of parsley, chopped

Directions:

1. Heat a pan with the oil over medium heat, add the shrimp and cook for 3 minutes on each side.
2. Add the rest of the ingredients, cook everything for 4 minutes more, divide into bowls, and serve.

Nutrition: 190calories, 26.2g protein, 8.3g carbohydrates, 5.5g fat, 0.7g fiber, 239g cholesterol, 279mg sodium, 267mg potassium

Creamy Shrimp

Prep time: 5 minutes | Cooking time: 8 minutes | Servings: 4

Ingredients:

- 1 pound shrimp, peeled and deveined
- 2 shallots, chopped
- 1 tablespoon olive oil
- 1 tablespoon chives, chopped
- 2 teaspoons prepared horseradish
- ¼ cup coconut cream
- Black pepper to the taste

Directions:

1. Heat a pan with the oil over medium heat, add the shallots and the horseradish, stir and sauté for 2 minutes.
2. Add the shrimp and the other ingredients, toss, cook for 6 minutes more, divide between plates and serve.

Nutrition: 204calories, 26.4g protein, 3.7g carbohydrates, 9g fat, 0.4g fiber, 239g cholesterol, 287mg sodium, 257mg potassium

Shrimp and Spinach Salad

Prep time: 4 minutes | Cooking time: 0 minutes | Servings: 4

Ingredients:

- 1 pound shrimp, cooked, peeled and deveined
- 1 tablespoon tarragon, chopped
- 1 tablespoon capers, drained
- 2 tablespoons olive oil
- Black pepper to the taste
- 2 cups baby spinach
- 1 tablespoon balsamic vinegar
- 1 small red onion, sliced
- 2 tablespoons lemon juice

Directions:

1. In a bowl, combine the shrimp with the tarragon and the other ingredients, toss and serve.

Nutrition: 210calories, 26.7g protein, 4.4g carbohydrates, 9.1g fat, 0.8g fiber, 239g cholesterol, 355mg sodium, 328mg potassium

Chives Tilapia

Prep time: 10 minutes | Cooking time: 15 minutes |
Servings: 4

Ingredients:

- 4 tilapia fillets, boneless
- 2 tablespoons olive oil
- 1 tablespoon lemon juice
- 2 teaspoons lemon zest, grated
- 2 red onions, roughly chopped
- 3 tablespoons chives, chopped

Directions:

1. Heat a pan with the oil over medium heat, add the onions, lemon zest, and lemon juice, toss and sauté for 5 minutes.
2. Add the fish and the chives, cook for 5 minutes on each side, divide between plates and serve.

Nutrition: 177calories, 21.8g protein, 5.5g carbohydrates, 8.1g fat, 1.3g fiber, 55g cholesterol, 43mg sodium, 95mg potassium

Sea Bass Pan

Prep time: 10 minutes | Cooking time: 13 minutes |
Servings: 4

Ingredients:

- 4 sea bass fillets, boneless
- 2 tablespoons olive oil
- Black pepper to the taste
- ½ cup white mushrooms, sliced
- 1 red onion, chopped
- 2 tablespoons balsamic vinegar
- 3 tablespoons cilantro, chopped

Directions:

1. Heat a pan with the oil over medium-high heat, add the onion and the mushrooms, stir and cook for 5 minutes.
2. Add the fish and the other ingredients, cook for 4 minutes on each side, divide everything between plates and serve.

Nutrition: 200calories, 24.5g protein, 3g carbohydrates, 9.7g fat, 0.7g fiber, 54g cholesterol, 90mg sodium, 409mg potassium

Paprika Scallops

Prep time: 3 minutes | Cooking time: 4 minutes |
Servings: 4

Ingredients:

- 12 scallops
- 2 tablespoons olive oil
- Black pepper to the taste
- 2 tablespoons chives, chopped
- 1 tablespoon sweet paprika

Directions:

1. Heat a pan with the oil over medium heat, add the scallops, paprika and the other ingredients, and cook for 2 minutes on each side.
2. Divide between plates and serve with a side salad.

Nutrition: 145calories, 15.4g protein, 3.2g carbohydrates, 7.9g fat, 0.7g fiber, 30g cholesterol, 146mg sodium, 335mg potassium

Shrimp with Coconut Asparagus Mix

Prep time: 10 minutes | Cooking time: 14 minutes |
Servings: 4

Ingredients:

- 1 asparagus bunch, halved
- 1 pound shrimp, peeled and deveined
- Black pepper to the taste
- 2 tablespoons olive oil
- 1 red onion, chopped
- 2 garlic cloves, minced
- 1 cup coconut cream

Directions:

1. Heat a pan with the oil over medium heat, add the onion, garlic, and the asparagus, toss and cook for 4 minutes.
2. Add the shrimp and the other ingredients, toss, simmer over medium heat for 10 minutes, divide everything into bowls and serve.

Nutrition: 353calories, 28.3g protein, 9.4g carbohydrates, 23.3g fat, 2.6g fiber, 239g cholesterol, 288mg sodium, 464mg potassium

Cod and Peas Pan

Prep time: 10 minutes | Cooking time: 20 minutes |
Servings: 4

Ingredients:

- 1 yellow onion, chopped
- 2 tablespoons olive oil
- ½ cup low-sodium chicken stock
- 4 cod fillets, boneless, skinless
- Black pepper to the taste
- 1 cup snow peas

Directions:

1. Heat a pot with the oil over medium heat, add the onion, stir and sauté for 4 minutes.
2. Add the fish and cook it for 3 minutes on each side.
3. Add the snow peas and the other ingredients, cook everything for 10 minutes more, divide between plates and serve.

Nutrition: 178calories, 21.7g protein, 5.4g carbohydrates, 8.1g fat, 1.7g fiber, 40g cholesterol, 100mg sodium, 36mg potassium

Desserts

Lime Cream

Prep time: 2 hours and 4 minutes | Cooking time: 0 minutes |
Servings: 4

Ingredients:

- 4 cups non-fat yogurt
- 1 cup coconut cream
- 3 tablespoons stevia
- 2 teaspoons lime zest, grated
- 1 tablespoon mint, chopped

Directions:

1. In a blender, combine the cream with the yogurt and the other ingredients, pulse well, divide into cups and keep in the fridge for 2 hours before serving.

Nutrition: 249calories, 6.4g protein, 22.6g carbohydrates, 14.3g fat, 1.5g fiber, 5g cholesterol, 94mg sodium, 166mg potassium

Almond Berry Pudding

Prep time: 10 minutes | Cooking time: 24 minutes |
Servings: 4

Ingredients:

- 1 cup raspberries
- 2 teaspoons coconut sugar
- 3 eggs, whisked
- 1 tablespoon avocado oil
- ½ cup almond milk
- ½ cup coconut flour
- ¼ cup non-fat yogurt

Directions:

1. In a bowl, combine the raspberries with the sugar and the other ingredients except the cooking spray and whisk well.
2. Grease a pudding pan with the cooking spray, add the raspberries mix, spread, bake in the oven at 400 degrees F for 24 minutes, divide between dessert plates and serve.

Nutrition: 221calories, 8.6g protein, 18g carbohydrates, 13.6g fat, 8.8g fiber, 123g cholesterol, 88mg sodium, 199mg potassium

Almond Cookies

Prep time: 10 minutes | Cooking time: 30 minutes |
Servings: 4

Ingredients:

- 1 cup almonds, crushed
- 2 eggs, whisked
- ½ cup almond milk
- 1 teaspoon vanilla extract
- 2/3 cup coconut sugar
- 2 cups whole flour
- 1 teaspoon baking powder
- Cooking spray

Directions:

1. In a bowl, combine the almonds with the eggs and the other ingredients except the cooking spray and stir well.
2. Pour this into a square pan greased with cooking spray, spread well, bake in the oven for 30 minutes, cool down, cut into bars and serve.

Nutrition: 594calories, 16.7g protein, 91.2g carbohydrates, 22.4g fat, 11g fiber, 82g cholesterol, 128mg sodium, 653mg potassium

Cinnamon Peaches

Prep time: 10 minutes | Cooking time: 30 minutes |
Servings: 4

Ingredients:

- 4 peaches, stones removed and halved
- 1 tablespoon coconut sugar
- 1 teaspoon vanilla extract
- ¼ teaspoon cinnamon powder
- 1 tablespoon avocado oil

Directions:

1. In a baking pan, combine the peaches with the sugar and the other ingredients, bake at 375 degrees F for 30 minutes, cool down and serve.

Nutrition: 78calories, 1.4g protein, 17.3g carbohydrates, 0.8g fat, 2.5g fiber, 0g cholesterol, 0mg sodium, 298mg potassium

Coconut Cake

Prep time: 10 minutes | Cooking time: 25 minutes |
Servings: 8

Ingredients:

- 3 cups almond flour
- 1 cup of coconut sugar
- 1 tablespoon vanilla extract
- ½ cup walnuts, chopped
- 2 teaspoons baking soda
- 2 cups of coconut milk
- ½ cup coconut oil, melted

Directions:

1. In a bowl, combine the almond flour with the sugar and the other ingredients, whisk well, pour into a cake pan, spread, introduce in the oven at 370 degrees F, bake for 25 minutes.
2. Leave the cake to cool down, slice, and serve.

Nutrition: 464calories, 5.5g protein, 30.6g carbohydrates, 37.8g fat, 3g fiber, 0g cholesterol, 328mg sodium, 201mg potassium

Cinnamon Apple Cake

Prep time: 10 minutes | Cooking time: 30 minutes |
Servings: 4

Ingredients:

- 2 cups almond flour
- 1 teaspoon baking soda
- 1 teaspoon baking powder
- ½ teaspoon cinnamon powder
- 2 tablespoons coconut sugar
- 1 cup almond milk
- 2 green apples, cored, peeled and chopped
- Cooking spray

Directions:

1. In a bowl, combine the flour with the baking soda, the apples, and the other ingredients except the cooking spray, and whisk well.
2. Pour this into a cake pan greased with the cooking spray, spread well, introduce in the oven, and bake at 360 degrees F for 30 minutes.
3. Cool the cake down, slice, and serve.

Nutrition: 305calories, 4.7g protein, 29.8g carbohydrates, 21.5g fat, 5.6g fiber, 0g cholesterol, 347mg sodium, 403mg potassium

Coconut Cream

Prep time: 2 hours | Cooking time: 10 minutes |
Servings: 4

Ingredients:

- 1 cup non-fat almond milk
- 1 cup coconut cream
- 2 cups of coconut sugar
- 2 tablespoons cinnamon powder
- 1 teaspoon vanilla extract

Directions:

1. Heat a pan with the almond milk over medium heat, add the rest of the ingredients, whisk, and cook for 10 minutes more.
2. Divide the mix into bowls, cool down, and keep in the fridge for 2 hours before serving.

Nutrition: 602calories, 1.6g protein, 125.5g carbohydrates, 14.9g fat, 1.3g fiber, 0g cholesterol, 308mg sodium, 159mg potassium

Strawberries and Yogurt Bowls

Prep time: 10 minutes | Cooking time: 0 minutes |
Servings: 4

Ingredients:

- 1 teaspoon vanilla extract
- 2 cups strawberries, chopped
- 1 teaspoon coconut sugar
- 8 ounces nonfat yogurt

Directions:

1. In a bowl, combine the strawberries with the vanilla and the other ingredients, toss, and serve cold.

Nutrition: 67calories, 2.2g protein, 13g carbohydrates, 0.2g fat, 1.4g fiber, 2g cholesterol, 29mg sodium, 112mg potassium

Pecan Cookies

Prep time: 10 minutes | Cooking time: 25 minutes |
Servings: 8

Ingredients:

- 1 cup pecans, chopped
- 3 tablespoons coconut sugar
- 2 tablespoons cocoa powder
- 3 eggs, whisked
- ¼ cup coconut oil, melted
- ½ teaspoon baking powder
- 2 teaspoons vanilla extract
- Cooking spray

Directions:

1. In your food processor, combine the pecans with the coconut sugar and the other ingredients except the cooking spray and pulse well.
2. Grease a square pan with cooking spray, add the brownies mix, spread, introduce in the oven, bake at 350 degrees F for 25 minutes, leave aside to cool down, slice, and serve.

Nutrition: 166calories, 3.3g protein, 6.9g carbohydrates, 14.9g fat, 1.4g fiber, 61g cholesterol, 24mg sodium, 125mg potassium

Strawberries and Coconut Cake

Prep time: 10 minutes | Cooking time: 25 minutes |
Servings: 6

Ingredients:

- 2 cups whole wheat flour
- 1 cup strawberries, chopped
- ½ teaspoon baking soda
- ½ cup of coconut sugar
- ¾ cup of coconut milk
- ¼ cup coconut oil, melted
- 2 eggs, whisked
- 1 teaspoon vanilla extract
- Cooking spray

Directions:

1. In a bowl, combine the flour with the strawberries and the other ingredients except the cooking spray and whisk well.
2. Grease a cake pan with cooking spray, pour the cake mix, spread, bake in the oven at 350 degrees F for 25 minutes, cool down, slice, and serve.

Nutrition: 390calories, 7g protein, 51.5g carbohydrates, 18.2g fat, 2.3g fiber, 55g cholesterol, 130mg sodium, 181mg potassium

Almond Cocoa Pudding

Prep time: 10 minutes | Cooking time: 10 minutes |
Servings: 4

Ingredients:

- 2 tablespoons coconut sugar
- 3 tablespoons coconut flour
- 2 tablespoons cocoa powder
- 2 cups almond milk
- 2 eggs, whisked
- ½ teaspoon vanilla extract

Directions:

1. Put the milk in a pan, add the cocoa and the other ingredients, whisk, simmer over medium heat for 10 minutes, pour into small cups, and serve cold.

Nutrition: 388calories, 7.5g protein, 21.9g carbohydrates, 32.7g fat, 7.2g fiber, 82g cholesterol, 88mg sodium, 414mg potassium

Walnuts Cream

Prep time: 10 minutes | Cooking time: 0 minutes |
Servings: 6

Ingredients:

- 3 cups non-fat milk
- 1 teaspoon nutmeg, ground
- 2 teaspoons vanilla extract
- 4 teaspoons coconut sugar
- 1 cup walnuts, chopped

Directions:

1. In a bowl, combine milk with the nutmeg and the other ingredients, whisk well, divide into small cups and serve cold.

Nutrition: 190calories, 9g protein, 11.1g carbohydrates, 12.4g fat, 1.5g fiber, 2g cholesterol, 66mg sodium, 302mg potassium

Coconut Avocado Cream

Prep time: 1 hour and 10 minutes | Cooking time: 0 minutes |
Servings: 4

Ingredients:

- 2 cups coconut cream
- 2 avocados, peeled, pitted and mashed
- 2 tablespoons coconut sugar
- 1 teaspoon vanilla extract

Directions:

1. In a blender, combine the cream with the avocados and the other ingredients, pulse well, divide into cups and keep in the fridge for 1 hour before serving.

Nutrition: 512calories, 4.7g protein, 22.9g carbohydrates, 48.2g fat, 9.4g fiber, 0g cholesterol, 41mg sodium, 805g potassium

Raspberries Cream Cheese Mix

Prep time: 10 minutes | Cooking time: 25 minutes |
Servings: 4

Ingredients:

- 2 tablespoons almond flour
- 1 cup coconut cream
- 3 cups raspberries
- 1 cup of coconut sugar
- 8 ounces low-fat cream cheese

Directions:

1. In a bowl, the flour with the cream and the other ingredients, whisk, transfer to a round pan, cook at 360 degrees F for 25 minutes, divide into bowls and serve.

Nutrition: 644calories, 9.8g protein, 66.8g carbohydrates, 41.7g fat, 8.8g fiber, 62g cholesterol, 183mg sodium, 365g potassium

Watermelon and Apples Salad

Prep time: 4 minutes | Cooking time: 0 minutes |
Servings: 4

Ingredients:

- 1 cup watermelon, peeled and cubed
- 2 apples, cored and cubed
- 1 tablespoon coconut cream
- 2 bananas, cut into chunks

Directions:

1. In a bowl, combine the watermelon with the apples and the other ingredients, toss and serve.

Nutrition: 131calories, 1.3g protein, 31.9g carbohydrates, 1.3g fat, 4.5g fiber, 0g cholesterol, 3mg sodium, 383g potassium

Lime Pears Mix

Prep time: 10 minutes | Cooking time: 10 minutes |
Servings: 4

Ingredients:

- 2 teaspoons lime juice
- ½ cup coconut cream
- ½ cup coconut, shredded
- 4 pears, cored and cubed
- 4 tablespoons coconut sugar

Directions:

1. In a pan, combine the pears with the lime juice and the other ingredients, stir, bring to a simmer over medium heat and cook for 10 minutes.
2. Divide into bowls and serve cold.

Nutrition: 281calories, 1.8g protein, 50g carbohydrates, 10.8g fat, 8g fiber, 0g cholesterol, 42mg sodium, 357g potassium

Orange Compote

Prep time: 10 minutes | Cooking time: 15 minutes | Servings: 4

Ingredients:

- 5 tablespoons coconut sugar
- 4 apples, cored and cubed
- 2 cups orange juice

Directions:

1. In a pot, combine apples with the sugar and the orange juice, toss, bring to a boil over medium heat, cook for 15 minutes, divide into bowls and serve cold.

Nutrition: 242calories, 1.5g protein, 62.5g carbohydrates, 0.7g fat, 5.7g fiber, 0g cholesterol, 44mg sodium, 487g potassium

Apricots Compote

Prep time: 10 minutes | Cooking time: 15 minutes | Servings: 4

Ingredients:

- 2 cups apricots, halved
- 2 tablespoons coconut sugar
- 2 cups of water
- 2 tablespoons lemon juice

Directions:

1. In a pot, combine the apricots with the water and the other ingredients, toss, cook over medium heat for 15 minutes, divide into bowls and serve.

Nutrition: 63calories, 1.1g protein, 14.7g carbohydrates, 0.6g fat, 1.5g fiber, 0g cholesterol, 6mg sodium, 211g potassium

Vanilla Cantaloupe Bowls

Prep time: 10 minutes | Cooking time: 10 minutes | Servings: 4

Ingredients:

- 2 cups cantaloupe, peeled and roughly cubed
- 2 teaspoons vanilla extract
- 4 tablespoons coconut sugar
- 2 teaspoons lemon juice

Directions:

1. In a small pan, combine the cantaloupe with the sugar and the other ingredients, toss, heat up over medium heat, cook for about 10 minutes, divide into bowls and serve cold.

Nutrition: 89calories, 0.7g protein, 21.7g carbohydrates, 0.2g fat, 0.7g fiber, 0g cholesterol, 46mg sodium, 215g potassium

Blackberries Salad

Prep time: 10 minutes | Cooking time: 0 minutes | Servings: 4

Ingredients:

- 1 cup cashews
- 1 teaspoon vanilla extract
- 2 cups blackberries
- ¾ cup coconut cream
- 1 tablespoon coconut sugar

Directions:

1. In a bowl, combine the cashews with the berries and the other ingredients, toss, divide into small bowls and serve.

Nutrition: 348calories, 7.3g protein, 24.5g carbohydrates, 27g fat, 5.8g fiber, 0g cholesterol, 21mg sodium, 430g potassium

Orange Bowls

Prep time: 4 minutes | Cooking time: 8 minutes | Servings: 4

Ingredients:

- 4 oranges, peeled and cut into segments
- Juice of 1 lime
- 2 tangerines, peeled and cut into segments
- 2 tablespoons coconut sugar
- 1 cup of water

Directions:

1. In a pan, combine the oranges with the tangerines and the other ingredients, bring to a simmer and cook over medium heat for 8 minutes.
2. Divide into bowls and serve cold.

Nutrition: 158calories, 2.6g protein, 37.6g carbohydrates, 0.4g fat, 5.5g fiber, 0g cholesterol, 23mg sodium, 409g potassium

Coconut Pumpkin Cream

Prep time: 2 hours | Cooking time: 0 minutes | Servings: 4

Ingredients:

- 2 cups coconut cream
- 3 tablespoons coconut sugar
- 1 cup pumpkin puree

Directions:

1. In a bowl, combine the cream with the pumpkin puree and the other ingredients, whisk well, divide into small bowls and keep in the fridge for 2 hours before serving.

Nutrition: 331calories, 3.4g protein, 20.6g carbohydrates, 28.8g fat, 4.4g fiber, 0g cholesterol, 21mg sodium, 442g potassium

Rhubarb and Figs Stew

Prep time: 6 minutes | Cooking time: 14 minutes | Servings: 4

Ingredients:

- 2 tablespoons coconut oil, melted
- 12 figs, halved
- 1 cup rhubarb, roughly chopped
- ¼ cup of coconut sugar
- 1 cup of water

Directions:

1. Heat up a pan with the oil over medium heat, add the figs and the rest of the ingredients, toss, cook for 14 minutes, divide into small cups and serve cold.

Nutrition: 252calories, 2.2g protein, 49.8g carbohydrates, 7.4g fat, 6.1g fiber, 0g cholesterol, 9mg sodium, 476g potassium

Nectarines Cocoa Squares

Prep time: 10 minutes | Cooking time: 20 minutes |
Servings: 4

Ingredients:

- 3 nectarines, pitted and chopped
- 1 tablespoon coconut sugar
- ½ teaspoon baking soda
- 1 cup almond flour
- 4 tablespoons coconut oil, melted
- 2 tablespoons cocoa powder

Directions:

1. In a blender, combine the nectarines with the sugar and the rest of the ingredients, pulse well, pour into a lined square pan, spread, bake in the oven at 375 degrees F for 20 minutes, leave the mix aside to cool down a bit, cut into squares and serve.

Nutrition: 221calories, 3.1g protein, 17.2g carbohydrates, 17.8g fat, 3.4g fiber, 0g cholesterol, 162mg sodium, 282g potassium

Grapes and Lime Compote

Prep time: 10 minutes | Cooking time: 20 minutes |
Servings: 4

Ingredients:

- 1 cup of green grapes
- Juice of ½ lime
- 2 tablespoons coconut sugar
- 1 and ½ cups of water
- 2 teaspoons cardamom powder

Directions:

1. Heat a pan with the water medium heat, add the grapes and the other ingredients, bring to a simmer, cook for 20 minutes, divide into bowls and serve.

Nutrition: 46calories, 0.5g protein, 12.4g carbohydrates, 0.2g fat, 1g fiber, 0g cholesterol, 3mg sodium, 75g potassium

Mandarin Cream

Prep time: 10 minutes | Cooking time: 20 minutes |
Servings: 4

Ingredients:

- 1 mandarin, peeled and chopped
- ½ pound plums, pitted and chopped
- 1 cup coconut cream
- Juice of 2 mandarins
- 2 tablespoons coconut sugar

Directions:

1. In a blender, combine the mandarin with the plums and the other ingredients, pulse well, divide into small ramekins, introduce in the oven, bake at 350 degrees F for 20 minutes, and serve cold.

Nutrition: 196calories, 1.7g protein, 18.1g carbohydrates, 14.5g fat, 1.6g fiber, 0g cholesterol, 26mg sodium, 281g potassium

Cherry Cream

Prep time: 10 minutes | Cooking time: 0 minutes |
Servings: 6

Ingredients:

- 1 pound cherries, pitted
- 1 cup strawberries, chopped
- ¼ cup of coconut sugar
- 2 cups coconut cream

Directions:

1. In a blender, combine the cherries with the other ingredients, pulse well, divide into bowls and serve cold.

Nutrition: 309calories, 2.3g protein, 35.4g carbohydrates, 19.2g fat, 2.7g fiber, 0g cholesterol, 26mg sodium, 327g potassium

Walnuts Pudding

Prep time: 5 minutes | Cooking time: 40 minutes |
Servings: 4

Ingredients:

- 1 cup basmati rice
- 3 cups almond milk
- 3 tablespoons coconut sugar
- ½ teaspoon cardamom powder
- ¼ cup walnuts, chopped

Directions:

1. In a pan, combine the rice with the milk and the other ingredients, stir, cook for 40 minutes over medium heat, divide into bowls and serve cold.

Nutrition: 666calories, 9.3g protein, 56.9g carbohydrates, 47.9g fat, 5.2g fiber, 0g cholesterol, 30mg sodium, 570g potassium

Fruity Bread

Prep time: 10 minutes | Cooking time: 30 minutes |
Servings: 4

Ingredients:

- 2 cups pears, cored and cubed
- 1 cup of coconut sugar
- 2 eggs, whisked
- 2 cups almond flour
- 1 tablespoon baking powder
- 1 tablespoon coconut oil, melted

Directions:

1. In a bowl, mix the pears with the sugar and the other ingredients, whisk, pour into a loaf pan, introduce in the oven, and bake at 350 degrees F for 30 minutes.
2. Slice and serve cold.

Nutrition: 371calories, 6.1g protein, 65.2g carbohydrates, 12.7g fat, 4.1g fiber, 82g cholesterol, 40mg sodium, 502g potassium

Vanilla Rice Pudding

Prep time: 10 minutes | Cooking time: 25 minutes |
Servings: 4

Ingredients:

- 1 tablespoon coconut oil, melted
- 1 cup white rice
- 3 cups almond milk
- ½ cup cherries, pitted and halved
- 3 tablespoons coconut sugar
- 1 teaspoon cinnamon powder
- 1 teaspoon vanilla extract

Directions:

1. In a pan, combine the oil with the rice and the other ingredients, stir, bring to a simmer, cook for 25 minutes over medium heat, divide into bowls and serve cold.

Nutrition: 291calories, 4.1g protein, 54.7g carbohydrates, 5.6g fat, 0.7g fiber, 0g cholesterol, 109mg sodium, 64g potassium

Lime Watermelon Compote

Prep time: 5 minutes | Cooking time: 8 minutes |
Servings: 4

Ingredients:

- Juice of 1 lime
- 1 teaspoon lime zest, grated
- 1 and ½ cup of coconut sugar
- 4 cups watermelon, peeled and cut into large chunks
- 1 and ½ cups of water

Directions:

1. In a pan, combine the watermelon with the lime zest, and the other ingredients, toss, bring to a simmer over medium heat, cook for 8 minutes, divide into bowls and serve cold.

Nutrition: 386calories, 1g protein, 103.3g carbohydrates, 0.2g fat, 1.1g fiber, 0.2g cholesterol, 200mg sodium, 187g potassium

Ginger Chia Pudding

Prep time: 1 hour | Cooking time: 0 minutes |
Servings: 4

Ingredients:

- 2 cups almond milk
- ½ cup coconut cream
- 2 tablespoons coconut sugar
- 1 tablespoon ginger, grated
- ¼ cup chia seeds

Directions:

1. In a bowl, combine the milk with the cream and the other ingredients, whisk well, divide into small cups and keep them in the fridge for 1 hour before serving.

Nutrition: 188calories, 3.2g protein, 16.1g carbohydrates, 13.4g fat, 3.8g fiber, 1g cholesterol, 11mg sodium, 126g potassium

Lemon Cashew Cream

Prep time: 2 hours | Cooking time: 0 minutes |
Servings: 4

Ingredients:

- 1 cup cashews, chopped
- 2 tablespoons coconut oil, melted
- 1 cup coconut cream
- tablespoons lemon juice
- 1 tablespoon coconut sugar

Directions:

1. In a blender, combine the cashews with the coconut oil and the other ingredients, pulse well, divide into small cups and keep in the fridge for 2 hours before serving.

Nutrition: 404calories, 6.6g protein, 17.5g carbohydrates, 37g fat, 2.4g fiber, 0g cholesterol, 14mg sodium, 351g potassium

Coconut Hemp and Almond Cookies

Prep time: 30 minutes | Cooking time: 0 minutes |
Servings: 6

Ingredients:

- 1 cup almonds, soaked overnight and drained
- 2 tablespoons cocoa powder
- 1 tablespoon coconut sugar
- ½ cup hemp seeds
- ¼ cup coconut, shredded
- ½ cup of water

Directions:

1. In your food processor, combine the almonds with the cocoa powder and the other ingredients, pulse well, press this on a lined baking sheet, keep in the fridge for 30 minutes, slice, and serve.

Nutrition: 185calories, 8g protein, 7.7g carbohydrates, 15g fat, 3.2g fiber, 0g cholesterol, 2mg sodium, 290g potassium

Coconut Pomegranate Bowls

Prep time: 2 hours | Cooking time: 0 minutes |
Servings: 4

Ingredients:

- ½ cup coconut cream
- 1 teaspoon vanilla extract
- 1 cup almonds, chopped
- 1 cup pomegranate seeds
- 1 tablespoon coconut sugar

Directions:

1. In a bowl, combine the almonds with the cream and the other ingredients, toss, divide into small bowls and serve.

Nutrition: 246calories, 6g protein, 15.9g carbohydrates, 19g fat, 3.9g fiber, 0g cholesterol, 5mg sodium, 255g potassium

Vanilla Chia Cream

Prep time: 10 minutes | Cooking time: 0 minutes |
Servings: 6

Ingredients:

- 2 cups coconut cream
- 2/3 cup coconut sugar
- 1 cup almond milk
- 3 tablespoons chia seeds, ground
- ½ teaspoon vanilla extract

Directions:

1. In a bowl, combine the cream with the chia seeds and the other ingredients, whisk well, divide into small bowls, leave aside for 10 minutes and serve.

Nutrition: 510calories, 5.3g protein, 54.7g carbohydrates, 33.6g fat, 7.5g fiber, 0g cholesterol, 143mg sodium, 374g potassium

Ginger Berries Bowls

Prep time: 5 minutes | Cooking time: 0 minutes |
Servings: 4

Ingredients:

- 1 cup blackberries
- 1 cup blueberries
- 1 tablespoon lime juice
- 1 cup strawberries, halved
- 1 tablespoon coconut sugar
- ½ teaspoon ginger powder
- ½ teaspoon vanilla extract

Directions:

1. In a bowl, combine the blackberries with the blueberries and the other ingredients, toss and serve.

Nutrition: 62calories, 1.1g protein, 15g carbohydrates, 0.4g fat, 3.6g fiber, 0g cholesterol, 2mg sodium, 148g potassium

Grapefruit and Coconut Cream

Prep time: 10 minutes | Cooking time: 10 minutes |
Servings: 4

Ingredients:

- 1 cup of coconut milk
- 2 tablespoons coconut sugar
- ½ cup coconut cream
- 1 teaspoon vanilla extract
- 4 grapefruits, peeled and roughly chopped

Directions:

1. In a pan, combine the milk with the grapefruits and the other ingredients, whisk, bring to a simmer and cook over medium heat for 10 minutes.
2. Blend using an immersion blender, divide into bowls and serve cold.

Nutrition: 204calories, 2.2g protein, 19.8g carbohydrates, 14.4g fat, 2.7g fiber, 0g cholesterol, 9mg sodium, 337g potassium

Rhubarb Cream

Prep time: 10 minutes | Cooking time: 14 minutes |
Servings: 4

Ingredients:

- 1/3 cup low-fat cream cheese
- ½ cup coconut cream
- 2-pound rhubarb, roughly
- chopped
- 3 tablespoons coconut sugar

Directions:

1. In a blender, combine the cream cheese with the cream and the other ingredients and pulse well.
2. Divide into small cups, introduce in the oven, and bake at 350 degrees F for 14 minutes.
3. Serve cold.

Nutrition: 218calories, 4.2g protein, 21.5g carbohydrates, 14.3g fat, 4.7g fiber, 21g cholesterol, 71mg sodium, 755g potassium

Mint Pineapple Mix

Prep time: 10 minutes | Cooking time: 0 minutes |
Servings: 4

Ingredients:

- 3 cups pineapple, peeled and cubed
- 1 teaspoon chia seeds
- 1 cup coconut cream
- 1 teaspoon vanilla extract
- 1 tablespoon mint, chopped

Directions:

1. In a bowl, combine the pineapple with the cream and the other ingredients, toss, divide into smaller bowls and keep in the fridge for 10 minutes before serving.

Nutrition: 215calories, 2.5g protein, 20.8g carbohydrates, 15.2g fat, 4g fiber, 0g cholesterol, 11mg sodium, 311g potassium

Berry Compote

Prep time: 10 minutes | Cooking time: 10 minutes |
Servings: 4

Ingredients:

- 2 tablespoons lemon juice
- 1 cup of water
- 3 tablespoons coconut sugar
- 12 ounces blueberries

Directions:

1. In a pan, combine the blueberries with the sugar and the other ingredients, bring to a gentle simmer and cook over medium heat for 10 minutes.
2. Divide into bowls and serve.

Nutrition: 87calories, 0.7g protein, 21.5g carbohydrates, 0.4g fat, 2.1g fiber, 0g cholesterol, 4mg sodium, 76g potassium

Lime Coconut Pudding

Prep time: 10 minutes | Cooking time: 15 minutes |
Servings: 4

Ingredients:

- 2 cups coconut cream
- Juice of 1 lime
- Zest of 1 lime, grated
- 3 tablespoons coconut oil,
- melted
- 1 egg, whisked
- 1 teaspoon baking powder

Directions:

1. In a bowl, combine the cream with the lime juice and the other ingredients and whisk well.
2. Divide into small ramekins, introduce in the oven, and bake at 360 degrees F for 15 minutes.
3. Serve the pudding cold.

Nutrition: 386calories, 4.4g protein, 9.1g carbohydrates, 39.9g fat, 3.2g fiber, 41g cholesterol, 35mg sodium, 475g potassium

Almond Cream

Prep time: 10 minutes | Cooking time: 0 minutes |
Servings: 4

Ingredients:

- 3 cups coconut cream
- 2 peaches, stones removed and chopped
- 1 teaspoon vanilla extract
- ½ cup almonds, chopped

Directions:

1. In a blender, combine the cream and the other ingredients, pulse well, divide into small bowls and serve cold.

Nutrition: 515calories, 7.3g protein, 19.7g carbohydrates, 49.1g fat, 6.6g fiber, 0g cholesterol, 27mg sodium, 705g potassium

Sweet Plums Mix

Prep time: 10 minutes | Cooking time: 15 minutes |
Servings: 4

Ingredients:

- 1 pound plums, stones removed and halved
- 2 tablespoons coconut sugar
- ½ teaspoon cinnamon powder
- 1 cup of water

Directions:

1. In a pan, combine the plums with the sugar and the other ingredients, bring to a simmer and cook over medium heat for 15 minutes.
2. Divide into bowls and serve cold.

Nutrition: 30calories, 0.1g protein, 8g carbohydrates, 0.1g fat, 0.2g fiber, 0g cholesterol, 2mg sodium, 27g potassium

Chia Apples Mix

Prep time: 10 minutes | Cooking time: 10 minutes |
Servings: 4

Ingredients:

- 2 cups apples, cored and cut into wedges
- 2 tablespoons chia seeds
- 1 teaspoon vanilla extract
- 2 cups naturally unsweetened apple juice

Directions:

1. In a small pot, combine the apples with the chia seeds and the other ingredients, toss, cook over medium heat for 10 minutes, divide into bowls and serve cold.

Nutrition: 155calories, 1.5g protein, 33.5g carbohydrates, 2.4g fat, 5.1g fiber, 0g cholesterol, 15mg sodium, 240g potassium

Rice Pudding

Prep time: 10 minutes | Cooking time: 25 minutes |
Servings: 4

Ingredients:

- 6 cups of water
- 1 cup of coconut sugar
- 2 cups black rice
- 2 pears, cored and cubed
- 2 teaspoons cinnamon powder

Directions:

1. Put the water in a pan, heat it over medium-high heat, add the rice, sugar and the other ingredients, stir, bring to a simmer, reduce heat to medium and cook for 25 minutes.
2. Divide into bowls and serve cold.

Nutrition: 340calories, 2.4g protein, 85.3g carbohydrates, 0.8g fat, 3.9g fiber, 0g cholesterol, 12mg sodium, 191g potassium

Rhubarb Compote

Prep time: 10 minutes | Cooking time: 15 minutes |
Servings: 4

Ingredients:

- 2 cups rhubarb, roughly chopped
- 3 tablespoons coconut sugar
- 1 teaspoon almond extract
- 2 cups of water

Directions:

1. In a pot, combine the rhubarb with the other ingredients, toss, bring to a boil over medium heat, cook for 15 minutes, divide into bowls and serve cold.

Nutrition: 52calories, 0.6g protein, 11.9g carbohydrates, 0.1g fat, 1.1g fiber, 0g cholesterol, 6mg sodium, 178g potassium

Coconut Rhubarb Cream

Prep time: 1 hour | Cooking time: 10 minutes |
Servings: 4

Ingredients:

- 2 cups coconut cream
- 1 cup rhubarb, chopped
- 3 eggs, whisked
- 3 tablespoons coconut sugar
- 1 tablespoon lime juice

Directions:

1. In a small pan, combine the cream with the rhubarb and the other ingredients, whisk well, simmer over medium heat for 10 minutes, blend using an immersion blender, divide into bowls and keep in the fridge for 1 hour before serving.

Nutrition: 363calories, 7.2g protein, 17.3g carbohydrates, 32g fat, 3.2g fiber, 123g cholesterol, 65mg sodium, 448g potassium

Minty Fruit Salad

Prep time: 5 minutes | Cooking time: 0 minutes |
Servings: 4

Ingredients:

- 2 cups blueberries
- 3 tablespoons mint, chopped
- 1 pear, cored and cubed
- 1 apple, cored, cubed
- 1 tablespoon coconut sugar

Directions:

1. In a bowl, combine the blueberries with the mint and the other ingredients, toss, and serve cold.

Nutrition: 104calories, 1g protein, 26.9g carbohydrates, 0.4g fat, 4.5g fiber, 123g cholesterol, 3mg sodium, 175g potassium

Dates Cream

Prep time: 5 minutes | Cooking time: 0 minutes |
Servings: 4

Ingredients:

- 1 cup almond milk
- 1 banana, peeled and sliced
- 1 teaspoon vanilla extract
- ½ cup coconut cream
- dates, chopped

Directions:

1. In a blender, combine the dates with the banana and the other ingredients, pulse well, divide into small cups and serve cold.

Nutrition: 119calories, 1.3g protein, 12.1g carbohydrates, 7.9g fat, 1.6g fiber, 0g cholesterol, 40mg sodium, 200g potassium

Almond Plum Muffins

Prep time: 10 minutes | Cooking time: 25 minutes |
Servings: 12

Ingredients:

- 3 tablespoons coconut oil, melted
- ½ cup almond milk
- 4 eggs, whisked
- 1 teaspoon vanilla extract
- 1 cup almond flour
- 2 teaspoons cinnamon powder
- ½ teaspoon baking powder
- 1 cup plums, pitted and chopped

Directions:

1. In a bowl, combine the coconut oil with the almond milk and the other ingredients and whisk well.
2. Divide into a muffin pan, introduce in the oven at 350 degrees F and bake for 25 minutes.
3. Serve the muffins cold.

Nutrition: 137calories, 2.1g protein, 3.1g carbohydrates, 12.3g fat, 1.3g fiber, 55g cholesterol, 22mg sodium, 76g potassium

Coconut Plums Bowls

Prep time: 10 minutes | Cooking time: 20 minutes |
Servings: 4

Ingredients:

- ½ pound plums, pitted and halved
- 2 tablespoons coconut sugar
- 4 tablespoons raisins
- 1 teaspoon vanilla extract
- 1 cup coconut cream

Directions:

1. In a pan, combine the plums with the sugar and the other ingredients, bring to a simmer and cook over medium heat for 20 minutes.
2. Divide into bowls and serve.

Nutrition: 194calories, 1.7g protein, 17.6g carbohydrates, 14.4g fat, 1.8g fiber, 0g cholesterol, 10mg sodium, 240g potassium

Seed Energy Bars

Prep time: 10 minutes | Cooking time: 20 minutes |
Servings: 6

Ingredients:

- 1 cup coconut flour
- ½ teaspoon baking soda
- 1 tablespoon flax seed
- 3 tablespoons almond milk
- 1 cup sunflower seeds
- 2 tablespoons coconut oil, melted
- 1 teaspoon vanilla extract

Directions:

1. In a bowl, mix the flour with the baking soda and the other ingredients, stir well, spread on a baking sheet, press well, bake in the oven at 350 degrees F for 20 minutes, leave aside to cool down, cut into bars and serve.

Nutrition: 189calories, 4.7g protein, 13g carbohydrates, 13.3g fat, 7.8g fiber, 0g cholesterol, 146mg sodium, 80g potassium

Nutmeg Baked Bananas

Prep time: 4 minutes | Cooking time: 15 minutes |
Servings: 4

Ingredients:

- 4 bananas, peeled and halved
- 1 teaspoon nutmeg, ground
- 1 teaspoon cinnamon powder
- Juice of 1 lime
- 4 tablespoons coconut sugar

Directions:

1. Arrange the bananas in a baking pan, add the nutmeg and the other ingredients, bake at 350 degrees F for 15 minutes.
2. Divide the baked bananas between plates and serve.

Nutrition: 118calories, 1.4g protein, 29.6g carbohydrates, 0.6g fat, 3.2g fiber, 0g cholesterol, 2mg sodium, 450g potassium

Cocoa Avocado Smoothie

Prep time: 5 minutes | Cooking time: 0 minutes |
Servings: 2

Ingredients:

- 2 teaspoons cocoa powder
- 1 avocado, pitted, peeled and mashed
- 1 cup almond milk
- 1 cup coconut cream

Directions:

1. In your blender, combine the almond milk with the cream and the other ingredients, pulse well, divide into cups, and serve cold.

Nutrition: 515calories, 5.5g protein, 20.3g carbohydrates, 49.7g fat, 9.9g fiber, 0g cholesterol, 94mg sodium, 848g potassium

Banana and Avocado Bars

Prep time: 30 minutes | Cooking time: 0 minutes |
Servings: 4

Ingredients:

- 1 cup coconut oil, melted
- 2 bananas, peeled and chopped
- 1 avocado, peeled, pitted and mashed
- ½ cup of coconut sugar
- ¼ cup lime juice
- 1 teaspoon lemon zest, grated
- Cooking spray

Directions:

1. In your food processor, mix the bananas with the oil and the other ingredients except the cooking spray and pulse well.
2. Grease a pan with the cooking spray, pour and spread the banana mix, spread, keep in the fridge for 30 minutes, cut into bars, and serve.

Nutrition: 734calories, 1.8g protein, 46g carbohydrates, 64.6g fat, 5.2g fiber, 0g cholesterol, 13mg sodium, 503g potassium

Cinnamon Bars

Prep time: 10 minutes | Cooking time: 25 minutes |
Servings: 6

Ingredients:

- 1 teaspoon cinnamon powder
- 2 cups almond flour
- 1 teaspoon baking powder
- ½ teaspoon nutmeg, ground
- 1 cup coconut oil, melted
- 1 cup of coconut sugar
- 1 egg, whisked
- 1 cup raisins

Directions:

1. In a bowl, combine the flour with the cinnamon and the other ingredients, stir well, spread on a lined baking sheet, introduce in the oven, bake at 380 degrees F for 25 minutes, cut into bars and serve cold.

Nutrition: 579calories, 3.7g protein, 53.7g carbohydrates, 41.9g fat, 2g fiber, 27g cholesterol, 17mg sodium, 275g potassium

Vanilla Green Tea Bars

Prep time: 10 minutes | Cooking time: 30 minutes |
Servings: 8

Ingredients:

- 2 tablespoons green tea powder
- 2 cups coconut milk, heated
- ½ cup coconut oil, melted
- 2 cups of coconut sugar
- 4 eggs, whisked
- 2 teaspoons vanilla extract
- 3 cups almond flour
- 1 teaspoon baking soda
- 2 teaspoons baking powder

Directions:

1. In a bowl, combine the coconut milk with the green tea powder and the rest of the ingredients, stir well, pour into a square pan, spread, introduce in the oven, bake at 350 degrees F for 30 minutes, cool down, cut into bars and serve.

Nutrition: 544calories, 6.6g protein, 54g carbohydrates, 35.4g fat, 2.7g fiber, 82g cholesterol, 203mg sodium, 322g potassium

Coconut Walnut Cream

Prep time: 2 hours | Cooking time: 0 minutes |
Servings: 4

Ingredients:

- 2 cups almond milk
- ½ cup coconut cream
- ½ cup walnuts, chopped
- 3 tablespoons coconut sugar
- 1 teaspoon vanilla extract

Directions:

1. In a bowl, combine the almond milk with the cream and the other ingredients, whisk well, divide into cups and keep in the fridge for 2 hours before serving.

Nutrition: 409calories, 6.5g protein, 17.3g carbohydrates, 37.8g fat, 3.7g fiber, 0g cholesterol, 18mg sodium, 399g potassium

Almond Lemon Cake

Prep time: 10 minutes | Cooking time: 35 minutes |
Servings: 6

Ingredients:

- 2 cups whole wheat flour
- 1 teaspoon baking powder
- 2 tablespoons coconut oil, melted
- 1 egg, whisked
- 3 tablespoons coconut sugar
- 1 cup almond milk
- Zest of 1 lemon, grated
- Juice of 1 lemon

Directions:

1. In a bowl, combine the flour with the oil and the other ingredients, whisk well, transfer this to a cake pan and bake at 360 degrees F for 35 minutes.
2. Slice and serve cold.

Nutrition: 324calories, 6.2g protein, 42.3g carbohydrates, 15.3g fat, 2.1g fiber, 27g cholesterol, 35mg sodium, 252g potassium

Recipe Index

A

almond

Almond Cookies, 6

Maple Almonds Bowl, 13

Lemon Spinach, 27

Almonds and Mango Salad, 31

Balsamic Beets, 34

Rice and Cranberries Mix, 35

Dill Dip, 38

Almonds Bowls, 42

Chicken and Almond Mushrooms, 50

Parsley Salmon Mix, 71

Almond Cookies, 74

Coconut Hemp and Almond Cookies, 78

Coconut Pomegranate Bowls, 78

Almond Cream, 79

almond butter

Almond Cookies, 6

almond milk

Chia Oats, 6

Cinnamon Oats, 7

Berries Pancakes, 7

Banana Muffins, 7

Almond Potato Waffles, 7

Coconut Quinoa, 8

Rice Bowls, 9

Strawberry Oats, 10

Almond Peach Mix, 10

Dates Ric, 10

Cherries Oatmeal, 10

Coconut Cocoa Oats, 11

Pomegranate Oats, 11

Lemon Chia Bowls, 12

Zucchini Almond Oatmeal, 13

Apple Oats, 14

Chia Bowls, 15

Almond Bars, 44

Almond Berry Pudding, 74

Cinnamon Apple Cake, 74

Almond Cookies, 74

Coconut Cream, 74

Almond Cocoa Pudding, 75

Walnuts Pudding, 77

Vanilla Rice Pudding, 77

Ginger Chia Pudding, 78

Vanilla Chia Cream, 78

Seed Energy Bars, 80

Dates Cream, 80

Almond Plum Muffins, 80

Cocoa Avocado Smoothie, 80

Coconut Walnut Cream, 81

Almond Lemon Cake, 81

apples

Minty Fruit Salad, 80

Cinnamon Oats, 7

Apples Bowls, 8

Apples Bowls, 10

Apple Oats, 14

Caraway Cabbage Mix, 30

Pumpkin Seeds Bowls, 41

Seeds Bowls, 43

Herbed Chicken Mix, 48

Chili Pork and Apples, 58

Cinnamon Apple Cake, 74

Watermelon and Apples Salad, 75

Orange Compote, 76

Chia Apples Mix, 79

apricots

Almond Scones, 6

Apricots Compote, 76

artichoke

Parsley Artichokes Mix, 34

Chili Chicken, 50

Eggs and Artichokes, 9

Dill Artichokes, 34

Creamy Turkey Mix, 45

Chicken and Artichokes, 51

Pork and Lemon Artichokes Mix, 59

Shrimp with Artichokes and Tomatoes, 69

arugula

Shrimp and Arugula Salad, 19

asparagus

Asparagus Salad, 17

Nutmeg Asparagus, 32

Lemon Asparagus, 33

Asparagus Snack Bowls, 39

Chicken and Tomatoes Mix, 46

Turkey and Asparagus, 53

Cod and Coconut Asparagus, 66

Shrimp with Coconut Asparagus Mix, 73

avocado

Mint Chickpeas Salad, 13

Shrimp and Arugula Salad, 19

Beef and Beans Salad, 22

Avocado Salad, 26

Zucchini Salsa, 35

Avocado Mix, 35

Cucumber Salad, 37

Peach and Olives Salsa, 38

Lemon Chicken Mix, 46

Cocoa Avocado Smoothie, 80

Banana and Avocado Bars, 81

Potato and Spinach Salad, 19

Lemon Spinach, 27

Grapes and Cucumber Salad, 27

Avocado, Tomato and Olives Salad, 34

Avocado Fries, 39

Avocado Dip, 41

Warm Pork Salad, 58

Trout and Avocado Salad, 66

Coconut Avocado Cream, 75

avocado oil

Carrots Salad, 28

Chili Corn Sauté, 31

Walnut Turnips Mix, 32

Paprika Rice Mix, 32

Coconut Olives Tapenade, 37

Figs Bowls, 39

Chili Walnuts, 40

Corn Spread, 41

Salmon and Spinach Bowls, 42

Pineapple Salsa, 44

Cumin Beets Chips, 44

Balsamic Chicken, 45

Turkey and Peach, 45

Chicken and Leeks, 47

Mustard Chicken, 48

Chicken and Greens, 48

Chicken Breast and Tomatoes, 50

Paprika Chicken, 51

Garlic Chicken Wings, 52

Pork and Zucchinis, 56

Pork with Mango and Tomatoes, 59

Lamb and Red Onions Mix, 60

Pork Meatballs and Sauce, 62

Lamb with Okra, 63

Coconut Sea Bass Mix, 70

Cinnamon Peaches, 74

B

bacon

Chives Risotto, 8

Spring Omelet, 14

banana

Dates Cream, 80

Almond Cookies, 6

Banana Muffins, 7

Watermelon and Apples Salad, 75

Nutmeg Baked Bananas, 80

Banana and Avocado Bars, 81

barley

Turkey and Barley, 52

Chives Pork and Barley, 61

beans
Beans Bake, 9
Green Beans Hash, 13
Corn and Beans Tortillas, 15
Raspberry Shrimp and Tomato Salad, 16
Cabbage Stew, 21
Beef and Beans Salad, 22
Pork Stew, 22
Beef Soup, 23
Parsley Green Beans Soup, 24
Green Beans Salad, 27
Balsamic Black Beans Mix, 29
Paprika Green Beans, 30
Green Beans Mix, 31
Thyme Black Beans Mix, 35
Broccoli Rice, 36
Oregano Beans Mix, 36
Beans and Tomato Salsa, 39
Lime Beans Salsa, 39
Coconut Beans Bars, 41
Beans Dip, 42
Chicken with Green Beans and Sauce, 46
Turkey and Olives, 54
Pork with Green Beans, 57
Pork and Green Beans, 63
Pork with Beans, 63
Hot Cod, 67
Salmon with Scallions and Green Beans, 67
Shrimp and Black Beans, 69

beef
Pork Soup, 16
Tomato Beef Stew, 17
Garlic Turkey Stew, 18
Ground Beef Skillet, 19
Coconut Broccoli Cream, 20
Beef and Cabbage Stew, 22
Beef and Beans Salad, 22
Beef and Scallions Mix, 23
Beef Soup, 23
Beef Skillet, 24
Thyme Beef and Tomatoes, 24
Turkey and Onion Mix, 45
Beet Salad, 28
Chives Dip, 37
Parsley Beets, 28
Balsamic Beets, 34
Roasted Sweet Potato Mix, 36
Coconut Beets, 36
Rosemary Beet Bites, 41
Cumin Beets Chips, 44
Turkey with Radishes, 52

Chives Chicken and Beets, 54
Coconut Pork with Beets, 61

bell pepper
Mozzarella Scramble, 8
Cheddar Hash Browns, 8
Beans Bake, 9
Cauliflower Salad, 10
Peppers Salad, 12
Chicken Hash, 13
Corn and Beans Tortillas, 15
Asparagus Salad, 17
Balsamic Chicken and Cauliflower, 18
Ground Beef Skillet, 19
Cilantro Peppers and Cauliflower Mix, 21
Chipotle Lentils, 25
Peppers Salad, 29
Bell Peppers Salsa, 41
Turkey and Chickpeas, 49
Chicken with Peppers, 53
Pork and Tomatoes, 57
Lamb with Veggies Mix, 61
Pork and Green Beans, 63
Salmon with Zucchini and Eggplant, 67
Spring Omelet, 14
Squash and Peppers Stew, 22
Turkey Tortillas, 22
Cheddar Cauliflower Bowls, 23
Mint Peppers, 35
Avocado Mix, 35
Coconut Peppers Dip, 40

blackberries
Coconut Berries, 10
Berries Rice, 11
Blackberries Salad, 76
Ginger Berries Bowls, 78

blueberries
Berries Pancakes, 7
Banana Muffins, 7
Coconut Berries, 10
Apples Bowls, 10
Ginger Berries Bowls, 78
Berry Compote, 79
Minty Fruit Salad, 80

bok choy
Lamb with Carrot and Bok Choy, 61

broccoli
Coconut Broccoli Cream, 20
Minty Shrimp and Olives Salad, 20
Chili Broccoli, 31
Broccoli Rice, 36
Oregano Broccoli Bars, 44

Basil Turkey and Broccoli, 46
Turkey and Broccoli, 51
Coconut Cod and Broccoli, 72

brussel sprouts
Paprika Brussels Sprouts, 29
Hot Brussels Sprouts, 31
Creamy Brussels Sprouts, 32
Brussels Sprouts Bowls, 40
Pork with Spring Onions and Sprouts, 63

C

cabbage
Cabbage and Leek Soup, 20
Cabbage Stew, 21
Beef and Cabbage Stew, 22
Tomato and Cabbage Mix, 28
Cabbage Salad, 28
Caraway Cabbage Mix, 30
Balsamic Cabbage, 33
Chives Cabbage Sauté, 35
Shrimp Salsa, 39
Chicken and Cabbage, 52
Thyme Lamb and Cabbage Stew, 61

cabbage (Savoy)
Turkey and Cabbage Mix, 47

capers
Almonds and Mango Salad, 31
Paprika Rice Mix, 32
Parsley Artichokes Mix, 34
Cucumber Salad, 37
Lime Beans Salsa, 39
Chives Pork and Barley, 61
Pork with Capers, 64
Dill Salmon, 66
Shrimp and Spinach Salad, 72

carrot
Cheddar Hash Browns, 8
Carrot and Peas Salad, 14
Zucchini Fritters, 16
Chicken Stew, 17
Chicken and Veggies, 51
Chicken with Tomatoes and Grapes, 54
Chives Chicken and Beets, 54
Cilantro Pork, 55
Lamb with Carrot and Bok Choy, 61
Eggs Salad, 12
Carrots Hash, 14
Corn and Beans Tortillas, 15
Pork Soup, 16
Turkey and Carrots Soup, 17
Trout Soup, 18
Tomato Soup, 18

Rosemary Carrot Stew, 21
Carrot Soup, 23
Shrimp Salad, 26
Carrots Salad, 28
Cabbage Salad, 28
Peppers Salad, 29
Paprika Carrots, 32
Lime Carrots, 33
Allspice Carrots, 34
Turmeric Carrot Chips, 38
Coconut Carrot Spread, 43
Chicken and Cabbage, 52
Pork and Carrots, 55
Salmon and Veggies Mix, 69

cashew
Cashew Parfait, 7
Creamy Brussels Sprouts, 32
Buttery Cashew Turkey, 50
Blackberries Salad, 76
Lemon Cashew Cream, 78

cauliflower
Cauliflower Salad, 10
Balsamic Chicken and Cauliflower, 18
Dill Cauliflower Soup, 20
Cilantro Peppers and Cauliflower Mix, 21
Cheddar Cauliflower Bowls, 23
Creamy Cauliflower Mash, 29
Rice and Cranberries Mix, 35
Cauliflower and Tomato Salsa, 38
Almond Bars, 44

celery
Dill Cauliflower Soup, 20
Carrot Soup, 23
Chili Chicken Mix, 48

cheese
Cheese Frittata, 9
Chives Dip, 37
Mint Cheesy Dip, 38
Cilantro Lemon Dip, 39
Cream Cheese and Leeks Dip, 41
Salmon Spread, 65
Raspberries Cream Cheese Mix, 75
Rhubarb Cream, 78

cheese (Cheddar)
Cheddar Hash Browns, 8
Eggs and Artichokes, 9
Mushroom and Rice Mix, 9
Coconut Hash, 12
Tomato Eggs, 12
Carrots Hash, 14
Zucchini Fritters, 16

Cheddar Cauliflower Bowls, 23
Almond Bars, 44
Turkey Sandwich, 52
Cheesy Turkey, 54

cheese (mozzarella)
Mozzarella Scramble, 8
Beans Bake, 9
Cod Tacos, 16
Turkey Tortillas, 22
Chicken and Tomato Mix, 25
Hot Brussels Sprouts, 31
Cheesy Spinach Dip, 37
Coconut Dip, 37
Salmon Muffins, 43
Pearl Onions Snack, 44
Oregano Broccoli Bars, 44
Creamy Turkey Mix, 45

cheese (Parmesan)
Chives Risotto, 8
Beef Skillet, 24
Garlic Tomatoes Mix, 29
Garlic Potato Pan, 31
Parmesan Eggplant Mix, 33
Parmesan Endives, 33
Coconut Turkey, 53
Parmesan Pork and Sauce, 59
Oregano Lamb Chops, 62
Cod and Green Onions Mix, 72

cherries
Cherries Bowls, 8
Cherries Oatmeal, 10
Vanilla Rice and Cherries, 15
Vanilla Rice Pudding, 77
Cherry Cream, 77

chia seeds
Chia Oats, 6
Lemon Chia Bowls, 12
Chia Bowls, 15
Coconut Beans Bars, 41
Seeds Bowls, 43
Ginger Chia Pudding, 78
Vanilla Chia Cream, 78
Mint Pineapple Mix, 79
Chia Apples Mix, 79

chicken
Chives Risotto, 8
Mushroom and Rice Mix, 9
Chicken Hash, 13
Chicken and Spinach Mix, 15
Chickpeas Stew, 16
Lemon Chicken Salad, 17

Chicken Stew, 17
Asparagus Salad, 17
Turkey and Carrots Soup, 17
Cilantro Chicken and Lentils, 17
Balsamic Chicken and Cauliflower, 18
Chili Chicken Soup, 19
Chicken and Sauce, 24
Turmeric Chicken Stew, 24
Chicken and Tomato Mix, 25
Turmeric Chicken Mix, 25
Paprika Rice Mix, 32
Rice and Cranberries Mix, 35
Thyme Black Beans Mix, 35
Broccoli Rice, 36
Coconut Chicken and Olives, 45
Balsamic Chicken, 45
Paprika Chicken and Spinach, 46
Chicken with Green Beans and Sauce, 46
Chicken and Tomatoes Mix, 46
Chicken with Zucchini, 46
Lemon Chicken Mix, 46
Chicken and Leeks, 47
Chives Chicken, 47
Turkey and Cabbage Mix, 47
Spiced Chicken Mix, 47
Mustard Chicken, 48
Chicken and Greens, 48
Chili Chicken Mix, 48
Herbed Chicken Mix, 48
Cumin Chicken, 48
Oregano Turkey and Tomato Mix, 49
Parsley Turkey and Quinoa, 49
Ginger Chicken, 49
Turkey and Parsnips, 49
Chicken and Green Onions, 49
Turkey and Chickpeas, 49
Chicken and Almond Mushrooms, 50
Chicken Breast and Tomatoes, 50
Chili Chicken, 50
Parsley Chicken and Peas, 51
Chicken and Artichokes, 51
Paprika Chicken, 51
Chicken and Veggies, 51
Garlic Chicken Wings, 52
Chicken and Cabbage, 52
Rosemary Chicken and Quinoa, 53
Chicken and Shrimp, 53
Chicken with Peppers, 53
Chicken with Tomatoes and Grapes, 54
Chives Chicken and Beets, 54
Lamb with Carrot and Bok Choy, 61

chickpeas

Quinoa Mix, 12

Mint Chickpeas Salad, 13

Garlic Chickpeas Fritters, 15

Chickpeas Stew, 16

Chickpeas Pan, 24

Chickpeas Spread, 37

Turkey and Chickpeas, 49

Cilantro Pork and Chickpeas, 60

chives

Chives Cabbage Sauté, 35

Chives Dip, 37

Paprika Potato Chips, 42

Chives Chicken, 47

Chives Pork and Barley, 61

Trout and Avocado Salad, 66

Thyme Shrimp, 67

Tuna and Chives Meatballs, 67

Chives Salmon and Olives, 69

Chives Sea Bass, 69

Allspice Shrimp, 71

Creamy Shrimp, 72

Chives Tilapia, 73

Paprika Scallops, 73

coconut

Cinnamon Plums, 8

Maple Almonds Bowl, 13

Vanilla Rice and Cherries, 15

Coconut Cranberry Crackers, 40

Almonds Bowls, 42

Chicken Breast and Tomatoes, 50

Coconut Pork Mix, 56

Coconut Hemp and Almond Cookies, 78

coconut butter

Berries Pancakes, 7

coconut cream

Cinnamon Plums, 8

Coconut Berries, 10

Apples Bowls, 10

Coconut Rice, 11

Baked Peach, 11

Coconut Hash, 12

Tomato Soup, 18

Cilantro Peppers and Cauliflower Mix, 21

Cheddar Cauliflower Bowls, 23

Chicken and Sauce, 24

Zucchini Soup, 25

Garlic Potato Pan, 31

Nutmeg Asparagus, 32

Creamy Brussels Sprouts, 32

Greens Sauté, 34

Coconut Beets, 36

Cheesy Spinach Dip, 37

Coconut Olives Tapenade, 37

Chives Dip, 37

Coconut Dip, 37

Pine Nuts Dip, 38

Shrimp Dip, 38

Sweet Potatoand and Coconut Dip, 39

Coconut Peppers Dip, 40

Coconut Beans Bars, 41

Avocado Dip, 41

Corn Spread, 41

Beans Dip, 42

Coconut Carrot Spread, 43

Coconut Kale Spread, 44

Creamy Turkey Mix, 45

Paprika Chicken and Spinach, 46

Chicken and Shrimp, 53

Turkey and Asparagus, 53

Peppercorn Pork, 56

Creamy Meatballs Mix, 60

Coconut Pork with Beets, 61

Coconut Lamb and Quinoa, 63

Coconut Flounder, 65

Dill Salmon, 66

Cod and Coconut Asparagus, 66

Cod and Coconut Sauce, 68

Creamy Salmon Curry, 68

Coconut Sea Bass Mix, 70

Creamy Shrimp, 72

Shrimp with Coconut Asparagus Mix, 73

Lime Cream, 74

Coconut Cream, 74

Coconut Avocado Cream, 75

Raspberries Cream Cheese Mix, 75

Watermelon and Apples Salad, 75

Lime Pears Mix, 75

Coconut Pumpkin Cream, 76

Blackberries Salad, 76

Mandarin Cream, 77

Cherry Cream, 77

Ginger Chia Pudding, 78

Vanilla Chia Cream, 78

Lemon Cashew Cream, 78

Grapefruit and Coconut Cream, 78

Coconut Pomegranate Bowls, 78

Rhubarb Cream, 78

Mint Pineapple Mix, 79

Lime Coconut Pudding, 79

Almond Cream, 79

Coconut Rhubarb Cream, 80

Coconut Plums Bowls, 80

Dates Cream, 80

Cocoa Avocado Smoothie, 80

Coconut Walnut Cream, 81

coconut milk

Almond Pancakes, 7

Cinnamon Porridge, 10

Berries Rice, 11

Coconut Rice, 11

Mango Oats, 11

Cinnamon Tapioca Pudding, 12

Quinoa Mix, 12

Millet Pudding, 13

Coconut Porridge, 13

Carrots Hash, 14

Coconut Toast, 14

Vanilla Rice and Cherries, 15

Potatoes Soup, 19

Coconut Broccoli Cream, 20

Creamy Cauliflower Mash, 29

Coconut Chicken and Olives, 45

Turkey and Broccoli, 51

Coconut Turkey, 53

Chicken with Peppers, 53

Creamy Pork Chops, 58

Pork and Olives, 64

Coconut Cake, 74

Strawberries and Coconut Cake, 75

Grapefruit and Coconut Cream, 78

Vanilla Green Tea Bars, 81

coconut oil

Almond Pancakes, 7

Asparagus Snack Bowls, 39

Turkey and Cabbage Mix, 47

Coconut Cake, 74

Pecan Cookies, 75

Strawberries and Coconut Cake, 75

Rhubarb and Figs Stew, 76

Nectarines Cocoa Squares, 77

Fruity Bread, 77

Vanilla Rice Pudding, 77

Seed Energy Bars, 80

Banana and Avocado Bars, 81

Cinnamon Bars, 81

Almond Lemon Cake, 81

Vanilla Green Tea Bars, 81

cod

Cod Tacos, 16

Shrimp Soup, 20

Citrus Cod, 66

Cod and Coconut Asparagus, 66

Hot Cod, 67

Turmeric Cod Mix, 67

Cod and Coconut Sauce, 68

Garlic Cod and Tomatoes, 70
Lemon and Mint Cod, 70
Coconut Cod and Broccoli, 72
Cod and Green Onions Mix, 72
Cod and Peas Pan, 73

corn
Corn and Beans Tortillas, 15
Shrimp and Spinach Salad, 16
Green Beans Salad, 27
Garlic Mushrooms, 30
Spinach Sauté, 30
Chili Corn Sauté, 31
Basil Olives Mix, 33
Rosemary Tomatoes, 34
Corn Spread, 41
Corn Salsa, 42
Chicken and Green Onions, 49
Lamb with Okra, 63
Minty Pork, 64

crab
Crab and Tomatoes Salad, 71

cranberries
Almond Scones, 6
Coconut Cranberry Crackers, 40
Turkey and Cranberries Mix, 50

cucumbers
Mint Chickpeas Salad, 13
Shrimp Salad, 26
Avocado Salad, 26
Green Beans Salad, 27
Spinach and Endives Salad, 27
Grapes and Cucumber Salad, 27
Tomatoes Salad, 29
Zucchini Salsa, 35
Olives Salsa, 37
Chives Salmon Salad, 66
Cucumber Salad, 37
Cucumbers Salsa Bowls, 38

D

dates
Dates Ric, 10
Chives Cabbage Sauté, 35
Dates Cream, 80

E

edamame
Chives Edamame Salad, 27

eggplant
Turmeric Chicken Stew, 24
Green Beans Mix, 31
Turkey Sandwich, 52
Chicken with Peppers, 53

Coconut Pork Mix, 56
Salmon with Zucchini and Eggplant, 67
Tomato Eggplant Soup, 18
Eggplant and Tomato Stew, 25
Parmesan Eggplant Mix, 33

eggs
Garlic Chickpeas Fritters, 15
Salmon Muffins, 43
Meatballs and Spinach, 60
Pork Meatballs and Sauce, 62
Tuna and Chives Meatballs, 67
Lime Coconut Pudding, 79
Cinnamon Bars, 81
Almond Lemon Cake, 81
Cheese Frittata, 9
Eggs and Artichokes, 9
Hash Browns Casserole, 9
Beans Bake, 9
Coconut Hash, 12
Tomato Eggs, 12
Eggs Salad, 12
Green Beans Hash, 13
Spring Omelet, 14
Carrots Hash, 14
Coconut Toast, 14
Scallions Omelet, 14
Squash Bites, 43
Almond Bars, 44
Oregano Broccoli Bars, 44
Creamy Meatballs Mix, 60
Almond Berry Pudding, 74
Almond Cookies, 74
Pecan Cookies, 75
Strawberries and Coconut Cake, 75
Almond Cocoa Pudding, 75
Fruity Bread, 77
Coconut Rhubarb Cream, 80
Almond Plum Muffins, 80
Vanilla Green Tea Bars, 81

endive
Shrimp and Spinach Salad, 16
Chicken Stew, 17
Spinach and Endives Salad, 27
Endives Salad, 27
Cilantro and Spring Onions Endives, 29
Turmeric Endives, 29
Parmesan Endives, 33
Pork with Chili Endives, 62

F

fennel
Garlic Turkey Stew, 18
Paprika Fennel Mix, 30

Chili Fennel Salsa, 42
Lamb with Veggies Mix, 61
Lemon Fennel and Salmon, 69

figs
Pomegranate Yogurt, 11
Figs Bowls, 39
Rhubarb and Figs Stew, 76

flounder
Coconut Flounder, 65

G

garlic
Green Beans Hash, 13
Carrot and Peas Salad, 14
Garlic Chickpeas Fritters, 15
Asparagus Salad, 17
Turkey and Carrots Soup, 17
Garlic Turkey Stew, 18
Potatoes Soup, 19
Salmon Skillet, 19
Minty Shrimp and Olives Salad, 20
Rosemary Carrot Stew, 21
Cabbage Stew, 21
Mushroom Soup, 21
Pork Stew, 22
Oregano Pork, 23
Beef Soup, 23
Chicken and Sauce, 24
Parsley Green Beans Soup, 24
Eggplant and Tomato Stew, 25
Rosemary Pork Chops, 25
Turmeric Chicken Mix, 25
Chives Edamame Salad, 27
Parsley Beets, 28
Beet Salad, 28
Garlic Tomatoes Mix, 29
Paprika Brussels Sprouts, 29
Garlic Mushrooms, 30
Parsley Mushrooms, 30
Chili Broccoli, 31
Hot Brussels Sprouts, 31
Garlic Potato Pan, 31
Garlic Potatoes, 32
Parmesan Eggplant Mix, 33
Balsamic Cabbage, 33
Coconut Kale Sauté, 34
Avocado Mix, 35
Cilantro Lemon Dip, 39
Lime Beans Salsa, 39
Brussels Sprouts Bowls, 40
Lentils Dip, 40
Dill Zucchini Spread, 43
Salmon Muffins, 43

Tomato Spread, 43
Turkey and Garlic Sauce, 45
Turkey and Onion Mix, 45
Basil Turkey and Broccoli, 46
Lemon Chicken Mix, 46
Turkey with Pepper and Rice, 47
Mustard Chicken, 48
Chili Chicken Mix, 48
Cumin Chicken, 48
Turkey and Broccoli, 51
Peppercorn Turkey, 51
Garlic Chicken Wings, 52
Chicken with Tomatoes and Grapes, 54
Balsamic Turkey, 54
Paprika Pork Mix, 55
Coriander Pork, 55
Cilantro Pork Skillet, 55
Parsley Pork and Tomatoes, 56
Lemon Pork Chops, 56
Coconut Pork Mix, 56
Lamb with Scallions and Mushrooms, 58
Chili Pork and Apples, 58
Hot Pork Chops, 58
Lamb and Radish Skillet, 59
Coconut Pork with Beets, 61
Thyme Lamb and Cabbage Stew, 61
Simple Pork and Leeks, 62
Pork and Radish Hash, 62
Pork and Onions Bowls, 63
Lime Lamb, 64
Pork and Cilantro Rice, 64
Thyme Shrimp, 67
Salmon with Scallions and Green Beans, 67
Turmeric Cod Mix, 67
Balsamic Salmon, 68
Balsamic Scallops and Scallions, 70
Garlic Trout, 70
Garlic Cod and Tomatoes, 70
Saffron Salmon and Onion, 71
Seafood and Tomato Bowls, 72

ginger
Rice Bowls, 9
Spinach and Tomato Stew, 21
Lime Turkey Stew, 22
Zucchini Soup, 25
Turmeric Chicken Mix, 25
Beet Salad, 28
Avocado, Tomato and Olives Salad, 34
Mint Cheesy Dip, 38
Bell Peppers Salsa, 41
Ginger Turkey Mix, 47

Spiced Chicken Mix, 47
Ginger Chicken, 49
Chicken and Artichokes, 51
Cilantro Pork, 55
Salmon with Scallions and Green Beans, 67
Turmeric Cod Mix, 67
Ginger Sea Bass, 72
Ginger Chia Pudding, 78
Ginger Berries Bowls, 78

grapes
Shrimp and Walnuts Salad, 26
Grapes and Cucumber Salad, 27
Chicken with Tomatoes and Grapes, 54
Grapes and Lime Compote, 77

H

halibut
Cilantro Halibut and Radishes, 68

hash
Coconut Hash, 12
Chicken Hash, 13

hash browns
Cheddar Hash Browns, 8
Hash Browns Casserole, 9

honey
Almond Potato Waffles, 7

K

kale
Endives Salad, 27
Spinach Mix, 31
Coconut Kale Sauté, 34
Coconut Kale Spread, 44
Lamb Chops and Greens, 60

L

lamb
Lamb and Cherry Tomatoes Mix, 57
Lamb with Scallions and Mushrooms, 58
Lamb and Radish Skillet, 59
Lamb Chops and Greens, 60
Lamb and Red Onions Mix, 60
Lamb with Veggies Mix, 61
Lamb with Carrot and Bok Choy, 61
Thyme Lamb and Cabbage Stew, 61
Oregano Lamb Chops, 62
Lamb with Okra, 63
Coconut Lamb and Quinoa, 63
Lime Lamb, 64

leek
Cabbage and Leek Soup, 20
Chicken and Leeks, 47
Parsley Pork Soup, 20

Shrimp Salad, 40
Cream Cheese and Leeks Dip, 41
Simple Pork and Leeks, 62

lemon
Lemon Chia Bowls, 12
Lemon Chicken Salad, 17
Garlic Tomatoes Mix, 29
Parmesan Endives, 33
Lentils Dip, 40
Lemon Chicken Mix, 46
Pork and Lemon Artichokes Mix, 59
Chives Salmon Salad, 66
Chives Sea Bass, 69
Lemon and Mint Cod, 70
Trout and Arugula Salad, 71
Shrimp and Sauce, 71
Parsley Shrimp and Pineapple Bowls, 72
Chives Tilapia, 73
Almond Lemon Cake, 81
Balsamic Shrimp Salad, 26

lentils
Cilantro Chicken and Lentils, 17
Chipotle Lentils, 25
Lentils Dip, 40
Turkey and Lentils, 52
Turmeric Pork Mix, 60

lime
Garlic Chickpeas Fritters, 15
Lime Turkey Stew, 22
Salmon Salad, 26
Endives Salad, 27
Lime Tomatoes, 30
Shrimp Salad, 40
Turkey and Potatoes, 48
Lime Pork, 57
Lime Lamb, 64
Hot Cod, 67
Shrimp and Black Beans, 69
Lime Cream, 74
Lime Pears Mix, 75
Orange Bowls, 76
Grapes and Lime Compote, 77
Lime Watermelon Compote, 77
Lime Coconut Pudding, 79
Nutmeg Baked Bananas, 80

M

mandarin
Mandarin Cream, 77

mango
Mango Oats, 11
Pomegranate Oats, 11

Chicken and Spinach Mix, 15
Almonds and Mango Salad, 31
Almonds and Mango Salad, 31
Almonds Bowls, 42
Pork with Mango and Tomatoes, 59
Lime Salmon and Mango, 65

maple syrup
Almond Peach Mix, 10
Maple Almonds Bowl, 13

milk
Walnuts Cream, 75

millet
Millet Pudding, 13

mushrooms (White)
Mushrooms Bowls, 42
Mushroom and Rice Mix, 9
Chili Chicken Soup, 19
Mushroom Soup, 21
Mushroom Salad, 23
Rosemary Pork Chops, 25
Garlic Mushrooms, 30
Parsley Mushrooms, 30
Turkey and Garlic Sauce, 45
Chicken and Almond Mushrooms, 50
Lamb with Scallions and Mushrooms, 58
Sea Bass Pan, 73

mussels
Seafood and Tomato Bowls, 72

N

nectarines
Nectarines Cocoa Squares, 77

O

oats
Chia Oats, 6
Almond Cookies, 6
Cinnamon Oats, 7
Almond Potato Waffles, 7
Strawberry Oats, 10
Cherries Oatmeal, 10
Coconut Cocoa Oats, 11
Mango Oats, 11
Pecan Bowls, 11
Pomegranate Oats, 11
Zucchini Almond Oatmeal, 13
Apple Oats, 14
Chia Bowls, 15
Coconut Cranberry Crackers, 40

okra
Pork with Olives, 61
Lamb with Okra, 63

olives
Peppers Salad, 12
Mushroom Salad, 23
Avocado Salad, 26
Salmon and Olives Salad, 26
Radish and Olives Salad, 27
Tomato Salsa, 28
Cilantro and Spring Onions Endives, 29
Basil Olives Mix, 33
Parsley Artichokes Mix, 34
Avocado, Tomato and Olives Salad, 34
Olives Salsa, 37
Coconut Olives Tapenade, 37
Cauliflower and Tomato Salsa, 38
Peach and Olives Salsa, 38
Lime Beans Salsa, 39
Pineapple Salsa, 44
Coconut Chicken and Olives, 45
Turkey and Olives, 54
Turkey Salad, 54
Pork with Olives, 61
Pork and Olives, 64
Chives Salmon Salad, 66
Chives Salmon and Olives, 69
Trout and Arugula Salad, 71

onion
Cheese Frittata, 9
Eggs and Artichokes, 9
Hash Browns Casserole, 9
Quinoa Mix, 12
Green Beans Hash, 13
Chicken Hash, 13
Carrot and Peas Salad, 14
Pork Soup, 16
Cod Tacos, 16
Zucchini Fritters, 16
Chickpeas Stew, 16
Chicken Stew, 17
Tomato Beef Stew, 17
Cilantro Chicken and Lentils, 17
Trout Soup, 18
Tomato Soup, 18
Tomato Eggplant Soup, 18
Chili Chicken Soup, 19
Ground Beef Skillet, 19
Salmon Skillet, 19
Coconut Broccoli Cream, 20
Parsley Pork Soup, 20
Cabbage and Leek Soup, 20
Dill Cauliflower Soup, 20
Balsamic Shrimp, 21
Oregano Pork, 23

Carrot Soup, 23
Chicken and Sauce, 24
Thyme Beef and Tomatoes, 24
Zucchini Soup, 25
Balsamic Shrimp Salad, 26
Shrimp Salad, 26
Salsa Seafood Bowls, 26
Pesto Zucchini Salad, 28
Tomato and Cabbage Mix, 28
Tomato Salsa, 28
Paprika Fennel Mix, 30
Paprika Green Beans, 30
Spinach Sauté, 30
Green Beans Mix, 31
Nutmeg Asparagus, 32
Paprika Carrots, 32
Coconut Kale Sauté, 34
Mint Peppers, 35
Thyme Black Beans Mix, 35
Cucumber Salad, 37
Olives Salsa, 37
Chili Fennel Salsa, 42
Turkey and Garlic Sauce, 45
Turkey and Onion Mix, 45
Coconut Chicken and Olives, 45
Turkey and Peach, 45
Chicken with Green Beans and Sauce, 46
Chicken with Zucchini, 46
Turkey and Potatoes, 48
Cumin Chicken, 48
Buttery Cashew Turkey, 50
Turkey and Greens, 50
Turkey and Cranberries Mix, 50
Parsley Chicken and Peas, 51
Turkey and Lentils, 52
Chicken and Cabbage, 52
Turkey and Barley, 52
Turkey with Radishes, 52
Paprika Pork Mix, 55
Pork and Carrots, 55
Cilantro Pork Skillet, 55
Parsley Pork and Tomatoes, 56
Pork and Tomatoes, 57
Coriander Pork, 57
Lamb and Cherry Tomatoes Mix, 57
Lamb with Scallions and Mushrooms, 58
Creamy Pork Chops, 58
Pork and Sweet Potatoes, 59
Cilantro Pork and Chickpeas, 60
Lamb Chops and Greens, 60
Turmeric Pork Mix, 60
Pork with Olives, 61

Pork with Chili Endives, 62
Oregano Lamb Chops, 62
Pork and Onions Bowls, 63
Pork with Beans, 63
Coconut Flounder, 65
Salmon Soup, 65
Lime Salmon and Mango, 65
Balsamic Scallops, 68
Creamy Salmon Curry, 68
Salmon and Veggies Mix, 69
Shrimp and Quinoa Bowls, 70
Saffron Salmon and Onion, 71
Coconut Cod and Broccoli, 72
Cod and Green Onions Mix, 72
Shrimp and Spinach Salad, 72
Shrimp with Coconut Asparagus Mix, 73
Sea Bass Pan, 73
Cod and Peas Pan, 73
Cauliflower Salad, 10
Eggs Salad, 12
Spring Omelet, 14
Chicken and Spinach Mix, 15
Potatoes Soup, 19
Beef and Cabbage Stew, 22
Chipotle Lentils, 25
Radish and Olives Salad, 27
Cilantro and Spring Onions Endives, 29
Tomatoes Salad, 29
Greens Sauté, 34
Chickpeas Spread, 37
Coconut Dip, 37
Shrimp Dip, 38
Shrimp Salsa, 39
Bell Peppers Salsa, 41
Dill Zucchini Spread, 43
Pearl Onions Snack, 44
Chicken and Tomatoes Mix, 46
Herbed Chicken Mix, 48
Chicken and Green Onions, 49
Turkey Salad, 54
Cilantro Pork, 55
Basil Pork Mix, 57
Creamy Meatballs Mix, 60
Lamb and Red Onions Mix, 60
Pork with Spring Onions and Sprouts, 63
Salmon Spread, 65
Citrus Cod, 66
Shrimp with Artichokes and Tomatoes, 69
Salmon and Spring Onions, 71

orange
    Shrimp and Arugula Salad, 19

Balsamic Chicken, 45
Citrus Cod, 66
Citrus Tuna, 68
Orange Compote, 76
Orange Bowls, 76

orange juice
    Pecan Bowls, 11

P

parsnips
    Turkey and Parsnips, 49

peaches
    Almond Peach Mix, 10
    Baked Peache, 11
    Peach and Olives Salsa, 38
    Turkey and Peach, 45
    Pork with Paprika Peaches, 59
    Salmon Salad, 66
    Cinnamon Peaches, 74
    Almond Cream, 79

pear
    Cashew Parfait, 7
    Pomegranate Yogurt, 11
    Pomegranate Yogurt, 11
    Minty Fruit Salad, 80
    Cherries Oatmeal, 10
    Lime Pears Mix, 75
    Fruity Bread, 77
    Rice Pudding, 79
    Carrot and Peas Salad, 14
    Beef and Scallions Mix, 23
    Parsley Chicken and Peas, 51
    Pork with Parsley Peas, 62
    Cod and Peas Pan, 73

pecans
    Pecan Bowls, 11
    Pecans Bowls, 42
    Pecan Cookies, 75

pepper (Chili)
    Mushroom Soup, 21
    Corn Salsa, 42
    Pork and Green Beans, 63
    Mushroom Salad, 23
    Chili Chicken Soup, 19
    Chili Chicken, 50
    Coriander Pork, 57

pepper (jalapeno)
    Basil Olives Mix, 33
    Pork and Lemon Artichokes Mix, 59

pepper (Serrano)
    Turkey with Pepper and Rice, 47

pine nuts
    Arugula Salad, 27
    Pine Nuts Dip, 38

pineapple
    Pineapple Salsa, 44
    Parsley Shrimp and Pineapple Bowls, 72
    Mint Pineapple Mix, 79

pistachios
    Coconut Quinoa, 8

plums
    Cinnamon Plums, 8
    Mandarin Cream, 77
    Sweet Plums Mix, 79
    Coconut Plums Bowls, 80
    Almond Plum Muffins, 80

pomegranate
    Pomegranate Yogurt, 11
    Pomegranate Oats, 11
    Chia Bowls, 15
    Arugula Salad, 27
    Coconut Pomegranate Bowls, 78

pork
    Pork Soup, 16
    Pork and Potatoes, 18
    Parsley Pork Soup, 20
    Pork Stew, 22
    Oregano Pork, 23
    Rosemary Pork Chops, 25
    Paprika Pork Mix, 55
    Coriander Pork, 55
    Pork and Carrots, 55
    Balsamic Pork, 55
    Cilantro Pork, 55
    Cilantro Pork Skillet, 55
    Pork and Zucchinis, 56
    Parsley Pork and Tomatoes, 56
    Nutmeg Pork, 56
    Lemon Pork Chops, 56
    Peppercorn Pork, 56
    Coconut Pork Mix, 56
    Lime Pork, 57
    Pork and Tomatoes, 57
    Coriander Pork, 57
    Basil Pork Mix, 57
    Pork with Green Beans, 57
    Chili Pork and Apples, 58
    Pork with Tomatoes and Spinach, 58
    Hot Pork Chops, 58
    Warm Pork Salad, 58
    Creamy Pork Chops, 58
    Pork with Paprika Peaches, 59

Parmesan Pork and Sauce, 59
Pork with Mango and Tomatoes, 59
Pork and Lemon Artichokes Mix, 59
Pork and Sweet Potatoes, 59
Cilantro Pork and Chickpeas, 60
Meatballs and Spinach, 60
Creamy Meatballs Mix, 60
Turmeric Pork Mix, 60
Coconut Pork with Beets, 61
Pork with Olives, 61
Chives Pork and Barley, 61
Simple Pork and Leeks, 62
Pork Meatballs and Sauce, 62
Pork with Parsley Peas, 62
Pork with Chili Endives, 62
Pork and Radish Hash, 62
Pork and Green Beans, 63
Pork with Spring Onions and Sprouts, 63
Pork and Onions Bowls, 63
Pork with Beans, 63
Pork with Capers, 64
Pork and Olives, 64
Minty Pork, 64
Pork and Cilantro Rice, 64
Tarragon Pork Roast, 64

potato
Almond Potato Waffles, 7
Beef Soup, 23
Pork and Potatoes, 18
Potatoes Soup, 19
Potato and Spinach Salad, 19
Chickpeas Pan, 24
Thyme Beef and Tomatoes, 24
Garlic Potato Pan, 31
Garlic Potatoes, 32
Roasted Sweet Potato Mix, 36
Sweet Potatoand and Coconut Dip, 39
Paprika Potato Chips, 42
Turkey and Potatoes, 48
Pork and Sweet Potatoes, 59

pumpkin
Cashew Parfait, 7
Tahini Pumpkin Dip, 37
Coconut Pumpkin Cream, 76

Q

quinoa
Coconut Quinoa, 8
Quinoa Mix, 12
Squash and Peppers Stew, 22
Parsley Turkey and Quinoa, 49
Rosemary Chicken and Quinoa, 53
Coconut Lamb and Quinoa, 63

Shrimp and Quinoa Bowls, 70

R

radishes
Radish and Olives Salad, 27
Chives Radishes, 28
Turmeric Radish Chips, 40
Turkey with Radishes, 52
Pork with Green Beans, 57
Lamb and Radish Skillet, 59
Pork and Radish Hash, 62
Shrimp and Radish Mix, 65
Cilantro Halibut and Radishes, 68

raisins
Almond Cookies, 6
Apples Bowls, 10
Maple Almonds Bowl, 13
Coconut Plums Bowls, 80
Cinnamon Bars, 81

raspberries
Chia Oats, 6
Almond Berry Pudding, 74
Raspberries Cream Cheese Mix, 75

rhubarb
Rhubarb and Figs Stew, 76
Rhubarb Cream, 78
Rhubarb Compote, 79
Coconut Rhubarb Cream, 80

rice
Chives Risotto, 8
Rice Bowls, 9
Mushroom and Rice Mix, 9
Dates Ric, 10
Berries Rice, 11
Coconut Rice, 11
Vanilla Rice and Cherries, 15
Paprika Rice Mix, 32
Rice and Cranberries Mix, 35
Thyme Black Beans Mix, 35
Broccoli Rice, 36
Turkey with Pepper and Rice, 47
Pork and Cilantro Rice, 64
Walnuts Pudding, 77
Vanilla Rice Pudding, 77
Rice Pudding, 79

S

salmon
Salmon Skillet, 19
Mushroom Salad, 23
Salmon Salad, 26
Salsa Seafood Bowls, 26
Salmon and Olives Salad, 26

Salmon and Spinach Bowls, 42
Salmon Muffins, 43
Salmon Soup, 65
Lime Salmon and Mango, 65
Salmon Spread, 65
Salmon Salad, 66
Dill Salmon, 66
Chives Salmon Salad, 66
Salmon with Zucchini and Eggplant, 67
Salmon with Scallions and Green Beans, 67
Balsamic Salmon, 68
Creamy Salmon Curry, 68
Chives Salmon and Olives, 69
Lemon Fennel and Salmon, 69
Salmon and Veggies Mix, 69
Salmon and Spring Onions, 71
Saffron Salmon and Onion, 71
Parsley Salmon Mix, 71

sausage
Hash Browns Casserole, 9

scallions
Scallions Omelet, 14
Beef and Scallions Mix, 23
Chili Corn Sauté, 31
Cucumbers Salsa Bowls, 38
Ginger Turkey Mix, 47
Spiced Chicken Mix, 47
Lime Pork, 57
Balsamic Scallops and Scallions, 70

scallops
Balsamic Scallops, 68
Balsamic Scallops and Scallions, 70
Paprika Scallops, 73

sea bass
Chives Sea Bass, 69
Coconut Sea Bass Mix, 70
Ginger Sea Bass, 72
Sea Bass Pan, 73

sesame
Almond Scones, 6

shallot
Turmeric Chicken Mix, 25
Arugula Salad, 27
Balsamic Cabbage, 33
Avocado Dip, 41
Coconut Kale Spread, 44
Cod and Coconut Sauce, 68
Shrimp and Black Beans, 69
Crab and Tomatoes Salad, 71
Parsley Salmon Mix, 71

Mozzarella Scramble, 8
Shrimp Soup, 20
Turmeric Chicken Stew, 24
Chickpeas Pan, 24
Rosemary Pork Chops, 25
Salmon and Olives Salad, 26
Chives Edamame Salad, 27
Cabbage Salad, 28
Balsamic Black Beans Mix, 29
Spinach Mix, 31
Chili Corn Sauté, 31
Creamy Brussels Sprouts, 32
Beans and Tomato Salsa, 39
Tomato Spread, 43
Squash Bites, 43
Balsamic Chicken, 45
Paprika Chicken and Spinach, 46
Basil Turkey and Broccoli, 46
Oregano Turkey and Tomato Mix, 49
Ginger Chicken, 49
Turkey and Parsnips, 49
Rosemary Chicken and Quinoa, 53
Peppercorn Pork, 56
Chili Pork and Apples, 58
Pork with Parsley Peas, 62
Coconut Lamb and Quinoa, 63
Tarragon Pork Roast, 64
Lime Tuna, 66
Citrus Tuna, 68
Cilantro Halibut and Radishes, 68

shrimp
Shrimp and Spinach Salad, 16
Raspberry Shrimp and Tomato Salad, 16
Shrimp and Arugula Salad, 19
Minty Shrimp and Olives Salad, 20
Shrimp Soup, 20
Balsamic Shrimp, 21
Balsamic Shrimp Salad, 26
Shrimp Salad, 26
Salsa Seafood Bowls, 26
Shrimp and Walnuts Salad, 26
Shrimp Dip, 38
Shrimp Salsa, 39
Shrimp Salad, 40
Chicken and Shrimp, 53
Cilantro and Nutmeg Shrimp, 65
Shrimp and Radish Mix, 65
Shrimp and Strawberries, 65
Thyme Shrimp, 67
Shrimp and Black Beans, 69
Shrimp with Artichokes and Tomatoes, 69

Shrimp and Quinoa Bowls, 70
Allspice Shrimp, 71
Shrimp and Sauce, 71
Shrimp and Basil Salad, 71
Seafood and Tomato Bowls, 72
Parsley Shrimp and Pineapple Bowls, 72
Creamy Shrimp, 72
Shrimp and Spinach Salad, 72
Shrimp with Coconut Asparagus Mix, 73

spinach
Tomato Eggs, 12
Chicken and Spinach Mix, 15
Shrimp and Spinach Salad, 16
Lemon Chicken Salad, 17
Asparagus Salad, 17
Potato and Spinach Salad, 19
Spinach and Tomato Stew, 21
Salmon Salad, 26
Avocado Salad, 26
Spinach and Endives Salad, 27
Lemon Spinach, 27
Grapes and Cucumber Salad, 27
Spinach Sauté, 30
Spinach Mix, 31
Cheesy Spinach Dip, 37
Salmon and Spinach Bowls, 42
Paprika Chicken and Spinach, 46
Pork with Tomatoes and Spinach, 58
Warm Pork Salad, 58
Meatballs and Spinach, 60
Salmon Salad, 66
Shrimp and Spinach Salad, 72

squash
Squash and Peppers Stew, 22
Chili Squash Mix, 30
Squash Bites, 43

stevia
Almond Pancakes, 7

strawberries
Coconut Berries, 10
Strawberry Oats, 10
Coconut Porridge, 13
Shrimp and Spinach Salad, 16
Shrimp and Strawberries, 65
Strawberries and Yogurt Bowls, 74
Strawberries and Coconut Cake, 75
Cherry Cream, 77
Ginger Berries Bowls, 78

T

tangerines
Orange Bowls, 76

tapioca
Cinnamon Tapioca Pudding, 12

tilapia
Chives Tilapia, 73

tomatoes
Peppers Salad, 12
Tomato Beef Stew, 17
Tomato and Cabbage Mix, 28
Chili Fennel Salsa, 42
Chicken and Veggies, 51
Lamb and Red Onions Mix, 60
Mint Chickpeas Salad, 13
Chickpeas Stew, 16
Lemon Chicken Salad, 17
Cilantro Chicken and Lentils, 17
Balsamic Chicken and Cauliflower, 18
Trout Soup, 18
Tomato Soup, 18
Potato and Spinach Salad, 19
Cabbage and Leek Soup, 20
Rosemary Carrot Stew, 21
Spinach and Tomato Stew, 21
Spinach and Tomato Stew, 21
Cabbage Stew, 21
Cilantro Peppers and Cauliflower Mix, 21
Mushroom Soup, 21
Beef and Cabbage Stew, 22
Squash and Peppers Stew, 22
Beef and Scallions Mix, 23
Parsley Green Beans Soup, 24
Turmeric Chicken Stew, 24
Beef Skillet, 24
Chickpeas Pan, 24
Thyme Beef and Tomatoes, 24
Eggplant and Tomato Stew, 25
Chipotle Lentils, 25
Salsa Seafood Bowls, 26
Spinach and Endives Salad, 27
Garlic Tomatoes Mix, 29
Tomatoes Salad, 29
Peppers Salad, 29
Garlic Mushrooms, 30
Lime Tomatoes, 30
Spinach Mix, 31
Rosemary Tomatoes, 34
Avocado, Tomato and Olives Salad, 34
Zucchini Salsa, 35
Cauliflower and Tomato Salsa, 38
Cucumbers Salsa Bowls, 38
Peach and Olives Salsa, 38
Shrimp Salsa, 39
Shrimp Salad, 40

Yogurt Dip, 41
Corn Salsa, 42
Tomato Spread, 43
Pineapple Salsa, 44
Chicken and Tomatoes Mix, 46
Chicken with Zucchini, 46
Chicken and Greens, 48
Herbed Chicken Mix, 48
Oregano Turkey and Tomato Mix, 49
Chicken and Almond Mushrooms, 50
Chicken Breast and Tomatoes, 50
Chili Chicken, 50
Chicken and Artichokes, 51
Peppercorn Turkey, 51
Paprika Chicken, 51
Turkey Tortillas, 53
Chicken with Tomatoes and Grapes, 54
Cheesy Turkey, 54
Pork and Tomatoes, 57
Pork with Green Beans, 57
Pork with Tomatoes and Spinach, 58
Pork with Mango and Tomatoes, 59
Cilantro Pork and Chickpeas, 60
Lamb with Veggies Mix, 61
Thyme Lamb and Cabbage Stew, 61
Pork and Radish Hash, 62
Pork with Beans, 63
Salmon Soup, 65
Shrimp and Strawberries, 65
Cilantro Halibut and Radishes, 68
Shrimp with Artichokes and Tomatoes, 69

tomatoes (Cherry)
Tomato Eggs, 12
Raspberry Shrimp and Tomato Salad, 16
Ground Beef Skillet, 19
Minty Shrimp and Olives Salad, 20
Balsamic Shrimp, 21
Chicken and Tomato Mix, 25
Tomato Salsa, 28
Balsamic Black Beans Mix, 29
Basil Olives Mix, 33
Beans and Tomato Salsa, 39
Coriander Pork, 55
Balsamic Pork, 55
Parsley Pork and Tomatoes, 56
Lamb and Cherry Tomatoes Mix, 57
Basil Pork Mix, 57
Warm Pork Salad, 58
Meatballs and Spinach, 60
Chives Sea Bass, 69
Garlic Cod and Tomatoes, 70

Crab and Tomatoes Salad, 71
Trout and Arugula Salad, 71
Seafood and Tomato Bowls, 72
Beef and Beans Salad, 22

tortillas
Turkey Tortillas, 22
Turkey Tortillas, 53

trout
Trout Soup, 18
Baked Trout, 65
Trout and Avocado Salad, 66
Garlic Trout, 70
Trout and Arugula Salad, 71

tuna
Lime Tuna, 66
Chili Tuna, 66
Tuna and Chives Meatballs, 67
Citrus Tuna, 68

turkey
Turkey and Carrots Soup, 17
Garlic Turkey Stew, 18
Lime Turkey Stew, 22
Turkey Tortillas, 22
Creamy Turkey Mix, 45
Turkey and Garlic Sauce, 45
Turkey and Onion Mix, 45
Turkey and Peach, 45
Basil Turkey and Broccoli, 46
Ginger Turkey Mix, 47
Turkey and Cabbage Mix, 47
Turkey with Pepper and Rice, 47
Turkey and Potatoes, 48
Oregano Turkey and Tomato Mix, 49
Parsley Turkey and Quinoa, 49
Turkey and Parsnips, 49
Turkey and Chickpeas, 49
Buttery Cashew Turkey, 50
Turkey and Greens, 50
Turkey and Cranberries Mix, 50
Turkey and Broccoli, 51
Peppercorn Turkey, 51
Turkey and Lentils, 52
Turkey and Barley, 52
Turkey Sandwich, 52
Turkey with Radishes, 52
Coconut Turkey, 53
Turkey Tortillas, 53
Turkey and Asparagus, 53
Cheesy Turkey, 54
Turkey and Olives, 54
Balsamic Turkey, 54
Turkey Salad, 54

turnip
Walnut Turnips Mix, 32

W

walnuts
Almond Scones, 6
Banana Muffins, 7
Shrimp and Walnuts Salad, 26
Parsley Beets, 28
Walnut Turnips Mix, 32
Walnuts Bowls, 40
Chili Walnuts, 40
Pecans Bowls, 42
Coconut Carrot Spread, 43
Coconut Cake, 74
Walnuts Cream, 75
Walnuts Pudding, 77
Coconut Walnut Cream, 81

watermelon
Shrimp and Basil Salad, 71
Watermelon and Apples Salad, 75
Lime Watermelon Compote, 77

yogurt
Cashew Parfait, 7
Berries Pancakes, 7
Cherries Bowls, 8
Apples Bowls, 8
Apple Oats, 14
Salmon Salad, 26
Coconut Beets, 36
Dill Dip, 38
Yogurt Dip, 41
Dill Zucchini Spread, 43
Turkey Salad, 54
Salmon Spread, 65
Trout and Avocado Salad, 66
Lime Cream, 74
Almond Berry Pudding, 74
Strawberries and Yogurt Bowls, 74

zucchini
Beef Skillet, 24
Chicken and Veggies, 51
Turkey Tortillas, 53
Salmon with Zucchini and Eggplant, 67
Zucchini Almond Oatmeal, 13
Zucchini Fritters, 16
Rosemary Carrot Stew, 21
Zucchini Soup, 25
Pesto Zucchini Salad, 28
Zucchini Salsa, 35
Dill Zucchini Spread, 43
Chicken with Zucchini, 46
Pork and Zucchinis, 56

Made in the USA
Middletown, DE
10 September 2020

18980705R00057